AN INTRODUCTION TO LAW AND BIOETHICS

AN INTRODUCTION TO LAW AND BIOETHICS

Banwari Lal

CYBER TECH PUBLICATIONS
4264/3, Ansari Road, Daryaganj, New Delhi-110002 (India)
Ph.: 011-23244078. Fax: 011-23280028
E-Mail: cyberpublicationsdelhi@yahoo.com

AN INTRODUCTION TO LAW AND BIOETHICS

Banwari Lal

First Edition 2009

Published by :

G.S. Rawat for **Cyber Tech Publications**
4264/3, Ansari Road, Daryaganj, New Delhi-110002 (India)
Ph.: 011-23244078. Fax: 011-23280028
E-Mail: cyberpublicationsdelhi@yahoo.com

Printed at : **Amit Enterprises**, Maujpur, Delhi, (9810878184)

Preface

The purpose of this book is to determine the extent to which existing law and legal policy is consistent with bioethical principles, and the extent to which it is adequately equipped to deal with emergent genetic technologies and the prenatal issues they raise. It should be noted that the parameters set by the topic of this paper require a comparative analysis of bioethics and the law. It therefore falls outside the scope of this paper to undertake a detailed analysis of feminist thought in the area of research. However, given the centrality of women to the issue of childbirth and pregnancy, it is submitted that one is (bio)ethically compelled to consider the interests of women in these areas. Thus, whilst not comprehensive, nor intended to be representative of all women's views, some of the most common criticisms and concerns encountered in feminist literature will be examined in the course of discussion. This will be done particularly with respect to the maternal/foetal relationship, and in the arguments against genetic testing based on the eugenic fear. Similarly, some of the most commonly expressed concerns regarding genetic testing raised by the disabled community will be addressed. In view of the technical nature of some aspects of this paper, a glossary of medical terms is provided. Discussion begins, with an outline of some of the most important current advances in genetic technology. The Human Genome Project represents one of the most ambitious and influential projects in biotechnology, introducing with it a range of technological advances that will influence both the type and scope of genetic knowledge.

—*Author*

CONTENTS

Introduction

Bioethics is the philosophical study of the ethical controversies brought about by advances in biology and medicine. Bioethicists are concerned with the ethical questions that arise in the relationships among life sciences, biotechnology, medicine, politics, law, philosophy, and theology.

SCOPE

While scientific research has produced social benefits, it has also posed some troubling ethical questions. Public attention was drawn to these questions by abuses of human subjects in biomedical experiments, especially during the Second World War. During the Nuremberg War Crime Trials, the Nuremberg code was drafted as a set of standards for judging physicians and scientists who had conducted biomedical experiments on concentration camp prisoners. This code is often credited with jump starting the interdisciplinary field now called bioethics.

On July 12, 1974, the National Research Act (Pub. L. 93-348) was signed into law in the United States, thereby creating the National Commission for the Protection of Human Subjects of Biomedical and Behavioral Research. One of the commission's charges was to identify the basic ethical principles that should underlie the conduct of biomedical and behavioral research involving human subjects, as well as to develop guidelines. After nearly five years of discussion and collaboration, these guidelines were published. In 1979, a statement of basic ethical principles and guidelines to assist decision-makers in resolving the ethical problems that surround the conduct of research with human subjects appeared in the Federal Register. This became known as the Belmont Report. The report centered around the following three important principles, or general prescriptive judgments:

1. Respect for autonomy of the Persons
2. Beneficence
3. Justice

Later principle of non-maleficence has been added to this list. To apply the general principles to the conduct of research involving humans, the Belmont Report suggested that the following requirements be considered: informed consent, risk/benefit assessment, and the just and fair selection of subjects of research. The Belmont Report remains a touchstone for many bioethicists.

With new challenges in public health and health policy, and with advances in bio-technology, today bioethics is a fast-growing academic and professional area of inquiry. Since the early 1980s, the field has generated at least a dozen English-language journals. In addition, many academic medical centers and some schools of law, engineering and the liberal arts offer degree programs with a specialization in bioethics. Such programs train physicians and nurses, attorneys, philosophers, theologians, health services researchers and even bench scientists.

As a field of inquiry, bioethics received another boost when President Clinton created an Advisory Committee on Human Radiation Experiments, chaired by Ruth Faden of the Johns Hopkins Berman Institute of Bioethics. The committee sought to analyze the following questions:

What is the federal government's responsibility for wrongs and harms to human subjects as a result of experiments with ionizing radiation? What remedies are appropriate for those wronged or harmed? And what lessons learned from studying research standards and practices in the past and present can be applied to the future?

President Clinton directed the Advisory Committee to uncover the U.S. history of human radiation experiments during the period 1944 through 1974. It was in 1944 that the first known human radiation experiment of interest was planned, and in 1974 that the U.S. Department of Health, Education and Welfare adopted regulations governing the conduct of human research, a watershed event in the history of federal protections for human subjects. In addition, the Advisory Committee examined cases in which the government had intentionally released radiation into the environment for research purposes. The Advisory Committee also identified ethical and scientific standards for evaluating these events, and made recommendations to help ensure that wrongdoing could not be repeated.

Today, the field of bioethics struggles with its proper scope. Should it concern itself with the ethical evaluation of all questions involving biology and medicine? Some bioethicists would narrow ethical evaluation only to the morality of medical treatments or technological innovations, and the timing of medical treatment of humans. Others would broaden the scope of ethical evaluation to include the morality of all actions that might help or harm organisms capable of feeling fear and pain, and include within bioethics all such actions if they bear a relation to medicine and biology.

THE PURPOSE OF BIOETHICS

The issues raised by bioethics as a distinct area of academic inquiry are largely answered by the needs of institutions. Bioethicists today are not hired or engaged in conversation (and thus "named") because of their opinions or because they have special skills of reasoning, but because they know and can put to work the enormous body of research and history of discussions about bioethics in a fair, honest and intelligent way, using tools from the different disciplines that "feed" the field. Training programs in bioethics differ in skill sets of faculty and size of program, but across the US, and increasingly globally, they do seem to share a commitment to that goal with few exceptions.

As a result, bioethics has been distinctively created, by institutions, specifically the multi-million dollar commitment of major and minor medical centers to the study of medical ethics as part of the development of curriculum and research efforts. Today it is all but impossible to create a major medical research effort without ethicists to assist. First in the regulatory review of research, the responsibility of the IRB, which can be staffed by persons not trained in ethics in any rigorous way, or trained specifically in the ethical and regulatory aspects of research with human subjects, rather than more comprehensively in bioethics. The second form of assistance is by those who can think in advance of the onset of research about its social, ethical and economic implications.

Ideology and Methodology

Bioethicists often focus on using philosophy to help analyze issues, and philosophical ethicists such as Peter Singer tend to treat the field as a branch of moral or ethical philosophy. However, this approach is sometimes challenged, and bioethics is becoming increasingly interdisciplinary. Many bioethicists come from backgrounds outside of academic philosophy, and some even claim that the methods of analytic philosophy have had a negative effect on the field's development. The percentage of bioethicists with professional backgrounds in health care, especially physicians, has been steadily increasing over time. In fact, the last two Presidents of the primary academic society for bioethicists in the U.S. (the American Society for Bioethics and Humanities) have been physicians. Some bioethicists, especially those who perform ethics consultation in clinical settings, emphasize the practical aspects of bioethics, and view the field as more closely related to clinical practice or public health than philosophy.

Religious bioethicists have developed rules and guidelines on how to deal with these issues from within the viewpoint of their respective faiths. Many religious bioethicists are Jewish, and Christian scholars. Since the Indian traditions of Hinduism, Buddhism, and Jainism considers the sanctity of all life, there is much literature related to the philosophy and ethics related to life in each of these traditions. A growing number of religious scholars from Islam have also become involved in this field. There has been some criticism by liberal Muslims that only the more religiously conservative voices in Islam are being heard on this issue.

Although there are a number of eminently qualified philosophers who approach bioethics from a religious perspective, some Western secular bioethicists are critical of the fact that religious bioethicists are often religious scholars without an academic degree or training in disciplines that pertain to the issues, such as philosophy (wherein the formal study of ethics is usually found), biology or medicine. From the standpoint of bioethicists whose work is secular, the central cause for caution as regards religious bioethics work is that tools and methods should be brought to bear on problems, rather than starting with conclusions, and then looking for justifications. Of course, this criticism does not apply solely, of even to all, forms of religious bioethical work.

In the case of most non-Western cultures a strict separation of religion from philosophy does not exist. In many Asian cultures, there is a lively (and often less dogmatic, but more pragmatic) discussion on bioethical issues. The discussion often refers to common demographic policies which are criticised, as in the case of China. Buddhist bioethics, in general, is characterised by a naturalistic outlook that leads to a rationalistic, pragmatic approach. Buddhist bioethicists include Damien Keown. In India, Vandana Shiva is the leading bioethicist whose speaks from the Hindu tradition. In Africa, and partly also in Latin America, the debate on bioethics frequently focus on its practical relevance in the context of underdevelopment and (national or global) power relations.

The intersection of medical technology, medical practice, and ethical principles has long been an important field of study, but the rapid advance of medical technology has made it perhaps the most important field of ethics today. Every human being is concerned with medicine and health, but they should also be concerned as to whether their health can be maintained in an ethical manner and an ethical environment.

Bioethics is an especially difficult field because it regularly concerns some of the most troubling topics: the nature of life, the nature of death, what sort of life is worth living, what constitutes murder, how we should treat people who are in especially vulnerable and painful circumstances, just what sort of responsibilities any of has to other human beings, and so on. Bioethics is not a wholly independent field - it must, obviously, draw a great deal from other ethical discussions.

At the same time, the way in which medical technology pushes the limits of what we humans can do also pushes the limits of our understanding of such discussions. Medicine today forces us to confront the nature of life and death in a manner that we are not normally accustomed to, but we have to get used to it because it's only going to get worse.

Medicine, Ethics, and Philosophy

Medicine and ethics are by no means strangers - on the contrary, medicine started out as an aspect of early philosophy. What this meant was that was a close integration of medical expertise and medical ethics existed. Those who engaged in research and experiments to determine what could be done in the fight against ill health were also the ones who led the debate over what should be done in that struggle - a very different situation from what we have today where the two tasks tend most often to be separated.

The Need for Bioethics

Is bioethics really such a critical issue for society today? Even if it didn't exist and we had to invent it today, it would involve the application of ethical principles and arguments to medical and biological issues. So what, if anything, is so special or unique about these issues that requires its own field of ethical inquiry?

Principles of Bioethics

Are there any basic principles which discussions of bioethics or medical ethics should ideally start with? The field of bioethics is, after all, very wide ranging - it encompasses just about every ethical issue involving medicine and biology. Without some basic and unifying principles, it would be difficult to imagine considering this a single field of study at all.

THE NEED FOR BIOETHICS

Ethical Dilemmas in Biology & Medicine

Is bioethics really such a critical issue for society today? Even if it didn't exist and we had to invent it today, it would involve the application of ethical principles and arguments to medical and biological issues. So what, if anything, is so special or unique about these issues that requires its own field of ethical inquiry?

Although medical professionals are educated to handle medical triage situations which involve technical questions about who has the best chance of living, neither they nor other members of society are necessarily trained for ethical triage situations. In our pluralistic society, we are faced with a wonderful diversity of values and ethical ideals, but we don't seem able to tell which values need to be employed when and which ethical dilemmas need our most immediate attention.

One of the results seems to be that we are forced to deal with one crisis after another. Our lack of sound reasoning and coherent values prevents us from engaging in the careful, advanced deliberations that would make it easier for us to handle new situations. Bioethics today is too much a matter of crisis management and not enough of reasoned discourse.

Just what are these crises which we keep facing? Probably the most immediately obvious type of crisis is the one occasioned by rapidly advancing medical technology. Our abilities to both understand and manipulate the very essence of who we are, whether that is identified with our DNA or our most private thoughts, improves on an almost daily basis.

For example, what will we do when the first cloned human is created in a laboratory? Much of the basic technology for such an achievement is already in place - it is conceivable that we might be able to do such a thing within the next century. Will it have the same rights as others? Should it even be permitted, legally?

While the advancement of medical technology creates the most obvious source of problems in bioethics, it is certainly not the only one. In the not-too-distant past, almost all of the medical ethics which a doctor had to deal with were confined to the very personal relationship and interaction between doctor and patient; whatever else existed in the field was minimal and of little general concern.

Today, however, the framework of medical ethics has been expanded to include much more. Medical practice is no longer constrained by the relationships within the individual medical practice. We have to deal with massive insurance companies, the allocation of limited medical resources, the amount of time medical residents are forced to work, the privacy of medical records, and so much more.

These issues will only continue to multiply alongside the increasing complexity of modern society. We can either try to deliberate about these issues in advance or we can wait until a crisis occurs and we are forced to deal with it right away, without the chance for careful discussion. Which makes more sense?

A special field of bioethics is needed because, for better or for worse, the coming century will probably be best described as the Biological Century or the Biological Age (in contrast to the Industrial Age that the West so recently experienced). Not only advances in medical science, but advances in many other fields will likely have biological components as well. We can't hide our heads in the sand and pretend that difficult questions aren't on their way - indeed, we already know about many of them, or at least their broad outlines.

A failure to address them now, while we still have time, would be a moral failure and a failure of courage. We should place very close attention to the advances made in medical technology and the changes made in how doctors are expected to work. We should be prepared to ask difficult questions about what is done with new technologies and how medical professionals operate. We all have an important stake in those answers. We deserve good answers.

Bioethics utilizes ethical theories in philosophy in order to approach some of the ethical dilemmas in contemporary clinical medicine. Major ethical systems - Kantian, utilitarian, virtue-centered, and care-oriented - all impact on contemporary bioethical discourse.

Some of the questions addressed by bioethics include: When should life-sustaining treatments like breathing machines or feeding tubes be started, continued or stopped? What should family members and health care professionals do if a patient refuses treatment that promises to be medically helpful? Who should make health care decisions for patients when they are unable to communicate or decide for themselves? What should patients do when they do not understand what professionals are saying and feel they are not offered the opportunity to participate in their own health care decisions?

Medical Ethics and the Law

This field concerns the relationship between clinical bioethics and the law that has evolved as clinical care has become increasingly complex with new medical technologies. It emphasizes legal theories and principles concerning ethical issues in the context of clinical care. Topics include advance directives, proxy decision-making, issues of consent and confidentiality, withholding and withdrawing care, the definition of death, mental competence and related matters.

Ethics of Research and Experimentation

This field concerns the principles of clinical and experimental research ethics and the regulation of research practices, particularly from the perspectives of the Nuremberg code and the Helsinki declaration. Topics include: scientific and research integrity; research with adult and pediatric human subjects; informed consent; vulnerable study populations; privacy and confidentiality of research and clinical records; conflicts of interest; research on animals; and research in third world nations.

Ethical Issues in Death and Dying

This field concerns the ethical issues associated with care of the terminally ill and with death issues more generally. Topics include: death; the definition and diagnosis of brain death; chronic vegetative states; loss of personhood; right-to-life/right-to-die; euthanasia; infanticide; physician-assisted suicide; palliative care; pain management; quality of life and related issues.

Ethical Issues in Health Care Allocation and Government Policy

This field concerns issues related to access to health care resources and on ways of understanding the issues of fairness and justice on an institutional system such as health care. Various models of paying for health care services and the ethical issues inherent in such systems, particularly in settings of limited resources are an important theme. Topics include: use of surrogates, transplantation policy, problems of financing, the allocation of resources, and experimentation.

Ethical Issues of Human Reproduction

This field concerns the various philosophical, legal and ethical issues dealing with human reproduction and considers differing philosophic and ethical positions relating to human reproduction. Topics include genetic engineering, reproductive technologies such as artificial insemination and in vitro fertilization, cloning, sanctity of life, the notion of family, etc.

Religion and Bioethics

This field concerns the various philosophical and ethical considerations of different religious faiths in the particular context of bioethics. Issues include: similarities and differences between religious faith and reasoned justification, the role of faith in morality and ethics, and the relationship of certain established faith traditions (e.g., Christianity, Judiasm, Islam) to particular issues in clinical and experimental medicine.

Ethical Relationships and the Health Care Team

This concerns the role of and relationships between various members of the health care team, focusing on their roles and responsibilities and how they influence decision making and communication regarding ethical issues. Issues concern the appropriate ways to resolve interpersonal difficulties such as challenging or disobeying a superior, reporting or stopping inappropriate behavior, and expressing moral or ethical judgments.

Bioethics Committees and Consulting

This field concerns the workings of hospital and university bioethics committees, institutional review boards, and bioethics consultants, focusing on understanding of nature, purpose and structure of these committees and of the role of bioethicists in such committees. National and international guidelines dealing with experimentation with human subjects, especially the Nuremberg code, are considered.

Ethical Issues in Genetics

This field concerns the bioethical issues present in the rapidly developing area of genetic technology, including the nature and methods of DNA analysis, the concept of genetic disease, genetic testing / screening for various diseases, genetic engineering of plants, animals and humans, and cloning. Social policy issues related to genetically modified foods are also important concerns.

PRINCIPLISM

One particulary popular approach to the analysis of bioethical problems is sometimes known as the "Georgetown School" of bioethics, named after Georgetown University where much of the early work on bioethics originated. This approach to bioethics emphasizes the principles of autonomy (respecting the decisions of autonomous persons), justice (fairness in the distribution of benefits and risks), nonmalfeasance (the duty to avoid causing harm); and beneficence (the duty to provide benefits and to balance benefits against risks). This approach is sometimes also known as "principlism".

BIOETHICS AND MORAL THEORY

Central to bioethics is moral theory. Moral theory can be approached from many viewpoints. The deontological approach to morality (from the Greek word deon, or duty) is based on specific obligations or duties. These can be positive (such as to care for our family) or negative (such as not to steal). This approach is also sometimes called nonconsequentialist since these principles are held to be obligatory regardless of any good or bad consequences of that might result. For example, it is wrong to kill even if it results in great benefit.

Philosophers have subdivided deontological theories into a number of categories, of which the concept of the "categorical imperative" developed by the 18th-century German philosopher Immanuel Kant is the best known. He said that we must "treat people as an end, and never as a means to an end", by which he meant that we should always treat people with humanity and dignity, and never use individuals as "mere instruments" as a means to our own happiness. Another version of the categorical imperative is: "Always act in such a way that the maxim of your action can be willed as a universal law." Other deontological approaches include "duty theory" (defining duties to God, duties to oneself, and duties to others), "rights theory" (concerned with rights that all people have, and which the rest of us must respect), and a more recent theory developed by W.D. Ross, which emphasizes prima facie duties.

The consequentialist approach to moral theory determines moral responsibility by weighing the consequences of one's actions. According to the consequentialist view, correct moral actions are determined by a cost-benefit analysis concerning the consequences of an action.

Several subtypes of consequentialism have been proposed: the view that an action is morally correct if its consequences are more positive or favorable than negative to the person performing the action (ethical egoism), the view that an action is morally correct if the consequences of that action are more positive than negative to everyone except the person doing the action (ethical altruism), and the view that an action is morally correct if the action's consequences are more positive than negative to everyone (utilitarianism).

Any good moral theory should have a set of traits that defines them as being good. These characteristics are needed to avoid a number of philosophical flaws that might otherwise occur. These include: bias, cultural imperialism / cultural ideology, prejudice, racism, sexism and other defects in logic and thinking. I would hold that the following are desirable traits of any good moral theory. It should be consistent – i.e., yielding similar results in similar settings. It should be universal - i.e., if the theory applies to one individual, then it should apply to all individuals. It should be intuitive – i.e., the theory fits our moral intuition.

Other individuals might add other characteristics to this list, such a need for the theory to be understandable by nonphilosophers (certainly a requirement for any practical theory), or the need for the theory not to be based on any religious teachings (although I feel that this is already covered by my requirement above). Others might add the requirements of being time-invariant (that the principles hold true over time) and trans-cultural (that the principles apply to all cultures), but I view these also as being covered by requirement. Still others might state that any moral theory must respect all forms of human life, no matter how degraded., while animal rights advocates might emphasize that a moral theory must necessitate respect for all sentient life forms, not just humans. Finally, Princeton's Professor Peter Singer would likely take issue with my third requirement that a moral theory be intuitive – his moral positions are often taken to be unintuitive and repugnant when first explained, especially in the matters of euthanasia and infanticide, although he makes his case forcefully and lucidly in his many writings.

Professor Paul Taylor, well-known for his writings in the domain of environmental ethics, argues that six characteristics are necessary for a philosophical principle to be a moral rule: generality, universality, priority, disinterestedness, publicity, and substantive impartiality. While his focus is on environmental ethics as opposed to bioethics, it can be seen that his views are substantially similar to mine once the meaning of the terms he uses are fully understood.

Beauchamp and Childress offer a number of useful notions on morality in the first chapter of their classic bioethics text, but their focus is not on developing a list of specific characteristics as, for example, Taylor has done. Still, their second chapter discusses this matter at some length, introducing requirements of clarity, coherence, completeness, simplicity, explanatory power, justificatory power and practicability. Finally, with respect to people's personal beliefs in the development of a good ethical theory, as discussed in requirement above, a good moral theory should be intuitive with respect to existing beliefs, but only when the personal beliefs meet the other requirements of consistency, time-invariance etc. as discussed above.

UTILITARIANISM

Why does the moral theory of Utilitarianism seem to falter when it is applied to questions of social or individual justice?

Utilitarianism is a school of philosophical thought frequently identified with the writings of Jeremy Bentham and John Stuart Mill. In more recent years it has undergone a number of refinements, such as "Preference Utilitarianism", advocated by Professor Peter Singer. Classical Utilitarianism advocates the principle of providing "the greatest happiness to the greatest number" as the basis for assessing the morality of various actions, while "Preference Utilitarianism" advocates the principle of meeting the preferences of the greatest number of people. Thus good variously consists in providing maximal happiness (or satisfying people's preferences, in the case of Preference Utilitarianism) and the rightness of an action depends directly or indirectly on its yielding such outcomes.

However, while Utilitarianism has had a strong influence of the intellectual landscape of philosophical discourse and, in particular, in ethical theory, Utilitarianism is often seen to falter when it is applied to questions of social or individual justice. In particular, Utilitarianism sometimes violates common-sense notions of justice. Because Utilitarianism seeks to maximize the total amount of a particular "utility" (like happiness or preferences) over an entire society or social group, it seeks whichever arrangement achieves maximum utility. But such an arrangement might be achieved by distributing benefits and burdens in a way that violates common notions of justice. For instance, the use of slaves might greatly help maximize the net happiness in a society, but common-sense notions of justice almost always take slavery to be wrong (with apologies to both Aristotle and Thomas Jefferson, who were both great intellectuals yet were slave owners).

Another serious criticism of Utilitarianism is that under the goal of maximizing happiness or some other utility, the wishes and desires of sadists and perverts are lumped in with the wishes and desires of everyone else when an overall determination of utility is made. By espousing a system in which the satisfaction of all desires are to be maximized, Utilitarianism can end up violating our intuitive precepts of natural justice.

John Rawls takes the position that we must reject Utilitarianism and instead develop a deeper understanding of what is right and wrong as a basis for making ethical decisions. What is needed, Rawls argues, is moral theory with justice at its core. That being said, other philosophers have proposed extensions to the classical utilitarian model to deal with some of the limitations identified above. One example is "Negative Utilitarianism", a moral philosophy aimed at producing the least amount of suffering throughout the world.

EQUITY ISSUES IN HEALTH CARE

In offering medical services there are often two kinds of health care systems to consider. First, in many countries there is a public system (funded primarily by taxes) that is usually accessible yet often limited in its resources. Then there is often also a private health care system, funded primarily via payments by private insurance or by occasional private individuals paying cash. Some countries have a predominantly public health care system (for instance, the Canadian system is almost entirely public, except for cosmetic procedures and the like), while some countries like the USA have a predominantly private health care system. The British system has both a public National Health Service as well as a thriving private system that has arisen in the face of the many shortcomings present in the National Health Service. While resource limitations are a problem with all health systems, the problem is usually far worse in the public systems funded through taxation. As a result, many individuals involved in health policy research are seeking to determine which clinical services are most valuable and appropriate and which ones are of more limited value. Their motivation is to make the best use of public funds by only offering those procedures known to be most effective, and not offering procedures that are of very limited or no benefit.

The fact is that some common medical practices have no rational clinical basis in the sense that they provide no benefit relative to the potential risks. Perhaps the best known example is that of newborn circumcision, which is still carried out in 27% of Canadian newborn boys. Other practices such as "female circumcision" can be frankly mutilating and even downright harmful, yet may be considered acceptable or even desirable in some cultures.

In a public health care system with limited resources, it makes sense either not to offer such procedures (in the case of male circumcision) or to explicitly forbid them when they are obviously harmful (as in the case of female circumcision). This is not to suggest that all clinically unnecessary procedures should always be unavailable – only that they should not be offered by the public health care system funded by tax money.

The Oregon Health Plan (OHP) has been widely heralded as a landmark innovation in public health care policy that rations public medical resources by a system of prioritizing funding for health care. This is done through a process of systematically ranking publicly offered medical services, an approach that has drawn substantial international interest as a rational model of medical resource allocation.

In 1989, Oregon enacted legislation to provide basic health care to all residents on Medicaid, their public health care system. This required that services be prioritized to determine what would or would not be covered – effectively establishing a rationing plan.

To do this, the Oregon legislature created a Health Services Commission charged with producing a list of health care services ranked in priority "according to comparative benefits of each service to the entire population being served." They heard testimony of numerous panels of physicians from every specialty and assessed how well each treatment that might be offered affected quality of life. From this they established a "cost-effectiveness value" for each "condition-treatment pair". The final product was a priority list of 709 condition-treatment pairs in ranked order. Based on the available state funds, a line was drawn on the list - any treatment above the line was covered; any treatment below the line was not. This turned out to be at the 587th condition-treatment pair.

While the Oregon system is not without its critics , the plan strikes me as a particularly fair and rational approach based on a process of public consultation coupled with clinical efficacy research. I would advocate this model as a good starting point for meeting the various needs and demands of a diverse population. This is not to suggest that the plan would necessarily apply to all residents – only those getting publicly-funded health care would be participate, and wealthier individuals with private insurance would participate in a different (more generous) plan.

Finally, there are a number of practices that are harmful to patients to the extent that they should be forbidden even when well-meaning individuals sometimes seek them. These include the previously mentioned practice of female circumcision, a number of dangerous quack remedies, and possibly the practice of euthanasia.

Deciding which ineffective or potentially harmful practices should be tolerated (as we do with male circumcision), and which ones should be forbidden (as with female circumcision) is not always an easy task, but application of the principle of nonmalfience is certainly one approach that has special merit.

Still, the principle of nonmalfience may sometimes be in direct conflict with the principle of patient autonomy in the cases of patients seeking ineffective or dangerous treatments. In my book, the principle of nonmalfience takes absolute priority. After all, was it not Hypocrites who said "First do no harm."

Appendix

The International Society for Equity in Health (www.iseqh.org) seeks to "promote equity in health and health services internationally through education, research, publication, communication and charitable support." It is concerned with exactly the sort of questions that have been raised here: How does one ensure fairness in access to health care resources? What procedures should not be made publicly available in a socialized health care system? How do we deal with cultural and economic factors that impact on the demand for health care services? They begin by offering two working definitions:

Equity in Health: The absence of systematic and potentially remediable differences in one or more aspects of health across populations or population groups defined socially, economically, demographically, or geographically.

Inequity in health: Systematic and potentially remediable differences in one or more aspects of health across populations or population groups defined socially, economically, demographically, or geographically. Also, the journal for the society, the International Journal for Equity in Healt, features a small number of articles that are helpful to address these issues. These and other sources identify a number of questions that need answering:

- How is fairness in a health care system to be assessed?
- Should health equity be measured at the individual or the group level?
- To what extent are health status inequalities sensitive to the type of health measure used?

The interested reader is referred to these resources for more information.

DISTRIBUTIVE JUSTICE

"In a situation of unmet need, with patients dying daily for the want of a donor liver, what is fair to all patients is to have approximately the same opportunity of receiving a donor liver." Jeffrey Crippin MD, Baylor University

Beauchamp and Childress (4th Edition, page 228) discuss various standards of fairness in the context of distributive justice. These are:

1. To each person an equal share
2. To each person according to need
3. To each person according to effort
4. To each person according to contribution
5. To each person according to merit
6. To each person according to free-market exchanges

These standards of fairness may be explored in the context of three commonly described models of distributive justice:

- Egalitarian model - where individuals have equal access to goods and services
- Utilitarian model - where goods and services are provided to those who are likely to benefit the most
- Libertarian model - where individuals rights and resources govern access to goods and services

Which model one agrees with most will depend to some extent on whether one views health care as a right (implying a right to universal access to health care), views health care as a need (where people with the greatest need have highest priority and people with similar needs treated similarly), or views health care as a market commodity.

Let us now consider the words of Dr. Crippin: "In a situation of unmet need, with patients dying daily for the want of a donor liver, what is fair to all patients is to have approximately the same opportunity of receiving a donor liver." While a single sentence of this kind is usually inadequate to express a complex philosophical position, Dr. Crippin's statement appears to be an expression of an Egalitarian model. In this model of social justice, one gives equal consideration to all interests while treating everyone as equals. As a result, individuals in need have equal access to goods and services. Note also that when Beauchamp and Childress write "To each person an equal share" they are invoking an Egalitarian model of medical services.

Notice that Crippin does not explicitly emphasize the degree of need in his statement. He does not say: "In a situation of unmet need, with patients dying daily for the want of a donor liver, what is fair to all patients is to have those individuals in greatest need to be given priority over those patients with a lesser need." Such an approach would reflect a Utilitarian model, in which medical resources are provided on the basis of maximal medical benefit. In the Libertarian model medical services are merely a market commodity subject to free-market conditions, and a fair distribution of medical resources occurs as long as they are distributed without force or fraud in a free-market economy. When Beauchamp and Childress write "To each person according to free-market exchanges" they are invoking a Libertarian model of medical services.

One common view is that any ethically appropriate model for organ allocation must take into account issues related to benefit and need., and that those patients who both have a strong need for a transplant and will strongly benefit from a transplant should get priority over patients with either less of a need or who would be expected to obtain less of a benefit. This is a Utilitarian viewpoint based primarily on clinical factors. And, in fact, this is more or less how things are done in the real clinical world. For instance, according to the American Medical Association criteria for organ allocation include:

1. The likelihood of benefit to the patient;
2. The impact of treatment in improving the quality of the patient's life;
3. The duration of benefits;
4. The urgency of the patient's condition; and
5. In some cases, the amount of resources required for successful treatment

This particular set of criteria for organ allocation appears to me to be a particularly well thought out set of Utilitarian principles that is superior to the simpler Egalitarian model advocated by Crippin in that if takes into factors like benefit, quality of life and urgency that are not explicitly addressed by the Egalitarian model. I would cast my vote for this approach.

MEDICAL FUTILITY THEORY

Helga Wanglie broke her hip in December 1989 after a fall in her home. She was 86. She was treated in hospital and moved to a nursing home, but a month later she was readmitted for respiratory complications and needed to be placed on a ventilator. Attempts to wean her were unsuccessful. As a result, she was transferred to a long-term care facility that specialized in ventilated patients. While there, she suffered a cardiac arrest with anoxia that resulted in severe, irreversible brain damage. She remained in a persistent vegetative state. Meanwhile, she also remained in a state of permanent ventilator dependency.

Because of her dismal prognosis, the medical staff suggested that her family consider termination of treatment. However, the family decided against any withdrawal of care, as she was apparently heard to have said "If anything happens to me, I want everything done". The matter went to court. In its decision, the court rejected the hospital's position and turned over full guardianship to Helga's 87 year-old husband. Helga Wanglie died of multisystem organ failure on July 4, 1991. Medical bills totaled approximately $750,000.

If one were searching for a case to use for starting a classroom discussion on futile care theory, this case would be an excellent starting point. Few clinicians would disagree that Helga Wanglie's case was completely hopeless, and almost all would also agree that there would be no clinical value in continuing extraordinary measures such as mechanical ventilation. Yet Helga Wanglie's husband fought for continued treatment of his wife despite these facts. His conflict with the medical profession highlights many of the issues involved in futile care ethics.

Medical Futility Theory

The concept of futility has had historic importance in medicine. According to Drane and Coulehan, for Hippocratic physicians, attempting a futile treatment was a display of ignorance. They also note that contemporary ethical standards published by the Council on Ethical and Judicial Affairs of the American Medical Association (AMA) show continuity with this tradition: "Physicians should not provide or seek compensation for services that are known to be unnecessary or worthless." Drane and Coulehan recognize, however, that patients and their families may not agree:

'Traditionally, applying the principle that physicians do not provide treatments when the interventions at their disposal do not produce medical benefits has been relatively straightforward. However, with the growing importance of patient autonomy and informed consent in treatment decisions, ethicists must now balance this principle with the principle of patient self-determination.'

'A patient's right to choose or refuse treatment is limited by the physician's right (and duty) to practice medicine responsibly. Bizarre or destructive choices made by a patient are not sacrosanct simply because the patient made them. In some cases, physicians may choose not to act on patient decisions that appear to be unreasonably destructive.'

'Physicians also have a right to refuse to provide futile treatments (i.e., interventions that might be physiologically effective in some sense but cannot benefit a patient). Patients themselves have a right to provide input into what would constitute a "benefit" for them, but physicians should be able to decide when a particular treatment is futile based on their knowledge of the treatment's effects and its likely impact on a patient's quality of life.'

Ethical principles dealing with medical futility can be developed based on the traditional bioethical principle of beneficence, as well based on traditional physician values identified above. Under the principle of beneficence, which directs physicians to apply their skill and knowledge only for the good of their patient, physicians should not provide treatment known not to produce clinical benefits. Some authors go further. For example, McGee et al. state: "Withholding futile treatments supports the ethical principles of both nonmaleficence (do no harm) and beneficence (relieve suffering)." Finally, the Catholic Health Association of the United States has issued a statement of principles on the issue that emphasizes similar principles. Modern arguments against futile care generally center on two issues. First, futile care has no possibility of achieving a good outcome and serves only to prolong death. No physical or spiritual benefit comes from such care. Futile care also prolongs the grieving process and frequently raises false hope. Also, futile care can be very difficult on caregivers, who may see themselves as forced to act against the best interests of their patient.

Secondly, in a setting of limited resources, futile care involves the expenditure of resources that could be used by other patients with a good likelihood of achieving a positive outcome. This second argument would appear to be strong in those nations with socialized health care systems.

Families Seeking Futile Care

The above not withstanding, families occasionally seek to ensure that their loved ones get heroic or extraordinary care even in the absence of any likelihood of clinical benefit. However, in most of these cases the family eventually comes to realize that there is no possibility of a good outcome from such efforts, and end up agreeing with the clinical team. But not always.

One famous case is that of Baby K, an anencephalic infant. The infant's mother wanted the hospital to continue with advanced supportive care (primarily ventilatory support) against the wishes of the clinical team, and sought legal support for her position. Ms. H. knew of her baby's condition from the second trimester of her pregnancy, but, motivated by a strong religious conviction that "all life is precious" and that God alone should decide how long the baby would live, she remained adamant that Baby K. be kept alive as long as possible.

The hospital's position was that such care would be futile. At the trial [Matter of Baby K. 16 F.3d 590 (4th Cir. 1994), n. 9 at 598.], expert testimony was given to demonstrate that provision of ventilator support for anencephalic infants goes beyond the accepted standard of care. The legal team for Baby K's mother adhered to a religious sanctity-of-life principle as the basis for their case. In the end, in a particularly controversial decision, the U. S. District Court ruled that the hospital caring for Baby K must put her on a mechanical ventilator whenever she had trouble breathing. In particular, the court interpreted the Emergency Medical Treatment and Active Labor Act (EMTALA) to require continued ventilation for the infant. The wording of this act requires that patients who present with a medical emergency must get "such treatment as may be required to stabilize the medical condition" before the patient is transferred to another facility. The court took the position that "it is beyond the limits of our judicial function to address the moral or ethical propriety of providing emergency stabilizing medical treatment to anencephalic infants. We are bound to interpret federal statutes in accordance with their plain language..." As a result of the decision, Baby K was kept alive much longer than most anencephalic babies, living to age 2½.

The cases of Baby K and Helga Wanglie vividly demonstrate how family and clinical caregivers may sometimes see matters very differently. Such differences usually reflect very different philosophical vistas, and cannot always simply be dismissed as being based on ignorance on the part of the family. For instance, some people take the "santity of life" argument to its extreme, arguing that all efforts to sustain life should be made wherever clinically possible, no matter how degraded that life may be. While much has been written to refute this position (see, for instance, the writings of Peter Singer), such (usually always secular) counterarguments generally have little or no impact on individuals invoking such arguments based on personal religious beliefs.

Some other individuals may argue that clinical care should be a market commodity that one should be able to purchase just like cruise vacations or luxury automobiles, as long as the purchaser of the clinical services has the necessary funds and as long as other patients are not being denied access to clinical resources as a result. In this model, Helga Wanglie should be able to get ICU care until funding vanished.

In my view, this market-oriented viewpoint is either naïve or wrong in several respects. First, in almost all such cases the funding comes from insurance carriers, who must avoid "wasting" funds to ensure that adequate funds are available for other clients. Secondly, competition for ICU resources can be intense, and providing ICU care to patients who will not benefit from them only makes access more difficult for patients for which ICU care would prove to be clinically beneficial. Finally, to view clinical care is a mere market commodity or service is to detach it from its underlying dignity and humanity.

The Case Against Medical Futility Theory

Are there, then, any potential problems with futile care theory? Could it be that the issues are not be as cut and dried as the clinical community would have it?

In this respect, it is helpful to consider matters from the perspective of those who disagree with the traditional clinical view regarding futile care. For Helga Wanglie and her husband, all human life - even a degraded and permanently unconscious human life – is still taken to be valuable, regardless of any considerations of quality of life. Similarly, the mother of Baby K no doubt saw her infant's life as infinitely valuable, even if incapable of a conscious existence.

One criticism of futile care theory is that the caregivers sometimes see things only from the perspective of their training, and thus seek to be the only decision-makers in these matters. However, as noted by Weijer and Elliott, for clinicians to be the sole decision-makers in these situations amounts to saying to families, "Your values don't count."

Weijer and Elliott go on to note that different viewpoints concerning the goals of treatment may form the basis for disagreements between families and clinicians:

> *"... judgments of futility make sense only in relation to a specified goal: an intervention may be futile if the aim is to cure an underlying disease but effective if the aim is to keep the patient alive. Yet in the most controversial cases in which futility is invoked the disagreement between doctors and families is not about the probability that an intervention will work but about the goals that it will serve."*

> *"... the concept of medical futility is a tarbaby. It cannot do what it is asked to do, and trying to force the issue*

won't produce a solution; it will produce a mess. When patients or families demand treatment that is unlikely to produce a good outcome doctors ought to disclose carefully the treatment options, the likely outcomes, and the probabilities of attaining those outcomes. Clearly, both the doctor's judgment and that of the patient (or family) are essential to the decision making process. ... This can be achieved only by an open and frank dialogue. Invoking futility ensures, if anything, that this will not occur."

Another problem confronting futile care theory is that invoking the principle of futility is sometimes direct conflict with the principle of patient autonomy. As the case of Helga Wanglie illustrates, when families make end-of-life decisions in conflict with caregivers, and the case ends up in courts, the courts are often strongly influenced by concerns for patient's right to autonomy. As Weijer and Elliott note : "Futility is not the ethical trump card that some would like it to be."

Another problem with futile care theory is that even defining the notion of clinical futility can be challenging. McGee et al emphasize that various definitions are used in the literature:

"The term medical futility has been used to describe life-or-death situations in which proposed treatments will fail to prolong quality life, achieve the patient's key goals for medical care, achieve a critical physiologic effect on the body, or result in a therapeutic benefit for the patient. Another definition of futility states that "if a treatment merely preserves permanent unconsciousness or cannot end dependence on intensive medical care, the treatment should be considered futile." In an attempt to give a quantitative definition of futility, some have suggested that treatments with less than a 1% chance of benefiting patients should be considered futile."

The Ethics Committee of The Society of Critical Care Medicine has attempted to clarify the concept of futility with a policy statement. They emphasize, among other things, that care that is extremely unlikely to be beneficial is not necessarily futile in nature]. They write:

> *"Treatments should be defined as futile only when they will not accomplish their intended goal. Treatments that are extremely unlikely to be beneficial, are extremely costly, or are of uncertain benefit may be considered inappropriate and hence inadvisable, but should not be labeled futile. Futile treatments constitute a small fraction of medical care. Thus, employing the concept of futile care in decision-making will not primarily contribute to a reduction in resource use. Nonetheless, communities have a legitimate interest in allocating medical resources by limiting inadvisable treatments. Communities should seek to do so using a rationale that is explicit, equitable, and democratic; that does not disadvantage the disabled, poor, or uninsured; and that recognizes the diversity of individual values and goals. Policies to limit inadvisable treatment should have the following characteristics: a) be disclosed in the public record; b) reflect moral values acceptable to the community; c) not be based exclusively on prognostic scoring systems; d) articulate appellate mechanisms; and e) be recognized by the courts. Healthcare organizations that control payment have a profound influence on treatment decisions and should formally address criteria for determining when treatments are inadvisable and should share accountability for those decisions."*

Finally, futility theory may be challenged on a statistical basis. While scenarios like providing ICU care to the brain dead patient or the anencephalic patient when organ harvesting is not possible or practical are easily identifiable as being completely futile, many other situations usually taken to be futile are far less clear. For instance, should surgeons attempt a heroic clinical rescue in a 99 year old unconscious patient with a ruptured abdominal aortic aneurysm, even though survival with a good outcome would be so very unlikely as to warrant publication of the case as a clinical case report? Various bleak clinical scenarios will vary in their degree of futility. For instance, when elderly patients sustain large third degree burns, mortality is almost guaranteed. This is similarly true for elderly patients sustaining massive trauma. But in many of these cases it can still be very difficult to accurately predict outcome.

As Weijer and Elliott note:

"... problems will arise with any criterion that allows doctors to rely solely on their own experience. Their recollections are biased towards cases with a poor outcome. Moreover, doctors' judgments about individual cases are not accurate enough to allow them to claim reliably that a given person has (for instance) less than a 1% chance of responding to treatment. While the agreement of several colleagues about a prognosis may improve the judgment's reliability, support from the literature may be lacking. Even if empirical data exist on a particular intervention, the vast majority of "negative" clinical trials have a sample size that is too small to provide strong enough evidence to rule out a small treatment effect."

VIRTUE IN HEALTH CARE

"Virtue is harder to be got than a knowledge of the world; and, if lost in a young man, is seldom recovered." John Locke

Wisdom is knowing what to do next; virtue is doing it. David Star Jordan

According to the Internet Encyclopedia of Philosophy "virtue theory is the view that the foundation of morality is the development of good character traits, or virtues". According to this model, a person is good or virtuous to the extent that he or she has virtues and lacks vices. Another way of looking at the matter is to state that there are certain ideals, such as the pursuit of excellence or dedication to the common good, which we should strive for and which permit the full development of our humanity. Virtues may be viewed as attitudes or character traits that enable us to develop this potential. The virtues of everyday life include generosity, fidelity, self-control, honesty, truthfulness, integrity, bravery, courage, justice, patience, prudence, fortitude, tolerance, and countless others. In fact, some virtue theorists have identified over 100 virtuous character traits.

However, different social groups may emphasize different "virtue sets". For instance, the Boy Scout virtues are " trustworthy, loyal, helpful, friendly, courteous, kind, obedient, cheerful, thrifty, brave, clean and reverend". By contrast, some other social groups (Satanists and Hell's Angels members come to mind) would not consider all of these character traits to be virtuous. Indeed one man's virtue may be another man's vice, as in the often-used term "generous to a fault".

Minogue details five virtues that are associated with medicine. He holds these to be:

1. Compassion
2. Courage
3. Tolerance
4. Honesty
5. Faithfulness (or Fidelity, or Loyalty)

Missing in this list is a trait that most patients want above all in a physician or nurse – competence. The importance of professional competence as a virtue has been emphasized elsewhere. For instance, the College of Human Medicine at Michigan State University has developed a set of "desirable professional attributes" that are used as examples of "professional virtue" for guiding medical students. These attributes fall into six categories:

1. Competence
2. Honesty
3. Compassion
4. Respect for Others
5. Professional Responsibility
6. Social Responsibility

While there is considerable overlap in these lists (for instance, both lists include compassion and honestly as desirable traits, and Minogue's "tolerance" trait is similar to the "respect for others" trait in the College of Human Medicine list), the differences are nonetheless striking. Also, some individuals do not regard "courage" as an especially important trait in clinical practice, except in the context that exercising honesty and responsibility in hostile settings can sometimes require considerable courage. Some individuals would argue that both these lists should be combined to make a list of virtues for physicians. The combined list one might then propose would be:

1. Competence
2. Honesty
3. Compassion
4. Respect for Others
5. Professional Responsibility
6. Social Responsibility
7. Courage
8. Loyalty

Yet it is also appropriate to consider even more virtues that might apply, such as resourcefulness, patience, integrity, wisdom and prudence. To the extent that these traits overlap with the list above it is not necessary to explicitly list them. Still, they are important clinical virtues.

One interesting issue is whether the traits of the virtuous physician and the traits of the virtuous nurse are similar. Many individuals would argue that they are indeed similar, that there are no more differences between the traits of the virtuous physician and the traits of the virtuous nurse then there are between the virtuous traits of the various medical specialties. There are, of course, differences between what nurses and physician do, just as there are differences between the various medical specialties do. But perhaps these differences are so great that different sets of virtues are necessarily implied. Both groups have the same goals in mind for their patient, and both groups share a similar clinical worldview. The fact that one group frequently implements orders from the other is not, in my view, an overriding issue. Nor perpahs should one regard it as particularly relevant that nurses are often said to come from a tradition of caring, while physicians are often said to come from a tradition of science and reason. The reality is that both traditions are major influences on both nurses and physicians in today's clinical world.

What is a Gene?

When Charles Darwin devised his theory of evolution through natural selection in 1859, it required that offspring inherit something from their parents. In 1865 Gregor Mendel described the basic principles of how this inheritance works, which he deduced from his famous observations on pea plants. Both men reached their conclusions with no knowledge of the molecules that underlie these principles, and it took much longer to establish the physical basis of inheritance. Although the term 'gene' was coined in the early 1900s to describe a unit of inheritance, it was not until the 1940s that work on bacteria proved that genes were contained in molecules of DNA (deoxyribonucleic acid).

James Watson and Francis Crick described the double helical structure of the DNA molecule in 1953, ushering in an age of molecular understanding of inheritance. In the ensuing years it became clear that all genes are encoded by DNA, which exists as enormously long molecules, packaged into chromosomes - dense bodies found in the nucleus of a cell that are visible through a microscope. A DNA molecule is made up of specific sequences of four different chemical units, called bases, abbreviated A, C, G and T [A = adenine; C = cytosine; G = guanine; T = thymine.]. These sequences contain the information that is inherited, and that help to determine the characteristics of an organism.

How does the information contained in genes get converted to black hair, or red flowers? Very basically, the DNA sequences are copied to molecules of RNA (ribonucleic acid), which can then act to string together proteins according to the original pattern. And proteins are essential to the structure and chemistry of all living cells. As our knowledge of the molecular basis of inheritance has grown, however, our definition of a gene has evolved. Most scientists would now agree that:

each gene is a region of DNA containing 'coding' sequences (which determine what products the gene produces), plus various control regions that regulate the activity of the geneall genes encode an RNA molecule, and the majority of these RNA molecules encode a protein product.

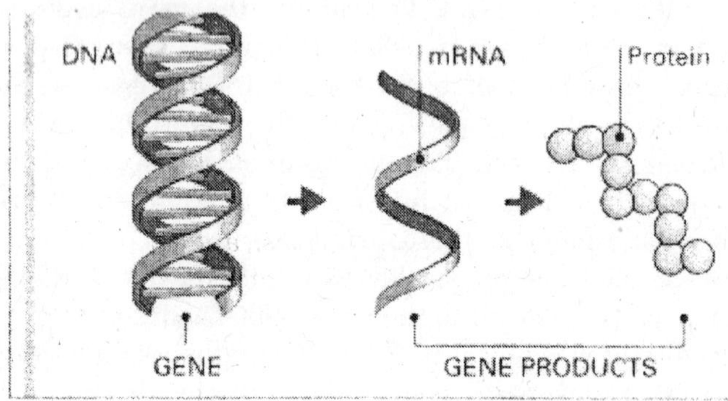

What we have learnt in the last few years is that quite a few important genes produce RNA that does not encode proteins, and many important functions have been found for these non-coding RNA molecules. So the molecular view of a gene is a region of DNA that encodes a gene product - either an RNA alone, or an RNA that ultimately encodes a protein.

In higher organisms the gene can be spread over large regions of DNA. Some DNA regions or sequences within a gene (exons) are reflected in the final RNA, but they are interspersed with DNA sequences (introns) that are not represented in the final RNA. Although the entire gene is copied into RNA, the RNA from intron regions is deleted by a process called splicing, leaving an RNA molecule (messenger RNA) which can then be used by the cell to produce a specific protein. It is very common for one gene to produce several RNAs that have undergone splicing in different ways, often resulting in the production of more than one protein by a gene.

A gene consists of not only of those regions that are copied into RNA, but also several elements or sections of DNA, often located adjacent to the gene, that regulate the copying of the gene into RNA. These control regions, called promoters and enhancers, are the sites where various molecules can bind to switch a gene on or off, or to adjust its level of activity.

Why are Genes of Interest?

As we have seen, genes are a set of instructions that guide the structure and chemistry of cells. Humans have about 30,000 genes, although each gene may produce several different RNA or protein products. Scientists strive to understand what genes are and how they work so that they can better appreciate the biology of living things, and how the natural variability of genes contributes to such things as population diversity, evolution, and the occurrence of disease. This knowledge can then be applied in many ways, such as in the detection or diagnosis of disease, for producing new drugs, or in new approaches to the treatment of disease.

Genes are a vital component of the hugely complex biological systems that we call life. Although they play a central role in the cell, their expression is moderated by interactions with various other components of the cell, such as proteins, hormones and other substances. The development and biology of an organism is also shaped by complex external influences. These include an organism's physical and social environments, which are in continual interplay with its genetic make-up. What an organism looks like, how it functions, and its role in any ecosystem is a continual interaction between all these influences.

The complexity of living systems means that genes do not operate in isolation, and they do not 'control' an organism's life. But they are a vital part of an organism's life, and we can understand biological systems better if we understand the role that genes play.

Why Carry out Genetic Modification?

Our ability to fully understand the structure and function of individual genes only came once techniques for isolating genes were available. This required removing DNA from the chromosomes of complex organisms (such as humans) and introducing small fragments of the isolated DNA into simple chromosomes, such as those contained in bacterial viruses (phages) or plasmids (small, circular DNA molecules that exist in many bacteria). These recombinant DNA methods, pioneered in the early 1970s, allowed the purification and detailed study of individual genes. Systematic application of recombinant DNA methods over the last 30 years, culminating in the Human Genome Project, has allowed a complete description of the sequence of three billion DNA bases that make up the 23 human chromosomes that contain our genes.

Thus a primary motivation for applying genetic modification techniques was to better understand the nature and function of genes. Biotechnological applications of these methods, in which genes are isolated, modified and expressed in genetically modified organisms for medical benefit, also became a very powerful motivating force.

How are Genes Isolated?

Some descriptions of genetic investigation seem to imply that scientists work with single genes, but in fact the original DNA must somehow be copied millions of times in order to get enough pure material to work with. This copying can be done in two main ways.

1. The first method, *recombinant DNA*, involves introducing the DNA into a living organism, and allowing that organism to replicate, thereby replicating the inserted DNA. To do this, the DNA is broken into pieces and introduced into a plasmid or phage (see above), which is capable of existing and replicating in a bacterial or yeast cell. As a result, each bacterial or yeast cell carries many copies of one recombinant DNA molecule, and the collection of cells which together carry all the DNA or genes of the donor organism is referred to as a library of DNA fragments. When these methods were first developed they were referred to as molecular cloning, as each fragment of DNA is 'cloned' (or copied) by the natural DNA-copying mechanism of the bacterium. Once a recombinant DNA library has been built up, it is possible to search through the yeast or bacterial cells

and separate out those that carry the desired DNA fragment. This provides a renewable source of the purified fragment, which may contain a whole gene, part of a gene or several genes. The libraries of millions of bacteria or yeast cells can be easily propagated or stored for many years in a frozen state. These recombinant bacteria and yeast are genetically modified organisms.

2. The second method, *polymerase chain reaction (PCR)*, requires detailed knowledge of the gene DNA sequence, and allows precise copying of a defined segment of DNA, such that many billions of copies can be produced in one or two hours. This process depends on a bacterial protein that naturally copies DNA, and does not require the genetic modification of any organisms.

There are two possible sources of DNA for the above approaches: DNA from chromosomes (genomic DNA), which is extracted by chemical methods, and complementary DNA (cDNA), which is synthesised using RNA purified from cells as a template to guide the copying. This cDNA doesn't usually exist in nature, because it is a copy of an RNA molecule that has been subjected to splicing, so all of the intron sequences are missing. The cDNA is produced in a test tube using a virus protein that can copy RNA into DNA.

There are two possible sources of DNA for the above approaches: DNA from chromosomes (genomic DNA), which is extracted by chemical methods, and complementary DNA (cDNA), which is synthesised using RNA purified from cells as a template to guide the copying. This cDNA doesn't usually exist in nature, because it is a copy of an RNA molecule that has been subjected to splicing, so all of the intron sequences are missing. The cDNA is produced in a test tube using a virus protein that can copy RNA into DNA.

What Happens when a Gene is Moved from one Organism to Another?

After a gene has been isolated, it can be modified before introducing it into another organism. These modifications will usually be carried out by a combination of methods, often involving PCR and the use of bacterial or yeast recombinant clones. Typically, a modification may involve replacing the normal control regions of the isolated gene so that the gene will function in a different organism or in different tissue. For example, if the goal is to express the gene in yeast to make a useful protein, control regions that normally function in yeast may be required. Similarly, if the gene product is to be expressed in cow's milk, control regions that normally function in the mammary gland may be inserted.

Most often, a cDNA copy of a gene is used to introduce a gene into another organism. This is because the intron sequences present in the genomic (chromosomal) version of a gene often make it too large to easily manage. The cDNA version is an abbreviated copy that usually contains all the information needed to make a gene product, but which is much simpler to handle than the genomic version. Further alterations are often made to the gene before introducing it into another organism.

Once the finalised version of the modified gene is ready it can be introduced into another organism by a wide variety of means, depending on the kind of organism, but in every case the DNA is scooped up by the organism's own cell machinery. For mice, we might inject the purified DNA into fertilised eggs, plants may be infected with bacteria carrying the modified gene, and cells in culture can be encouraged to take up the modified DNA by pulsing them with electricity or treating them with chemicals.

The modified DNA will usually be picked up and integrated into the chromosome of the host organism somewhat randomly. Often the modified DNA becomes inserted into the large regions of chromosomal DNA that lie between genes, but it can be integrated within or close to a gene and either disrupt that gene or alter its normal expression. This may have unexpected effects, usually by causing a mutation, which means the transgenic organism will differ unpredictably from a non-transgenic organism. At least two strategies are used to minimise these effects. First, the position at which a recombinant DNA molecule is integrated into the chromosome of a transgenic organism can be established using PCR or other means. This allows an assessment of the impact on nearby genes of the genetic modification, and transgenic organisms produced in an experiment can be screened in this way. Second, methods have been developed for inserting DNA at precise chromosomal locations, less likely to cause unpredictable effects, but these cannot be used in all circumstances.

What is Produced in the Other Organism?

Once the 'transgene' is introduced into another organism, and assuming it functions (is recognised by the cell as a gene, and RNA is produced from it), the nature of the products will depend on:

the design of the experiment (including the modifications to the gene) the organisms in question.

If a full and accurate cDNA copy of a gene from any organism is introduced (with appropriate control regions) into a bacterium, a yeast, a plant or an animal, we would expect that it should produce the correct RNA. If the RNA normally encodes a protein, it is likely that the protein will also be produced, and that the chemical make-up of the protein will be very similar in all organisms. The gene may well be expressed in tissues in which it is not normally expressed, although this is often by design (for example, a blood protein in milk).

However, proteins can naturally undergo an extraordinary range of modifications once they have been produced, including processing (being broken into pieces by enzymes in the cell), being joined with other proteins and RNA molecules, or coating with sugars and other molecules. These modifications can be specific to the cell, the tissue and the organism in which they are made. For example, a human protein made in yeast should still retain the same sequence of sub-units (amino acids), but it will have quite a different pattern of sugars attached. If the same protein was made in bacteria, it would lack these sugars altogether.

These modifications can be crucial to the correct functioning of a protein, so it is common for genes expressed in divergent species to not work properly. This is much less of a problem when transferring genes between closely related species, such as human and mouse. However, some human genes have been made to work very well in organisms as different as yeasts and fruit flies. So, when a gene is transferred into another organism, it should still make the same RNA and protein it did in its host organism, but the final nature of the protein, and the way it functions, may be somewhat different due to these specific and important modifications.

What does it Mean for one Gene to be Identical to Another?

We mentioned above that mice and humans are closely related species. At face value this seems absurd, but we are talking here in genetic terms. So what does it mean to be genetically similar, or even the same? Scientists often examine similarity between genes from different species by measuring the degree of *identity* between their DNA sequences. Essentially the same complement of genes occurs in all organisms, reflecting the evolutionary relatedness of species (we all derive from a common ancestor). Simple organisms may have relatively few genes, but these genes will look similar in their DNA sequence to those in higher organisms. It is possible to trace the evolutionary origins of the genes in human chromosomes by comparing them with genes of more and more distantly related species. For example, almost all genes in the human genome can be clearly discerned in the mouse genome, often with relatively minor differences in DNA sequence or gene structure. Therefore, scientists often talk of the mouse and other organisms as having the 'same' genes as occur in humans, but rarely (if ever) would the genes be identical.

Differences in the sequence of human DNA occur at a rate of about 1 in every 1200 bases, meaning that human genomes differ by about 2.5 million bases between individuals. This means that when one gene is examined in many individuals it is common to see several different forms of the gene. So, even the 'same' human genes will not necessarily be identical.

A gene introduced into a transgenic organism may be similar to that of the host organism or the organism from which it was derived, but it is unlikely to be identical to either. During the process of developing the transgenic organism, the sequence of the gene may have been modified, and it will most likely have been coupled with a control region that does not come from the original gene. Therefore, in most situations it would be more correct to refer to 'equivalent genes' rather than the same genes. There are several levels of equivalence.

The genes could have very similar DNA sequences, and we might infer that they will have equivalent functions.

The genes may differ in DNA sequence, but encode similar or even identical proteins.

Some aspect of the function of the genes may be measured, and judged to be equivalent.

Perhaps the ultimate test of equivalence comes, ironically, from transgenic experiments in which human genes are used to replace the equivalent gene in a mouse, a fruit fly, or a yeast. These types of experiments have demonstrated that many genes are functionally interchangeable between species.

What do Scientists mean by 'Human Genes'?

Scientists use the term 'human genes' in several ways, depending on the context in which it is used. The common use refers to those genes naturally found on human chromosomes, but in other circumstances the term may be applied to:

chromosomal DNA sequences isolated from human material but 'stored' in a recombinant bacterial library

a recombinant DNA molecule derived by molecular cloning of a human gene, and inserted into the chromosome of another organism

a recombinant DNA molecule produced as a cDNA copy of a human gene (even though this is substantially different to any gene normally found in a human cell, as it lacks the introns and doesn't exist in nature) the precise sequence of bases (A, C, G and T units) that make up a gene, recorded in a computer database (or on paper).

If we move a human gene into some other organism, does this make the transgenic organism somehow more like a human?

Some people are worried that if a 'human gene' occurs in a food product, say, then in some sense they are eating something human, or more like a human. This worry is unfounded. First, as we have seen, humans have many of the same genes as other organisms, and even if the gene is unique to humans the actual DNA will not have been physically derived from a human, but will have been replicated in one of several ways.

Second, 'human genes' in another organism result in proteins that are often different from human proteins, due to a variety of modifications brought about by the very different physical environment.

Finally, because an organism reflects the activity and interaction of:

- the many thousands of genes in its genome
- the co-ordinated behaviour of the cells and tissues of which it is composed
- the complex environmental influences to which the organism is exposed, adding one or a few human genes into this immensely complex system is not going to 'make the organism more human', just as eating a steak does not make me more cow. Every organism is already adapted to cope with a considerable degree of genetic variability, as shown by the genetic diversity inherent in every population of living things. Adding new genes to some extent simply mimics this natural diversity. The addition of large numbers of human genes into another organism would most probably severely disrupt the biology of the transgenic organism, with disabling consequences. An organism affected in this way would still not be in any way human (or even human-like).

2

Bioethics and Tobacco

Tobacco is a legal product and smoking it is a legal practice, at least in most locales. Yet it is understood by all to be unhealthy and a cause of/contributing factor to several diseases leading to disability and death. One interesting question is whether the life-long smoker's right to national health insurance (such as the US Medicare system) to cover the treatment of lung cancer should be forfeited because of this self-destructive behavior.

According to the World Health Organization one out of every two long-term smokers will ultimately be killed by tobacco. They note that "in developed countries, half will be killed in old age, after age seventy, but the other half will be killed in middle age, before age seventy, and those who die from smoking before age seventy will lose more than 20 years of life expectancy". In the USA, a 1998 study by Leonard Miller, professor of social welfare at the University of California Berkeley and Dorothy Rice, professor emeritus of health economics at the UCSF School of Nursing found that "smoking-related Medicaid costs amount to $12.9 billion per year, or $322 billion in 25 years without inflation", a figure that they noted "does not include the financial impact of cigarette smoking on Medicare or private insurance companies".

About 75% of Americans do not smoke, yet everyone pays for the cost of treating tobacco-related illnesses via higher insurance premiums and taxes. Many people argue that it is not fair that non-smokers have to pay many billions of dollars in health insurance premiums and taxes for the medical treatment of smokers. Given the well-established link between long-term tobacco use and lung cancer, this has led some individuals to suggest that life-long smokers should be denied Medicare or Medicaid health insurance coverage for the treatment of lung cancer.

However, such a policy may be both impractical and unethical.

First, while there is no doubt that health care costs are higher for smokers, the extra health care costs to Medicare and Medicaid associated with smoking can be recovered simply by increasing the price of cigarettes. This would be a particularly effective alternative to denying Medicare services to smokers, since there is strong data to suggest that raising the cost of cigarettes is one of the most effective ways of reducing consumption.

Secondly, tobacco smoking is hardly the only form of self-destructive behavior. Other self-destructive practices that one might focus one include the following:

- excessive alcohol consumption
- not wearing seatbelts while driving
- participation in unsafe sexual practices
- excessive food consumption leading to morbid obesity
- use of dangerous recreational drugs such as cocaine or heroin
- participation in dangerous sports without sufficient attention to safety issues

In the interests of fairness, if one were to deny Medicare services to smokers, it would also be necessary to deny Medicare services to individuals who sustain clinical insults as a result of other self-destructive behavior. It should be apparent that this would be a logistical nightmare.

Third, if life-long smokers on Medicare health insurance should be denied coverage for the treatment of lung cancer, they should also be denied coverage for other diseases strongly linked to smoking: coronary heart disease, cerebrovascular disease, peripheral vascular disease, emphysema, chronic obstructive pulmonary disease, bladder cancer, and even age-related macular degeneration (AMD), a leading cause of blindness.

Fourth, the US government has not made a concerted effort to reduce tobacco use. Industry commentators often point out that there is an incestuous relationship between the tobacco industry and US government. While the idea of regulating tobacco use and creating a "smoke-free" society remains a popular dream in Washington, the reality is that the federal government and the 50 states eagerly consume a steady flow of sin taxes generated by the sale and consumption of tobacco products. Furthermore, and most amazingly, Washington continues to subsidize the growth of tobacco. Some critics suggest that the US federal government should clean up its own house first before implementing draconian Medicare policies of the nature suggested.

Fifth, there are many causes of lung cancer besides tobacco smoking, and some forms of lung cancer (e.g. small cell cancer) are not related to smoking at all. Radon exposure, exposure to asbestos, and even dietary factors may account for many cases of lung cancer. In fact, the only form of lung cancer that is unequivocally linked to smoking is squamous cell carcinoma.

Finally, medicine has a humane tradition of being nonjudgmental and caring for all regardless of social worth or social standing. Public policy should reflect this. Some critics suggest that setting into place a policy whereby a life-long smoker's access to Medicare for the treatment of lung cancer should be forfeited is inhumane in the extreme. Such action says to the patient that he or she is unworthy of our clinical attention, and is in clear violation of the principle of beneficence.

Neuroethics has emerged as a separate area of study over the last decade. It has developed in response to rapidly increasing understanding of the biological function and activities of the brain, the development of technologies that enable imaging of brain activity, medications to treat brain-based diseases, and the linking of brain and machine. All these developments offer the promise of new means to not only treat human disease, but also to enhance human capacities – whether that of children, the 'well', or the military.

The body of literature is still quite small. A few authors appear frequently, and many of the articles offer an overview of the field and endeavour to alert readers to the new concerns. Only some of the papers are within the bioethics literature. Ethical issues are being drawn to the attention of the neuroscience and medical communities.

Authors come from a range of disciplines, and frame the issues accordingly. Some have identified ethical issues within their professional practice and write from that perspective. Others are responding to the issues from experience in other fields of bioethics, philosophy, or sociology.

Running through much of the literature is a concern with the language used to describe the relationship between the biological brain and the sense of self, mind, identity or personhood. Conversations about self, mind, identity and personhood long pre-date the biological understanding of the brain, but now there is a struggle to bring together the language of philosophy and science, when similar (or at times the same) vocabulary is used, and the bioethics conversations require attention to both.

A number of the issues discussed are not new to bioethics but may be new to a community of professionals (e.g. managing incidental findings through use of scanning technologies), or there may be new dimensions to older issues (e.g. innovative treatments, or cognitive 'privacy').

The technology that is the major concern is neuro-imaging. Challenges from this technology include: how to interpret brain scans, the translation of research to clinic or court, and whether or not better understanding of brain activity and function will challenge legal understandings of responsibility.

There is considerable anxiety about the potential for neuroscience (particularly pharmaceutical treatments and mind/machine interfaces) to be used to enhance rather than to treat. There are pragmatic concerns about the safety of these interventions, but also about threats to autonomy – will people be allowed to choose to use these technologies for enhancement or have their autonomy constrained; will it become acceptable for the military to require the use of these technologies by their soldiers, or the courts be able to require their application in some situations? Others discuss whether and to what extent enhancement will affect our sense of self and identity, and others how it will play out in the social arena, for instance how uptake and benefit will interact with social inequalities.

Finally, there is some limited discussion about who needs to be involved in conversations about the emerging possibilities of neuroscience.

INTRODUCTION AND SCOPE OF REVIEW

This literature review has been prepared for Toi te Taiao: the New Zealand Bioethics Council. Its purpose is to identify key publications in the peer reviewed medical and bioethics literature and from international Neuroethics research groups, and review the issues raised and ethical approaches used. Neuroethics is understood as the study of the ethics of neuroscience.

The boundaries of 'neuroethics' are not clearly defined, and it is important to note some exclusions in this review. This paper does not review

The neuroscience of ethics – studies of the neural basis of ethical thinking

The ethical literature within the philosophical literature (which would have required searches of additional databases)

Papers focussed on neuroscience, but which review long-standing, and well discussed ethical issues e.g. informed consent for participation in research trials. Papers which cover long-standing discussions are only included if they explore ethical dimensions of the issue that are particular to neuroscience.

Method

The New Zealand Health Technology Assessment Clearing House (NZHTA) was commissioned to carry out the literature search. It was asked to search

a. the wider medical and social science literature (e.g. Medline and Science and Social Citation Index) against key words (bioethics/ethics/ethical AND neuroscience/ neurology/brain scanning/brain imaging/brain/ plus neuroscience AND society)

b. key bioethics journals for any articles around neuroscience per se (which may identify a broader range of issues than those captured in a. above.) Suggested journals were: Hastings Center Report, AJOB, Journal of Medical Ethics, Biosocieties, Journal of Law, Medicine and Ethics, Bioethics, Journal of Clinical Ethics. Journal of Medical Humanities, Kennedy Institute of Ethics Journal, Bioethics Review (formally Monash Bioethics Review), Science Technology Studies, Science and Engineering Ethics, Theoretical Medicine and Bioethics

The abstracts of the papers were reviewed, those deemed relevant to the search identified, and then sourced by the Bioethics Secretariat. Those that were available were then forwarded to the author for further selection, then review and analysis.

In selecting papers, the following exclusions were applied:

- neuroscience of ethics – the material/biological basis of moral thought
- applications of well-discussed/rehearsed issues in bioethics, applied to neuroscience situations e.g. informed consent requirements for research or for organ banks
- description and discussion of the science or clinical interventions per se
- papers in languages other than English
- professional codes and expectations for groups or health professionals.

In addition, news reports and editorials on the subject were read, but only included in the reference list when they contained data or issues not reported elsewhere. The reference list contains a full list of papers reviewed. A number of books read as background to the project are also referred to within the text and included in the references. Neuroethics is emerging as an area of interest where many streams of thought and research are converging and mixing. Neuroscience itself is becoming a discipline that incorporates different scientific traditions. Genetics, development studies, immunology, bioengineering, as well as traditional anatomy and neuroscience are all becoming important, and bring their own particular sets of analytical tools and conceptual assumptions. Scientific thinking about the brain and associated neural systems in not settled territory but is constantly developing, and increasingly multi-faceted.

That said, the literature reviewed for this paper identified particular scientific developments that require ethics attention. These include brain scanning technologies, implantation of stem cells or neural tissues in the brain (and the possible future scenario of brain transplants) and drugs able to target particular brain activity or functions. (The writing on implantation of stem or neural cells into the brain largely dates from the 1990s, and the trialling of techniques to treat Parkinson's disease.) In addition, some established scientific understandings or technologies were recognised to have implications that are specific for the use in association with brain function e.g. genetic testing for mental or degenerative cognitive conditions.

Bioethics is a discourse that has always drawn on multiple theoretical disciplines – philosophy, law and theology were the early ones, but now also disciplines such as sociology, feminist theory, history of science and philosophy, political studies, anthropology, and public health. Since its early days in the 1970s bioethics has moved well out from the initial focus on protection of individuals in the research context, and attention on the doctor-patient relationship. Thinking has been extended by developments in genetics, the challenges of new birth technologies and stem cell research, threats of global pandemics, and the moral demands to address health inequalities, particularly in the developing world. It has however, largely remained focused on research with human subjects, and health applications of biotechnology.

In addition to conversations in bioethics there are conversations in philosophy (that have been running in parallel with bioethics) that are now being brought into the bioethics discussions about neuroscience – in particular understandings of free will and responsibility, and how (if at all) this thinking is affected by material understanding of the brain, and the relationships between brain, mind and 'self'.

Neurophilosophy has emerged as an area interested in neuroscience and philosophy of mind – looking for a unified theory of mind and brain (Evers 05).

This confluence of so many strands of thought therefore requires analysis of multiple discourses – scientific, ethical, socio-cultural, and philosophical (Illes and Racine 05, Evers 2005, Singh and Rose 2006) – each of which comes to the discussion with its own history, and all of which play a part in shaping the current landscape of the bioethical discussions of neuroscience.

This review reports predominantly on those strands of the conversation that are found in the bioethics and medical literature captured within particular databases. However, it does signal areas (referred to in that literature) that are explored in other communities of knowledge and investigation, particularly in philosophy and sociology.

It is also important to note that only a very small proportion of the papers reviewed for this literature survey came from the peer reviewed bioethics literature per se. Neuroethics has only a small (though growing) presence in the bioethics journals. There is a small cluster of papers from around 1996 (at the time when fetal transplants into the brain for the treatment of Parkinson's disease was being trailed), and then later clusters of papers as journals such as the AJOB run special issues, and invited commentaries on lead papers.

These lead writers (e.g. J Illes, M J Farah, and P R Wolpe) often turn up in the general medical literature, and/or are to be special editors of forthcoming special issues in other journals.

Thus, a great deal of this literature is in the wider medical literature captured by the Medline database. Much of it is of a preliminary nature – alerting readers to the developing technologies and possible ethical implications, and inviting professionals to become involved in the discussions.

DESCRIBING THE LANDSCAPE (THE GEOLOGICAL HISTORY!)

Neuroethics is situated in an historical and political landscape with at least three key features that affect how current conversations are pursued in different contexts.

The history of the neuroscience, and its use for political agenda

The history of other disciplines concerned with related areas e.g. philosophy, sociology – how certain language and ideas have been used and developed

Other areas of science (genetics) and of ethics enquiry (e.g. human enhancement) that raise similar or parallel concerns

It is at the confluence of these and other streams of thought that 'Neuroethics' is developing as a particular conversation – the territory is being mapped out, and certain participants are choosing to join. This is not necessarily happening in a coherent or self-conscious way. The conversations are as yet quite tentative (and largely descriptive of the issues that need to be discussed rather than in-depth discussions), and led by a small number of writers. But indications are there of the fault lines of enquiry.

Science

Our current understanding of the brain as central to our human abilities and identity is of recent origin. Only in the seventeenth century were the connections made between the soft matter in the head and our ability to think and reason (Zimmer 2004). In subsequent centuries this progressed into craniometry and phrenology (study of the shape of the skull as a measure of the development of 'organs' within the brain – which in their turn enabled the determination of character and intellect). In addition to being used to detect the character of the individual, measurements were also used to create intelligence hierarchies within and between races.

Surgical techniques were developed last century, including the infamous lobotomy, devised as means of controlling aggressive or violent behaviour. In more recent decades there have been surgical interventions for obsessive- compulsive disorder and for Parkinson's and other movement disorders. And of course there has been the development of pharmaceutical interventions for treating a range of psychiatric disorders (Finns 2003, Illes and Racine 2005, Williams 2002, Wolpe 2002b). Most recently, the development of various scanning techniques has allowed insight into the biological activities of the brain, and with fMRI the ability to follow these in real time.

The future directions of science are always difficult to predict, but some look forward to greater ability to treat mental illness and enhance human mental capacities, including through neurotechnology.

Some hold very high hopes. The emergent technologies will create new industries and products, provide competitive advantage (both via treatment of mental illness and through enhancement of mental capacities of workers) and drive a debate about the right of individuals to enhance themselves. There is also the possibility of new behaviours, as we learn to 'see things differently' through shifts in mental perspectives. There will be a new type of human society, a post-industrial, post-informational neurosociety (Lynch 2004)!

Philosophy

Philosophy has long concerned itself with ethics, and with broader analysis of concepts such as self, identity, freedom and responsibility. Philosophers have also been concerned to understand the nature of the mind, mental events, mental functions, mental properties and consciousness, and of the nature of their relationship with the physical body: the so-called 'mind–body' problem. This area of work (philosophy of the mind) and neuroscience converged in the field of neurophilosophy in the 1980s, which draws together the methods of analytic philosophy with empirical neuroscience methods to seek a unified theory of mind/brain (Evers 2005).

Other areas of Bioethics Enquiry

Bioethics as a discipline or area of study, is of relatively recent origin. Its early work focused on the ethics of research with human subjects (driven in large part by various scandals where vulnerable populations were exploited in research, but building on reflections on research carried out in Nazi Germany), and the use of innovative clinical technologies such as organ donation and end of life decision-making (Rothman 1991). In the last 10-15 years, bioethics' attention has widened out from the doctor-patient relationship to encompass the ethical, social and legal challenges raised by genetics, and the public health issues of HIV and other potential pandemics. There is also increasing recognition of the need to address issues specific to particular countries or political dynamics e.g. ethics of research in the developing world.

There is thus a track record now of bioethics considering both the research and clinical implications of new technologies, and their social, ethical, legal, policy and political ramifications.

'Neuroethics' History

References to 'neuroethics' and neuroethical issues made their first appearances in the late 1980 and early 1990s, around issues to do with the role of the neurologist at end of life decisions, philosophical perspectives on the brain and the self (possibly in association with trials of transplantation of brain tissue to treat Parkinson's disease), and the neurophysiological and neuropsychological influences on child rearing and education (Illes and Raffin 2002).

But a new level of activity and intensity of focus seems to have emerged since 2002. The Economist picked up on the topic in 2002, as did Francis Fukuyama in his Our Posthuman Future. A first world conference, Neuroethics: Mapping the field was held in the US in that year and later initiatives have included a special conference on Neuroscience and the Law in 2004, and the US President's Council on Bioethics attention to the topic in 2004 (Illes and Raffin 2002, Kennedy 2004, Farah 2002).

By 2002 the field was being divided into 'the ethics of neuroscience' (both ethical issues raised in the course of designing and instituting neuroscientific studies, and the evaluation of the ethical and social impact of the results of those studies) and the 'neuroscience of ethics' – what can be learnt about traditional philosophical notions such as free will, self-control, personal identity, and intention by studying the brain (Roskies 2002).

Neuroethics is now expanding as a sub-field with established journals extending their coverage to deliberately include neuroethics (e.g. the Journal of Cognitive Science), or putting out special issues (e.g. The AJOB will be devoting 3 special issues to neuroethics in 2007). Special neuroethics research centres have been established (for example the Centre for Cognitive Neuroscience at the University of Pennsylvania, and the Stanford Center for Biomedical Ethics). The (US) President's Council on Bioethics website holds transcripts of discussions held on neuroethics, and a European initiative, The Meeting of the Minds, is a two year project to help citizens learn about the impact of brain science and support greater involvement of the public in the debate on future research, technological decision making and governance. However, it will be interesting to see to what extent the bioethics community shapes the discourse of neuroethics. The discussions are being profiled in other bodies of literature, and the discourse being strongly shaped by individuals and institutions whose training is in neuroscience (e.g. Farah) or who are grounded in other disciplines such as sociology (e.g. Singh).

FAULT LINES IN THE CONVERSATIONS

The ethical issues in neuroscience relate to researcher obligations, the clinical and non-clinical impacts of the technology, and the philosophical and theoretical issues (Illes et al 2006). These overlap and inform one another.

This section firsts discusses conceptual issues (the fluidity of language and concepts running through the discussions), and then the key issues – those that are familiar within bioethics, and those that are recent or new to bioethics.

CONCEPTUAL ISSUES

Fluidity of Language and Concepts

The field of neuroethics is characterised by a lack of tight boundaries at a number of different levels. The territory is fluid and ever changing. The areas of science that neuroethics covers are increasingly diverse as neuroscience draws on knowledge from areas such as genetics, immunology, anatomy, stem cell and developmental work, psychology, and medical engineering.

Older categories of thought such as human/non-human are gaining an ethical significance as new re-arrangements of biological material becomes possible – there are interfaces between humans/animals (chimeras), and also between humans and machines (cyborgs).

These interfaces are both in the form of prosthesis that can be controlled by neural impulses, and machines that are embedded in the brain.

The language used in the discussions can have different meanings and/or connotations when used by people in different communities of knowledge or practice, and there are long standing discussions that remain unresolved; and the significance of the line between human and not-human is also under discussion.

The Science

The science that is the focus for neuroethics is diverse.

Pharmaceutical research is identifying drugs that can treat mental disorder of emotion, cognition, behaviour and perception. Some of these drugs may also be of value for enhancing so-called 'healthy' people.

There are major conversations around the use of brain imaging technologies- an area where the technologies are developing rapidly, and raise the possibility of being able to 'read' the mind in various ways and for diverse social and medical purposes.

Not only are a range of biological sciences being brought to bear on understanding and manipulating the brain (e.g. stem cells and tissue regeneration, pharmacology, immunology, development and genetics) but engineering and IT are also involved in developing the scanning techniques and prosthetics that interface with the neural system.

Human or Not?

The 'boundaries' between human and machine, or human and animal, are increasingly permeable. Prosthesis can be embedded in the neural system, either within the brain itself (e.g. a cochlear implant), or via control mechanisms mediated through the peripheral nervous system. And discussions proceed about to what extent it is ethically acceptable to implant animal neural tissue in human brains, or human neural tissue in animals (Greene et al 2005, Karpowicz et al 2005, Moreno 2003). The attention here is on such concerns as; whether introducing human cells into non-human primate brains affects moral status, arguments for deciding what (human) mental capacities are significant in determining moral status; and whether the grafting of human cells into non-human primate brains could result in significant changes in morally relevant moral capacities.

Overlapping Language Conversations

The conversations about all these issues are embedded in various forms of language, and there remains considerable diversity of working assumptions about what the language may mean or imply.

There is a metaphorical landscape of how one conceives of the brain itself - as a biological organ (the anatomic brain) or the brain as concept (the metaphoric brain) (Gindro and Mordini 1998). Metaphors operate at a different level when thinking of the brain as a biological 'thing' (neural pathways and network, blood flows, bridges, channels and docking sites), images that themselves need to relate to the rest of the body – is the brain separate, embedded, interconnected? Then how does one relate all that structure to function, and then to behaviour (Singh and Rose 2006)? What is the relationship between psychological and physiological processes, and how that relates to brain structures? What is the significance of any thing one measures (Hancock and Szalma 2003)? And what are the implications of different ways of relating each to the other? These issues become critical when considering the interpretation and uses of imaging technologies.

And then there is the language landscape, which requires attention not only to the way in which key notions and terms are used in different contexts and disciplines (Evers 2005), but also to the social and political contexts that shape the meaning of the words and how they are interpreted. For instance, individual capacities can be conceptualised as internal to or belonging to the individual – memory, cognition, emotion, desire or the effects of drugs. Or they can be seen as distributed functions – "shaped, organised, facilitated and given meaning and salience by the particularities of their interactive, spatial, pragmatic and linguistic context" (Singh and Rose 2006:97).

Certain concepts, and the relationships between them, come up in discussions again and again. Brain, mind, person, self, personal identity can all come loaded with different assumptions about what they refer to and how they could or should function in a conversation.

For some, the brain is the "defining organ of human behaviour and personality" (Mahowald 1998:50), or personal identity is the person-of-the-living-brain (Gillon 1996). Yet, what is it about the brain that makes it so, and why? In exploring this (and similar issues), the difficulty is that people refer to other terms, that themselves have multiple meaning and usages – terms such as personhood, or identity.

A number of issues raised in the literature are related to the use of language to do with brain, mind, identity and personhood.

There is a concern with 'identity'. What sorts of brain interventions will change identity? In general we are comfortable with temporary interventions (e.g. Prozac) but what about permanent changes, such a permanently altering the brain stem to produce more serotonin? Or psychosurgery or brain trauma (it would seem that some does and some does not affect identity, but what is the important difference)? (Moreno 2003). Is identity about biological continuity, or psychological continuity (Budford and Allford 2005)?

People talk of identity as 'brain identity' or as 'personal identity'. Northoff (1996) demonstrates the complexity of the issues in his detailed exploration of the language used to describe 'identity' in relation to brain and/or tissue transplantation. When thinking about transplanting brain tissue from one person (or fetus) to another person, multiple questions arise: how much change in the brain changes its (the brain's? the person's) identity? A whole brain transplant would, but if not a whole brain is transplanted, how much is sufficient to change identity? Does adding tissue to a brain make a different sort of change to brain identify than taking tissue away? Does the location of new tissue within the brain have any influence on whether or not brain identity is changed? What is the line between brain preservation and the alteration of brain identity? Does it rest on biological material present, or functionality?

When considering 'personal identity', is one thinking of a qualitative thing (not altered by fixing lesions) or a numerical thing (any new material would be a change in identity)? How is the brain/body interface affected by a tissue transplantation? Not at all if identity is not affected by the tissue transplant, but considerably if identity is affected by the presence of new tissue.

DeGrazia (2005) also notes the potential for conceptual confusion in our languages around 'identity'. He distinguishes between 'numerical identity' and 'narrative identity'. The analytical philosophical tradition, he argues, focuses on numerical identity (which allows for change over time, in the sense that a plant is the same plant despite growth, flowering and decline). But that could also rely on either psychological continuity or biological continuity. By contrast, many people would operate from a sense of 'narrative identity' where the individual's identity is linked to a story they can tell about themselves.

And at what point in development does personal identity appear? Possibilities include at conception (identity is genetic), at a critical stage of brain development, at sentience, consciousness, birth, or self-consciousness. That some mental states or functions have more ethical significant to personhood or identity than others is implicit in Burgess and Tawia's (1996) paper on locating the beginning of consciousness. While they deliberately step around the issue, nevertheless there is a firm implication that there is something ethically important about what ends or begins at the point of consciousness (a human? a person?)

There are discussions about how mind is related to body, or mind to brain (if brain is something other than body). Northoff points out the multiple positions amongst philosophers about how brain is related to mind, and whether mental states are related to the brain, or to psychological functions. There is also no agreement among philosophers about how psychological continuity relates to personal identity, nor whether a change in brain identity necessarily leads to a change in personal identity

Moreno (2003) tries to draw some distinctions between mind and brain, and explores how different understandings of the relationship between brain and mind relate to notions of free will and responsibility. Can the mental be reduced to the physical? If so, does that imply that there is no freedom of will? And if the mental can be controlled by the physical manipulation, does that imply there is no freedom of will? He rejects all these positions, and notes that most thinkers come down on the side of 'soft determinism', the view that we are capable of entering into the chain of causes of our thoughts and actions.

Roskies (2004) takes a pragmatic approach, and rejects the idea that people on the street will believe our behaviour is determined, and argues that people will continue to maintain a person is morally responsible for their actions. She also argues that "the idea of moral responsibility is a social one, one that applies to people in virtue of their role in society and their capacities as agents and not because they exercise some sort of metaphysical freedom. Given this understanding, it is not surprising that people judge agents to be morally responsible despite a stipulation of determinism" (Roskies 2004:4).

"Personhood' is a concept that has been given ethical significance in some previous bioethics discussions (e.g. to do with end of life decision-making and termination of pregnancy). Is personhood tied to particular parts of the brain, or to particular functions? When discussing the significance of tissue transplants into the brain, Mahowald (1998) states that not all parts of the brain used or the site transplanted into raise the same ethical or philosophical questions. Those involved with higher functions appear more significant in some ways, and are associated with personhood. (This is a distinction already made when defining brain death, where a distinction may be made between death of the brain stem and that of the cerebral cortex or upper brain.) There would seem to be an implicit view that there is some unit smaller than the brain (or is it some functions of the brain?) that has particular (ethical) significance. There is an elision between biological description (certain tissue) and particular function (certain mental capacities) that is then used to make ethical judgements.

Zwanziger (2003) and Jedlièka (2005) both point out the need to distinguish between reductionism as a metaphysical explanation (the individual is no more or less than a complete physical description of the body, and that body determines what the individual decides to do) and reductionism as a heuristic of explanation (which can tie an observation at the organism level to a phenomena at say a biochemical level, but not reduce the organism to 'mere' biochemistry.)

Functionality also surfaces in Burd et al's paper (1998) in which they tease out possible ethical questions about the research use of human brain tissue. When would growing brain tissue develop properties of mind? Does a brain-mind need a body to be a person? Can a person give consent to grow brain tissue in the lab if it could later develop independent capacity to respond?

Framing

Writers approach the issues in neuroethics from particular directions. For some, the issues are about medical ethics, for example how best to get informed consent in the context of genetic testing for risk of loss of certain cognitive functionality. For others the issue may be about whether or not a particular use of neuroscience is medicalising a human trait such as hyperactivity, significantly shifting a social practice such as the legal understanding of responsibility, or providing a tool to reinforce attitudes and behaviours that will further entrench social inequalities.

Different enquiries may require different sets of questions, and take the enquirer into quite different domains of knowledge. Understandings of legal responsibility might be concerned with analysis of the law, or with philosophical understandings of the 'self' – or with both . Wondering if dosing for ADHD reinforces social inequalities and allows for amplification of certain cultural practices of competition tends more to a sociological analysis.

In the literature reviewed here, there is little coherence or consistency of approach. Rather, a rich and diverse set of concerns is approached in diverse ways, often without direct reference to one another. The writers are often embedded in quite different and at times very distinct discourses.

A small number of papers do explicitly discuss the relationships between disciplines involved in neuroethics, and/or argue for contributions from particular disciplines. Illes and Racine (2005) open up some discussions about the epistemological and ethical challenges of reading neuroimaging data, and identify the need to consider not only traditional bioethics but wider perspectives on the construction of knowledge. De Vries (2005) questions the differences between neuroethics, and a sociology of neuroscience. He argues that not only are their different disciplinary tools, but that sociology of neuroscience is more reflective – while neuroethics studies neuroscience, a sociology of neuroscience studies all of neuroscience, neuroethics and the relationship between the two, including the consequences of a separate and distinct field of neuroethics.

Sociology and bioethics are clearly in this conversation together. The new publication Biosocieties has made neuroscience one of its early topics of interest, and is already offering analyses informed from sociology. Singh and Rose (2006) for instance, draw on the history and sociology of the normal, and remind the reader that the lab and clinic are not empty spaces but are structured in particular ways that enable or eliminate certain interactions. Debates in neuroethics need to draw on the empirical evidence about the social, ethical, psychological, legal and governmental implications of the operation of neuroscience.

Evers (2005) is concerned that the philosophical level of analysis be sufficient in neuroethics. She notes that bioethics interprets scientific data within the ethical, legal and social contexts, but what is also needed is a general philosophical level of analysis, broad and thorough conceptual analysis of key notions. This, she thinks, will come from traditional philosophy of mind, and the more modern neurophilosophy.

KEY ISSUES

That said, some overarching themes do emerge. These are teased out below, but it important to note that these themes are an artificial construction, an imposition of order for ease of discussion. In practice, these themes are interlocked, and writers contribute in different places, in different ways. Quite a lot of papers are generic and descriptive, teasing out the landscape of the discussions in an effort to alert various readerships to an emerging area.

I have followed Farah (2004) in making a distinction between practical and philosophical issues familiar to bioethics, and those that are recent or new to bioethics, and largely of interest because of the developments in neuroscience. This is not an uncomplicated division. While there are a set of issues that are generally accepted to be 'old' issues for bioethics, there are others that some would see as traditional issues in a new context.

Some of the so- called 'new' issues are also highly speculative– a scientific possibility that may not be realised for some time. It may not even be particularly useful or responsible to be teasing them out at this stage (Schick 2005). Inflating the powers of neuroscience and speculating about their implications for free will or normalcy (with insufficient attention to the real powers of technologies or the social life of their fictions) may lead neuroethics to become "part of a culture of hype and hope, futurology and fear" (Singh and Rose 2006).

Practical and Philosophical Issues Familiar to Bioethics

The search explicitly excluded papers whose focus were issues that are well rehearsed elsewhere in the literature, and merely applied to a neuroscience context – for example how to get consent for people to donate tissues to brain banks, use of diagnostic tools in the absence of clinical treatment, resource allocation, and the ethics of clinical drug trials. However, there were references to such issues in many papers. There are also issues that are related to others in bioethics, but have a particular salience for brain science.

Issues New to a Community of Professionals

There are issues that are familiar elsewhere, but new to a particular community of professionals.

Illes (2002) is particularly concerned that practitioners in brain scanning may not be sufficiently alert to the ethical situations that may arise in the course of their research. It is possible that in the course of conducting brain scans for medical or research purposes, that incidental findings happen. How will these be dealt with? Is the possibility raised with the subject at the consent stage? Are their channels through which the subject can be referred if medical follow up is necessary? And what sort of 'reading' would be of sufficient concern to lead to an alert? (See also Check 2005.) Such issues have been canvassed in relation to genetic testing. The issues may not be new, but the community of practitioners likely to be dealing with them could be. Similarly, there ethical issues associated with pre-disposition genetic testing for degenerative brain conditions with which neurologists need to be familiar (Paulson 2002), and added dimensions of care when genetics and neurology converge (Slosar 2006).

Fresh Dimensions to Established Issues

There are issues that are familiar elsewhere, but where brain science introduces some fresh dimensions.

Novel Clinical Interventions in the Brain

New technologies offer the promise of new dimensions to clinical treatment. There are possibilities of Central Nervous

System (CNS) stem cell transplants (from humans or animals) (Burd et al 1998, Grisolia 2001, 2002) gene transfer in the brain (Lesch 1999), psychosurgery, and neuromodulation or deep brain stimulation (Fins 2003, 2004 Schiff et al 2002).

Many of these interventions are only at the innovative or research stage, and participants are likely to be people with few other clinical options, or very poor prognoses. Elsewhere in the ethics literature there are well rehearsed discussions about the ethical issues associated with innovative treatment, including in relation to research on people who are not able to give consent, and the potential risk/benefit ratio for people with different clinical diagnoses (Fins 2000). In relation to interventions in the brain, it is to be hoped that there have been learnings from earlier experience with psychosurgery, which was poorly regulated and unresponsive to ethical and clinical criticism, but it appears that a 1977 report on psychosurgery, issued by the National Commission for the Protection of Human Subjects in Biomedical and Behavioral Research has largely been lost from public memory (Fins 2003, 2004).

However, there is also a wider question that emerges - "How much can we reweave the cerebral tapestry without creating a new self, a new identity?" (Grisolia 2002;823) Further discussion of this and related issues is in section 4.2.2.3, Neuroenhancement.

Models of the Self

Many authors touch on dimensions of the 'self' or personhood, and there is some discussion about the language used. But the tension through many of the conversations is to do with the extent to which the brain holds, captures or is the site of the self/the person. The biological purpose and function of the brain was only identified in the seventeenth century (Zimmer 2004) and so philosophical thinking about the ideas of self and personhood were developed in isolation from biological considerations, and more in relation to theology and the soul. Now, scanning can give us a window into what is happening as we think and feel, and pharmacology give us new options for treating and manipulating the brain – which can also be understood as the mind, or even the self. Yet mind is both brain (and hence body) but also 'more than the brain'. What is the true self – the person before or after treatment for brain malfunction, before or after drugs to enhance mood or cognition (Singh 2004, Northoff 1996)?

This tension permeates many of the discussions on the use of neuroscience, particularly to do with neuroenhancement, and ideas of responsibility. More futuristic discussions on potential mind-machine interfaces raise this issue in a different way – what will brain-machine interfaces do to our sense of self as our mental abilities are enhanced or networked to other humans also using machines? Will it fracture our 'unitary consciousness (Hancock and Szalma 2003)? Concerns about models of the self also surface in discussions on informed consent from people whose mental state (biological state?) may be compromised in some way, not 'normal'.

Informed Consent and the Biological Model of the Self

Some interventions in brain function raise issues that are consistent with those raised elsewhere in the ethics literature - for instance, questions of informed consent for participation in drug trials, or for brain or psychosurgery (Williams 2002, Alfano and Brunetti 1997, Kulynych 2002), require attention to the capacity of the participant to understand what is being proposed, and to make a choice about whether or not to participate.

But developments in neuroscience also open the possibility of a biological rather than social model of the self. We are getting a better understanding of the biological basis for changes in mental states, cognitive function, and responses to pharmacological intervention and other drugs. At times changes in brain activity in response to external events can be visualised via various brain scanning technologies.

If the person in question is understood not to be functioning in a usual or 'normal' way, a biological model of the self can imply that the person's choices are a function of the state of their brain, as determined by a particular combination of neural states and connections – all of which may compromise their ability to make choices.

Several writers explore the implications for research with addicts. While there is an established concern to protect vulnerable people who participate in brain research (Cook-Deegan 2000, Gur et al 2002), questions are now being raised about the extent to which those whose behaviour is controlled by the state of their brain receptors and neurotransmitter systems (ie addicts), can give free and informed consent for research. Is the person able to make a choice, or are their choices totally shaped by the current state of their brains?

Hall et al(2003, 2004) argue (in response to colleagues questioning if or what forms of drug research can be carried out with addicts (Cohen 2004)) that the challenge is to develop theories of addiction that both take seriously the neurological basis for drug effects and addition, while not also depicting addicts as automatons who behaviour is under the control of the drugs. Uhl (2003) argues, in response to Hall, that addiction is not an all or nothing switch, and that research can be considered on a case-by-case basis that recognises that addicts are not devoid of free will. It is important to balance understanding of areas or circumstances where they might be impaired, with their rights of self-determination to participate in research.

Effects on Public Interventions to Deal with Addictions

A biological model of addiction also has social and political implications. While Hall et al (2004) are concerned that a biological rather than social model of addiction could result in severe restrictions on the type of neuroscience research that can be carried out, they also warn against causal accounts of addiction being used to justify legal coercion to use pharmacotherapies and drug vaccines – what they would regard as a 'simple minded social policy'. They also recognise the potential for advances in neuroimaging that might enable identification of 'addicts' or prediction of future addiction, leading to concerns about invasion of privacy, third-party use of imaging data, and consumer protection against over interpretation of test results. Similar issues arise around interventions to reduce smoking. Caron et al (2005) review the science that demonstrates an association between specific genetic profiles and susceptibility to smoking and nicotine addiction. Such work is leading to a market for pharmaceutically based nicotine maintenance, but it also raises questions about how ideas such as causality, choice and free will will be articulated in relation to smoking? A medicalised understanding of smoking see addicts as passive agents in a disease process they cannot control, and which requires medical intervention. For others smoking is a free choice, and medical professionals have little role in breaking the habit. Different models of addiction will lead to different public health interventions, with a risk that an individualisation or medicalisation of smoking undermine current public health strategies that focus on preventing or reducing tobacco exposure.

Social and Political uses of Research

Neuroscience is taking research into areas that generate considerable societal discomfort. Researchers are investigating the biological basis for violence (Enserink 2000), the neurobiology of intelligence (Gray and Thompson 2004), and the neurobiology of sexuality (Wolpe 2004). While the researchers pursue these areas with the hope of finding treatments, there is the possibility the research will feed deterministic understandings of human social behaviour and abilities, and associated policy, legal, and cultural choices. For instance, if the technology claims to be able to predict future behaviour, or the risk of a condition that elevates risk of a behaviour, if or when can compulsory treatment orders be made? The courts already order social interventions, e.g. to address violent behaviour – why not interventions directly in the central nervous system, such as drug treatments (Farah 2002)? Morse (2004) notes that the criteria for abnormality are socially decided, and we are at a time when there is a tendency to pathologise troublesome behaviour.

Anxiety about such possibilities is not totally unreasonable. Earlier biological understandings of social behaviour (such as phrenology) have had a chequered history (Enserink 2000), and the discussions have often been set up (or reported) as nature vs nurture, rather than recognising the degree to which research is uncovering some of the complex interactions between genetics and environment, and how they can play out in terms of human development (Masters 1996).

Illes (2003) recognises that there may be questions about the moral and social responsibility of some research topics and designs. For instance, are all studies of normative neurobehavioural phenomena ethically acceptable? Leshner (2004) also recognises that some may not even want to investigate some aspects of the brain, but argues that "we [the scientific community] have an obligation to apply the full power of science to solving the toughest problems facing humanity, even if they are potentially contentious....scientists have a duty to be extremely sensitive to the potential implications and uses of the results of their work, and that they need to engage fully with other members of the public...in developing a moral consensus and guidelines about how we will proceed" (Leshner 2004 p.3).

This call for the scientists to be involved in the social and ethical discussions with the wider community is present in a number of papers (e.g. Racine et all 2005, Doucet 2005, Hall et al 2004).

Privacy and Confidentiality

Issues of privacy and confidentiality are also thought through elsewhere in the ethics literature. However, one dimension is new in relation to brain research and that is the issue of 'mental privacy'.

There is well established thinking about how to deal with issues of privacy in relation to say the collection of genetic data. Here one would respect privacy by not collecting information, and confidentiality by not sharing that information, without permission of the person. Such an approach can be applied to the information gathered by neuroimaging. Farah (2002, 2005) considers information about psychological traits and states should be subject to the same sorts of protections.

But Reid and Baylis (2005) argue that potential for neuroimaging to violate our 'privacy of thought', introduces a new dimension to the conversations. 'Thoughts' are quite different constructs to 'genes'. They regard thoughts as more central to our sense of self than genes can ever be. Thoughts are the raw materials of our stories and language, through which we construct our selves, our identities. To allow such a process to be subject to external reading would be of quite a different order than allowing our genetic makeup to enter the public domain. Wolpe et al (2005) talk of this in terms of 'cognitive liberty'. Sententia (2004) explores this idea too in relation to the convergence of nano-bio-info-cogno technologies that will affect or monitor cognition. He argues:

"Cognitive liberty is every person's fundamental right to think independently, to use the full spectrum of his or her mind, and to have autonomy over his or her own brain chemistry. Cognitive liberty concerns the ethic and legality of safeguarding one's own thought processes, and by necessity, one's electrochemical brain states. The individual, not corporate or government interests, should have sole jurisdiction over the control and/or modulation of his or her brain states and mental processes" (Sententia 2004: 223).

Practical and Philosophical Issues Recent or New to Bioethics

Is Neuroethics New or is it Not?

A brief flurry of discussion on whether or not neuroethics is in fact 'new' can be found in the special issue of AJOB, in the responses to Illes and Racine's (2005) paper on neuroimaging. In that paper they argue that while ethics of genetics is a legitimate starting point for considering the ethical issues raised by neuroscience, it is not sufficient. In particular they are of the view that the difficulty of 'carefully and properly interpreting the relationship between brain findings and our own self-concept is unprecedented" (2005:6). The complexity of neuroscience research poses challenges for the integration of knowledge and meaningful interpretation, and there is a need to address the challenges of interpretation, and the cultural and anthropological frameworks that shape our understandings of self and personhood.

Respondents take various approaches.

Scheick (2005), for instance, argues that the challenges that Illes and Racine identify may not all be similar to those that have arisen in genetics, but where that is the case (e.g.

the use of physiological tests of truth telling) there are other debates to draw on (such as the use of other lie-detection technologies). The difficulty of neuroethical enquiry may not arise from its newness, as much as from the need to master vast and enduring debates about the relationship between mind and body.

Knoppers (2005) is unconvinced by Illes and Racines' arguments that neuroethics faces particular challenges, but rather is concerned that neuroethics learn from the genethics debates as it frames the issues for the neurosciences. She alerts readers to the historical parallels and challenges, including an overly simplistic approach to the science and the too easy adoption of early models of understanding genes.

Wilfond (2005) rejects the argument that neuroethics either raises new issues, or requires a different 'approach'. The issues raised by neuroscience have parallels in various other areas, and while the context of an issue may require particular consideration, there is no need for new conceptual tools or theories. Any differentiation of sub-disciplines within an area is understandable for reason of common methodologies, or common areas of focus. It may also be useful socially (to create a professional identity or respond to needs for funding). But coining new terms such as neuroethics may be distracting, or obscure rather than clarify issues. He argues against the need to create sub-disciplines for different streams of ethics (genethics, neuroethics, etc).

Applications of Neuroimaging

New imaging research – what it may enable : Recent developments in brain imaging techniques (e.g. functional magnetic resonance imaging (fMRI) and positron emission tomography (PET) allow clear images of the state of the brain structures. They also enable replicable experimental designs to investigate the relationship between brain function/activity and cognitive behaviour, for instance to understand cognitive changes in people with Alzheimer's disease (Illes and Racine 2005, Rosen et al 2002). But the technology can also be used for similar research on the relationship between brain function/

activity and social dimensions such as emotion and personality. Such work has been carried out on normal healthy people, and also those who have come to the attention of forensic services, say for violence. Investigations have been on topics such violence, racial attitudes, preferences, and specific thoughts (Canli and Amin 2002, Farah 2002).

Much work is focussed on understanding and description, with making the links between biological behaviour (neural activity) and the processing of cognitive and emotional activity.

As understanding develops, there is interest in finding clinical applications, and there are also a number of potential applications outside health -- forensic uses to predict violence or future illegal behaviour such as paedophilia, to guide court directed treatment strategy, to detect lying, or to determine ability to accept legal responsibility (Canli and Amin 2002, Farah 2002,Glannon 2006, Wild 2005). There is also the likelihood of the use of scanning techniques in interrogation, possibly as an alternative to torture (Thompson 2005).

Some authors signal caution that such practical applications are near to practical or commercial reality. For instance, there is much work still to be done to understand the interactions of different parts of the memory system as well as the processes required to formulate or implement behaviours intended to mislead – yet alone how all this links to use of language. Such work would need to happen before any lie detection processes would be robust (Illes 2004).

Such caution is perhaps reinforced by research into media coverage of fMRI. Racine et al identify three trends in the press coverage – neuro-realism, neuro-essentialism, and neuro-policy. Neuro-realism "describes how coverage of fMRI investigations can make the phenomenon real, objective or effective in the eyes of the public" (2005:160). The images provide visual proof, with no recognition of the complexities and uncertainties underneath the data collection and image processing. Neuro-essentialism leads to subjectivity and personal identity being reduced to the brain (Dumit 2003), and neuro-policy attempts to use fMRI results to promote political or personal agendas, such as to 'prove' that pornography is addictive. All these trends overlook the complexities behind the technology and its interpretation, which challenge any simple response to or use of the research results.

Challenges: There are some challenges that relate directly to the research itself, for instance, selection of patients (both healthy volunteers and those with neuropsychiatric disorders, or other variations from the 'norm'), privacy in management of data, and management of incidental findings arising from the research (Illes et al 2002, Alfano and Brunetti 1997).

But underlying these issues are wider conceptual and methodological challenges – what would 'normal' look like (in terms of neural activity, social behaviour, cognition, and brain images)? How to interpret images? To what extent and under what circumstances, can findings be translated to the clinic or to other practical applications?

Interpreting images, and 'Normality': While the technology can produce wonderful images of activity in the brain, the question remains about what the images 'mean', especially if the evidence from one group of people is used to generalise to other populations.

Firstly, it important that brain images are recognised not as realities, but only as representations of reality – and as such are subject to limitations that lie in the technologies themselves, and limitations that result from the interpretation of the images and the meaning with which they are inscribed. There are epistemological limits to how the images are produced (e.g. variability in research design, statistical treatment of data and resolution), and the images can only produce a model of the brain, and any model needs to be treated with caution. Also cultural and anthropological frameworks bind any interpretation of neuroimaging studies. Ideas about emotions and the self, for instance, are culturally determined (Illes and Racine 2005).

Dumit (2003) discusses how the presentation of brain images in magazines and books can change people's understanding of their selves, of their bodies. People with depression, who understand themselves as having neurotransmitter imbalances, must negotiate a relationship between self and brain – if there is something wrong with my brain, is there something wrong with me? Even avoiding the sense of 'wrong' as a moral judgement about oneself, one is left to negotiate the meaning of a sick brain for one's autonomy, and the extent to which one becomes a "pharmaceutical self" in that one needs chemical assistance to have the brain that is one's 'own'.

Secondly, what is the relationship between structure and function, or brain activity and behaviour? While certain structures are usually involved in particular activities such as memory and emotion, it is also the case that the brain has enormous plasticity, some non-visible (to the scan) structures may be important to function, and it is not clear just what effects on function can be predicted from particular changes in structure (Stevenson and Goldsmith 2002, Rosen et al 2002). Nor does a correlation between activity and function, or activity and behaviour, necessarily establish causality (Desmond and Chen 2002, Canli and Amin 2002).

Thirdly, what is a 'normal' brain? Not only are there few normative scans available from healthy populations on which to base any comparison, it is also not clear how the normal brain changes with time, especially in relation to the development of foetuses and children. It is especially difficult to get base line normative data for children since they are not so easily or often enrolled in research. Often scans from children who have been scanned as part of medically necessary diagnostic work-ups and identified as 'negative' are studied as a means toward understanding 'normal' brain structure and function (Desmond and Chen 2002, Hinton 2002).

Not only are there few templates of normal brains with which to compare those suspected of not being normal, it is not even clear what brain measure should be used as a norm, and which brain structure one is measuring in any particular use of the idea of normality. Also, a measure of normal is statistical and not absolute (Canli and Amin 2002).

And when linking brain activity with behaviour, 'normality' is a social judgement. Deviance, or example, is socially constructed , and reflects social norms and values. It is not inherent in either behaviour or brain (Howard 2002).

Thirdly, Stevenson and Goldworth draw attention to how questions of interpretation can slide between bio-hermeneutics and bioethics. While interpretation of brain images may give some indications of the current state of a brain, and possibly be used to make judgements about likely future outcomes for that person, such images do not relieve the circumstances of "the complexities or ambiguities of personal being" (2002;451) and should not be confused with the need for the interpretation of circumstances and choices that is required of bioethics.

Can one translate from research to clinic or court?

There are some obvious possible clinical benefits of brain imaging. It may enable clinicians to distinguish between subtypes of a condition that may present in similar ways, but have different underlying pathologies. It may enable clinicians to identify those who will benefit from pharmacological intervention or early treatment, ensure early access to treatment, and in some situations (e.g. Alzheimer's) provide an opportunity for people to plan for later deterioration (Hinton 2002, Rosen et al 2002).

At a forensic level, techniques based on scanning may enable lie detection, provide a tool to assess the likelihood of someone re-offending, or inform a court-ordered direction for mental health treatment (Wolpe et al 2005).

But there are several issues still to be worked through before these things are practicable or reliable.

A number of dimensions need to be considered in translating scanning research from lab to clinic or court. For instance, the technology may not be able to be used with a clinical population as it is with a research population. Scanning requires that the participant be able to co-operate in particular ways, such as keeping still, but this may not be possible with some groups of people, for example those with Alzheimer's disease. Also clinicians need to understand the limits of interpretation and the types of statistical errors that may arise, and may need education about how to interpret brain research. In addition, when caring for older patients, there may be additional safety screening requirements (Rosen et al 2002).

Farah (2002) argues that scans do not yet have a place in psychiatric diagnosis. Those abnormalities that characterise particular groups are not yet diagnostic at the individual level. In addition, there is still a limited understanding of the links between physiological and psychological data – neural correlates are only the first step in understanding.

While scans may be able to say something about the current state of a person's brain, great caution is required in using that information to predict future outcomes. Such associations are not validated in the case of Alzheimer's disease and much greater sensitivity and specificity is required to predict future from a current brain state and functionality (Rosen et al 2002). With neonates and young children, little is known about normal brain development and what should be regarded as within the range of normal at any particular stage of development. In addition, there is considerable brain plasticity- current brain activity may not predict future outcome (Hinton 2002, Stevenson and Goldworth 2002).

DiPietro (2005) notes that the use of neurobehavioral assessment before birth can be distinguished from clinical fetal assessment. The latter is focused on good birth outcomes, while the former is orientated towards outcomes for child and his/her development post-birth, and comes with all the challenges of prediction.

Non-clinical use of scanning may also be making assumptions about prediction. Corporates may want to use scanning one day to inform their choice of staff, and assume that certain traits are what is needed in their workplace (Moreno 2003). Or a scan might inform a decision about whether or not to restrict someone's activity, such as driving. But it is problematic to link brain activation with a behaviour of interest (Rosen et al 2002).

In a forensic environment, scanning could be used to predict violence, determine a felon's ability to control their behaviour, to monitor mental health treatment of a convicted psychopath. Or could it be used along the lines of 'notifiable diseases' with respect to psychopathy, paedophilia and related disorders that put the public at risk? However, one can not assume that certain brain behaviour will lead to actual feared behaviour e.g. not all men aroused by images of pubescent girls will go on to be sex offenders (Canli and Amin 2002,Howard 2002).

Popma and Raine discuss the implications of brain imaging for the forensic assessment of anti-social behaviour, as more links are made between biology and behaviour. They note the gaps in the knowledge about the relationship between biology and antisocial behaviour, and call for "prudence and due circumspection" in translating knowledge from correlational and risk research to clinical practice (2006:436).

In a security or court situation, there may also be interest in using some of the emerging lie-detection technologies, based on brain scanning. Indeed, in some parts of the world, security concerns may provide an incentive for (possibly too) early adoption of the technologies (Moreno 2005). Wolpe et al (2005) note the technical limitations of current technologies. For instance, the validity of the technologies is yet to be established –does the test give information about what it claims to test, and to what extent do various methods used in the test control for possible confounding effects? They note that a test developed under lab conditions may not be as reliable when transferred to different test populations, and that sensitivity and specificity may change with different sub-groups of people.

Fischbach and Fischbach (2005) point out that imaging relies on changes in blood flow as a surrogate for neuronal activity, and does not have the temporal resolution to detect what may be a fleeting brain state. But perhaps more challenging to the use of lie detection technologies is that lying is a complex activity - not only may it be morally justified in some situations, it also may involve quite different brain activities whether it involves deception, falsification, fabrication or misrepresentation. Lying is a social activity (e.g. 'of course father Christmas exists'), and cultural factors play a role in determining what is or is not a 'lie'. Could it be that what one detects is not the lie, but the thought that one should not lie (Buller 2005)?

As early as 1996, there was anxiety amongst professionals about the transition from research to practical use of scanning technologies, and the Society of Nuclear Medicine prepared guidelines that provide guidance for professionals preparing forensic reports on elements essential to a complete and useful clinical report, and provides standards to differentiate well established clinical applications from research uses (Society of Nuclear Medicine 1996).

Effect of neuroscience on legal understandings of responsibility, and court decisions.

Pharmaceutical interventions, brain scan results and the possibilities of neurosurgery offer new strategies for use in the legal system – some of which have precedents. There may be changes to how the courts even understand or interpret 'responsibility' where some brain scans may provide evidence of abnormal brain activity; and scans may indicate what sorts of treatments may address the underlying cause of antisocial or illegal behaviour such as violence.

There are a few papers specifically examining how neuroscience will affect the law, and most are within the same publication – that of the Royal Society's Philosophical Transactions special issue on Law and the Brain. Some papers fall outside the scope of this report as they look at the material and biological basis of legal thought, including neuroscientific models of normative behaviour, or evidence of underlying biological activity when we make legal judgements such as how we sort deception from self-deception or understand what is happening to decision-making under provocation (Goodenough and Prehn 2004, O'Hara 2004).

Legal understandings of responsibility: There is an emerging dialogue about whether or not legal understandings of responsibility will be shifted by neuroscience. As understandings of the biological base of behaviour expands, it is possible that arguments will be made in courts that a person's understanding and/or ability to distinguish between right and wrong is compromised because of the particularities of their brain. Moreno (2003) suggests that further legal categories will need to be developed to capture different senses of culpability, as has already been done in cases that involve psychoactive drugs. And courts are likely to depend on expert advice on the state of a person's brain. As discussed above, there are real challenges in translating research to the courts.

Morse (2004) does not think that legal understandings of the law will be compromised by neuroscience. He argues that the law "views human action as reason-governed and treats people as intentional agents, not simply part of biophysical flotsam and jetsam of the causal universe." The law assumes adults are capable of minimal rationality and responsibility, and while that assumption can be rebutted in appropriate cases the criteria for non-responsibility are demanding and infrequently used. Morse also rejects the idea that responsibility is tied to free will. Causation per se has nothing to do with free will – it is not the same as compulsion or lack of capacity for rationality, and it is diminished rationality that concerns the law.

Green and Cohen agree that the current framework for assessment of criminal responsibility is not changed by neuroscience. But they also argue that neuroscience will affect moral intuitions that relate to the punishment that a crime deserves – "rationality is a presumed correlate of what most people really care about. What people really just want to know is if the accused, as opposed to something else is responsible for the crime, where that 'something else' could be the accused's brain, genes or environment" (2004:1780). As the new science progresses it will undermine people's sense of free will, and the idea of distinguishing between the truly guilty and those who are victims of neuronal circumstances will seem pointless. They project a move away from retributive punishment (giving people what they deserve) to a more consequential view of law – we hold people responsible because doing so seems on balance to be beneficial (deterrence, containment etc).

Morse also reminds the reader of the social context for understanding responsibility - neuroscience cannot tell us how much rationality is required for responsibility. That is a social, moral, political and legal call. And Glannon reminds readers that the main reason for questioning the use of neuroimaging to make legal (and ethical) judgements is that "it involves a move from empirical claims about the brain to normative claims about how people ought to behave. Free will and responsibility are not primarily empirical, but normative notions reflecting social conventions and expectations about how people can and should act" (2005:41).

Threats to civil liberties: Neuroscience may also raise threats to our civil liberties. If brain scanning delivers what it promises, there is the potential for invasion of privacy, the 'reading' of our thoughts. There may be new treatments for a wider range of brain-related 'conditions'. What constitutional or legal limits should be placed on the use of the technologies? For what conditions and what treatments is it acceptable for the court to require treatment, perhaps so that one is capable of standing trial (Morse 2004)?

Neuroenhancment: Enhancement is frequently mentioned in the literature reviewed for this paper, and a number of themes emerge. Enhancement is not of course confined to neuroscience, but there appears to be an intuition that there is something distinct about enhancing mental, cognitive, or behavioural functions and intervening directly in the brain (Wolpe 2002a), arising no doubt from the cultural understanding of the brain as central to the self or identity or person. Many of the issues discussed, however, are generic to all opportunities for enhancement.

In general, most papers are an over-view of the area, summarising the issues and calling for discussion of the issues. A few of the papers provided an insight into the different approaches apparent within different academic disciplines (Hyman 2005, Singh and Rose 2006). One paper (Mauron 2003) approached the issue from a wider perspective, and placed the issue of enhancement within an historical and philosophical framework.

What the science is making possible : Discussions of enhancement have had some exposure in recent years – but have not been confined to neuroenhancement. The US President's Bioethics Council, for instance released a report in that covered the full range of enhancement possibilities and Carl Ellliot's (2003) book Better than Well has promoted considerable discussion of technologies that include cosmetic surgery and the use of glasses as well Prozac and Ritalin. In relation to cognition, mood or emotion, people have always sought enhancement whether through education, coffee, hard work, or alcohol. But a new range of techniques are becoming available. Drugs and prosthetic devices developed primarily for medical application now are seen to have uses that fall outside the traditional 'medical' realm.

In recent decades, drugs have been developed for treatment of psychiatric disorders, be they to do with cognition and behaviour, emotion or perception. Many of these drugs can also be used to treat mild symptoms and improve on cognitive and emotional states that fall within the current range of 'normal' – e.g. drugs that improve attention and memory, mood and effect (Turner and Sahakian 2006, Hyman 2006, Chatterjee 2004a). Some are also of interest for athletic enhancement e.g. medication to enhance neural plasticity (Hyman 2006).

Positive effects on mood may also come from use of some engineering technologies. There is some evidence that repetitive transcranial magnetic stimulation (rTMS) can have a therapeutic effect on depression. Could it affect mood of normal people on 'off' days (Chatterjee 2004)?

Advances in machine and IT technologies also offer the possibility of human/machine interfaces that will be not only for 'treatment' but also for 'enhancement purposes'. Prosthetics are being developed for hearing and vision (e.g. the cochlear implant), and techniques being developed for 'applied neural control (e.g. Parkinson's pace-maker like device for brain). Wearable computer-person interfaces are under development and also an implantable brain chip, which raises the possibilities of networking brains between people. Early users for some of these newer possibilities are likely to be people with a disability, but the military have considerable interest in this field (Chatterjee 2004, Maguire and Mcgee 1999, Hyman 2005, Breithaupt and Weigmann 2004). While some question whether the technical barriers can be overcome (White 1999), there is a new discipline emerging, neuroergonomics, that studies how brain mechanisms are involved in human performance in interaction with technology (Hancock and Szalma 2003).

What is enhancement (and what is treatment)?: It has proved impossible to define a clear line between therapy and enhancement. It is apparent that where one draws that line is dependent on the context and the purpose of making the distinction. The same treatment may be therapeutic in one context (severe depression, extreme behavioural difficulties) and an enhancement in another (a 'healthy' person wanting to feel 'better than well, a child needing to concentrate better to achieve at school; breast surgery following mastectomy for cancer, and breast surgery to improve one's figure).

The purpose for drawing the distinction may lie in deciding what is or is not a medical treatment, and needing to be paid for as such. (This may relate to what is obligatory for society to provide in way of care (Wolpe 2002).) While at first glance an obvious task, in practice it is a challenging distinction to. When, for instance, is a child sufficiently short that treatment with growth hormone is a medical treatment, and when a social enhancement? And there is a difficulty in even deciding what an illness is – is shyness, for instance? Not only are many mental health conditions on a continuum with 'normal' , but objective tests for presence or degree of illness are sill missing in many cases. Direct-to-consumer marketing may also expand diagnostic zones in minds of people about what needs to be treated (Hyman 2006).

Deciding what counts as a medical treatment is not the same as what services a health professional may provide. This may well evolve into areas that have not traditionally been the domain of health professionals. Chatterjee (2006) notes that some psychologists already act as coaches in pursuit of happiness – how long before neurologists take up this role, using the tools that science provides to enhance well-being and happiness?

An alternative purpose for drawing the distinction is one of public policy – in some jurisdictions this will in part be about health funding, but it could also be to do with sport (what enhancements are acceptable for athletes to use?), education (what enhancements can assist children to concentrate or achieve success, be it medically prescribed Ritalin or off-label methylphenidate?), or policy to regulate access to drugs (whether through rules, oversight of physicians and engagement of the public on discussion of issues) (Kennedy 2004, Hyman 2006).

A third reason for drawing a distinction between therapy and enhancement is to do with deciding what is species–typical functioning. (Treatment gets one into the range of normal, enhancement lifts one above it.) This determination of what counts as 'normal' could either be to define what is 'natural', or to use as a convenient baseline to determine what society owes its members, what treatments should be offered (Wolpe 2002).

There are some challenges around defining 'normal'. It is yet another term that can have different meanings, and where the meanings can be put to various political purposes. 'Normal' can describe a statistical value, the distribution of a characteristic across a population. The driver for this definition has often been to understand a continuum within a population, which can then be converted to distinct categories in the interests of managing populations. This will also interact with social understanding of where responsibility lies for dealing with those who fall outside the 'norm'. Hyman (2005) notes that with the variation from the norm based on population statistics, health can be seen as fitness of a particular sort. Early public health, hygiene and eugenics programmes were based on population responses to dealing with variation from the norm, but these have now given way to self-help programmes, where responsibility has been shifted to the individual who can choose behaviour and practices.

But 'normal" can also be a social and subjective judgement. It can develop a moral value – the norm what we 'ought' to be, something to strive for. In this usage, average comes to be seen as deficient (Hogle 05). Treatment may be what enables one to reach one's potential. And if one is prepared to offer the treatment (as treatment not enhancement) to those who start at the bottom or middle of the distribution curve then why not also the 'already-clever' people who choose to enhance (Singh 2005, Turner and Sahakian 2006)?

The difficulty of making a water-tight distinction between therapy and enhancement could lead to a view that since we cannot make a distinction between treatment and therapy, no meaningful line can be drawn. Dees (2004), however, rejects this position. Just because it is difficult, does not mean we leave it to the market or the military to decide – that is to surrender ethics to power.

Caplan (2004) argues that none of the arguments offered to resist enhancement are sufficient for an in-principle rejection. Singh (2005) rejects the adequacy of abstract philosophical reasoning in isolation from empirical studies of the particular situation. Only detailed study of the particular technology in particular contexts can uncover the drivers of and values involved in uses of enhancement.

Other considerations/issues: A number of other issues are also raised in relation to enhancement. Some of these are pragmatic concerns – for instance, lets not get carried away and forget the practical issue of safety. Others are more philosophical – concerns about self and identity.

Some issues are mentioned, but not explored; for example, that enhancement is to be 'playing God' (Maguire and Mcgee 1999), or unnatural (but so are so many medical interventions) (Caplan 2003); or that there are concerns about bodily integrity and intuitions about the sanctity of the body (Maguire and Mcgee 1999).

Safety: There are a number of safety concerns about the use of drugs for neuroenhancement:

There is little known about the long-term effects of drugs on neural plasticity, and to what extent any such effects are different than those affected by experience. (Hyman 2006)

The effect of drugs are known on the research population (the population with the illness for which it was developed) but not necessarily on the general population or on the cognitively intact. What possible other (collateral) effects are not looked for in the development of the drug? For example, does a drug enhance memory but affect the selection process about what we remember? What effects are there on personality over time, especially with children, for which there is a general shortage of data on effects of drugs? Drug trials are usually over a short time while treatment may be over a longer period – what effects might this longer use have (Hyman 2006, Turner and Sahakian 2006, Wolpe 2002a)?

The effects of drugs are not necessarily predictable or guaranteed. Our understanding of pharmacogenomics is still limited, and there is some evidence that optimal levels of some medications may depend on the baseline levels of performance, and that it may vary with different patient groups e.g. adults vs children.

It is important to avoid unwarranted claims of efficacy results (Turner and Sahakian 2006). Chatterjee (2004a) does not think that safety issues are a great concern. There are incentives in place for treatments with minimal side effects.

How one assesses these risks will be affected by whether or not the person is 'ill'. Hyman (2006) points out that at the population level, the greatest risk is that drugs will be underused in treatment of mental disorders. But the risk/benefit calculus does shift when a person is not already ill.

Threats to autonomy: Given the potential risks, it may be wise to restrict use of some medications and technologies until more is known. However, an argument is also made that one should allow an individual to choose based on good information. This position is based on libertarian assumptions that all have access to information, and the skills to interpret it. It also fails to be concerned about the impacts of the drugs in societies without civil liberties or good education systems, or recognise the current limited access to all clinical trial results (Turner and Sahakian 2006).

Additional concerns about threats of some of these 'enhancements' to autonomy are raised in the context of court mandated implants. Forced drug administration is already allowed in court systems, for example when a person is dangerous to themselves or others, and already in the US an individual has been ordered to take medication so as to be fit state to stand trial - this is a social purpose rather than one driven by concern for the health of the individual per se (Maguire and Mcgee 1999, Turner and Sahakian 2006). Enhancement may be used on soldiers. Are their any limits on what the state can do to its own soldiers (assuming a 'just' war) (Wilson 2004, Wolpe 2002)?

In the case of enhancement via neural connections to machines, there may be a different threat to freedom. If the human becomes an extension of the machine, who controls the individual's mental state – the person or external authority who has access to the machine-human interface? And what will it mean for autonomy as machines become more 'human', able to read human minds, adjust their interfaces with humans to make life more pleasurable, or to relieve boredom (Hancock and Szalma 2003)?

Self and identity: Discussions of self and identity in relation to enhancement run the spectrum from abstract philosophical reasoning, to empirical studies of situations where drugs are being used in a context that can be understood as enhancement. DeGrazia (2005), for instance, teases out the language used to discuss identity in relation to enhancement. Whether or not altering a person's identity is problematic depends on whether one is referring to numerical or narrative identity. Altering a numerical identity, with its associated psychological continuity, may be problematic, but DeGrazia sees no issue with changing one's narrative identity – any intervention (enhancement or otherwise) will affect one's story about oneself, one's sense of where one fits in the world and how one got to be there. He recognises that there is some concern that enhancement might affect some 'core' traits that are central to a person's narrative identity, be they psychological style (e.g. suspicious or confident), personality or intelligence. However, he argues that such reasoning is suspect and enhancement techniques are "unlikely to affect traits that are plausibly considered inviolable" (2005:280)

Singh (2005) argues for studies that identify how understandings of self and personhood are culturally shaped. There is a need to pay attention to how issues are playing out in particular situations. It is important to reconcile and understand how people think about persons and brains, and persons and physical systems (Farah and Wolpe 2004), but too often the issues are discussed in the abstract rather than in relation to a particular drug or its use, and the bioethics discussions isolated from other disciplines . This results in the 'self' and 'identity' being thought of as "identifiable, coherent and stable", encouraging an essentialist view of the self. Singh proposes instead that self and identity are "fragile, fragmented and embedded" and empirical studies are needed to understand how these concepts play out in actual lives (Singh 2005:35).

He uncovers some of this cultural shaping in his work on ADHD, where mothers and fathers understood the treatment in quite different terms as they were asked to think about the relationship between neurochemistry and personhood. Mothers saw ADHD behaviours as 'part' of who their sons are, and treatment as opening the possibility for their sons of a better understanding of themselves. Mothers situated their understanding within a success narrative that itself provides a moral imperative to treat – treatment enabled the actions of a freed authentic self in a culturally valued story of male development that included success at school. But while they saw the drugs as enabling the authentic boy to act during the week, there were dilemmas for weekend treatment – then there was a desire to let child be itself, unmodified by drugs. On weekends, however, the boys do not need treatment to be 'free'. Through all this runs a tension about how to relate self and brain to the body, how to distinguish between behaviour and the child's real self.

Fathers understand treatment options within a different frame. They do not see the disruptive behaviour as part of underlying pathology, but rather that 'boys will be boys'. Their behaviour is seen as evidence of this. Fathers are sceptical of diagnosis and the use of medication, but also see how the boy's behaviour disadvantages their sons. This is of particular concern in sports and physical activities. For fathers biology not a morally neutral zone – it can be weak and flawed (and needing medication) and thus (via genetic links) implicate fathers.

Singh also notes from his study that shifts in context will shift the moral debate e.g. as long-acting medications for ADHD become available, some of the moral dilemmas of dosing and how to involve/inform others such as teachers become less intense.

Context can shape understandings of self and identity in various ways. For instance, in a culture where identity is linked to what one consumes, combined with increased attention to bodily practice, it is a challenge to work out who is the authentic self - the one before or after one has altered the body (Hyman 2005)?

But whether the overall effects of enhancement are beneficial or not, whether it undermines or re-enforces a sense of personal agency, is also dependent on context. For a child, for instance, who has interpreted himself through "the prism of severe symptoms, such as feelings of worthlessness, prior to treatment,...change would, to a great degree, be the long-tern goal of therapy" (Hyman 2006:108). It is important to remember that not all changes in personhood are bad. It is possible to recognise great good in some religious epiphanies, the re-invention of ourselves in non-medical ways, and the 'finding' of ourselves through treatment of depression (Chatterjee 2004a).

It may be that in all these issues, our responses are shaped by our view of the teleology of the technology and our view of human life. Do we see humans as animals that will use any technology, or is the use of neuroenhancement an affront to our humanity (Wolpe 2002)? What kind of society should we become (Dees 2004)?

Social issues: The social practice of enhancement may have effects on both individuals, and on wider communities (Maguire and Mcgee 1999, Turner and Singh 2006). There is a concern for social justice, in relation to the unequal distribution and effect of enhancement technologies (Butcher 2003, Hyman 2002, Maguire and Mcgee 1999, Turner and Sahakian 2006). However, this is not a new issue - the use of prescription drugs to both treat and improve function already appears greater among the advantaged (Hyman 2006), and people already have access to many things that enhance inequality e.g. music camps and maths tutors (Caplan 2003). And is the issue access or availability (Chatterjee 2004a)? It is likely that the use of enhancement technologies will act to re-inforce current cultural patterns. Singh (2005) offers evidence of this in his study of the use of ADHD medications and the concerns of parents that their children be able to 'compete'. Others identify concerns that the availability of enhancement technologies will change values, such as the value of hard work, and applying oneself. But they note that we already have ways of moderating the 'pain' of living, such a taking drugs to treat headaches, the use of heating to keep warm and healthy, and technology to travel (Chatterjee 2004a, Turner and Sahakian 2006).

And then there is the threat of social coercion, and will the possibility of enhancement promote diversity or sameness (Butcher 2003)? This might take the form of demand for superior performance by others e.g. pilots to take medication because evidence shows that those on donepezil perform better in emergencies; or doctors so they can perform better after long hours of work? The reason for coercion in such situations is not so much to benefit the taker of the medication, as the benefit of others (Chatterjee 2004a, Hyman 2006). Caplan (2003) has a different take – we owe it to our children and society to optimise abilities. The answer is not to avoid enhancement but ensure it is always a choice.

Different analytical approaches to enhancement : Apparent in all this literature is a range of analytical approaches to enhancement. Some are explicit about their approach (e.g. Degrazia arguing out of the analytical tradition of philosophy, or Singh as a sociologist), but most are not.

Hogel (2005) reviews the literature on enhancement (not confined to but including neuroenhancement) and identifies that there is no coherent body of literature, but work in areas of anthropology, social studies of science, technology and medicine, bioethics, and disability studies. The bioethics literature tends to extrapolate the situations of individuals to society and then universalise across cultures, societies and time frames – it excludes analysis of social disparities, differences in local conditions, and differing value systems. On the other hand anthropologists tend to look at the relation of modern forms of power and how they operate through bodily disciplines and modifications. They explore such things as how body enhancements are not only about commodification but also about changing ways of understanding biological and social life, and the cyborg literature challenges romanticised notions of pure or natural self that should not be tampered with – the body becomes a set of relations rather than a package with some form of agency. She also notes that cognitive enhancement relies on reductionist assumptions that all behaviour, interactions and psychological functions are related to neuronal structures – it makes the social invisible.

Hogel also identifies that the enhancement literature in general tends to focus on some technologies and avoid consideration of others. Computerised prosthetics (other than cochlear implants) are one such gap.

Mauron's paper takes a broad historical and philosophical approach as he discusses the significance of neural enhancement. He places the issue in the context not only of recent discussions of genetic determinism, but also within the wider cultural debates about humanism and the extent to which the views embedded in that tradition feed into any initiatives to biologically engineer mankind (including eugenics). To what extent is it legitimate to re-engineer human nature, whether by cultural or biological means? He goes on to argue that the link between self and the brain is much stronger than between genes and personal identity, that recent discoveries in neuroscience are more likely to bring turbulence to classical philosophical concepts such as free will and ascriptions of responsibility, and that more attention could be devoted to the "troubling implications of wilfully shaping the human brain"(2003:250).

Who should be Talking about all this?

It is notable that so many of the papers reviewed for this report are authored by scientists or clinicians, or published for clinical audiences. Only a small fraction of the papers are published in bioethics journals. There is a clear call for scientists and clinicians who work in the area of neuroscience to familiarise themselves with the ethical and social issues that their work raises, and to take an active role in the wider discussions with the community. Some writers offered an 'alert' or challenge to particular professional groups – to neurologists (Chatterjee 2004), to neuropsychologists (Bush et al 2002), to researchers funded by a defence agency (Anon 2003), to neuroscientists or scientists in general (Doucet 2005, Moreno 2003, Illes 2006), or to neuroimaging experts (Illes 2002). Topics cover areas as diverse as neurogenomics (Hancock and Szalma 2003), cosmetic neurology (Chatterjee 2004a), the goals of medicine (Hogle 2005),and public understandings of science, intelligence, and sexuality (Hall et al 200, Gray and Thompson 2004,Wolpe 2004).

Yet other papers were reminding readers of the need for a pre-emptive public discussion about the emerging issues (Butcher 2003, Turner and Sahakian 2006, Maguire and McGee 1999, Racine et al 2005) and/or calling for scientists' participation in the debates (Leshner 2004). Other's focus is simply on the public communication of results (Bloom 2002, Kulynych 2002, Wolpe 2004). And a very few papers are reminding readers that we make sense of technological possibilities in the light of our own cultural and religious traditions (Paladin 1998, Albright 1996).

CONCLUSION

Neuroscience is raising some fascinating questions. How will we integrate new neurotechnologies into our lives and social practices? How will we come to understand ourselves, our sense of agency and of responsibility as the biological basis of our mental activities is better understood? How will be come to think about the enhancement of our cognitive and emotional life as the technologies developed to treat medical conditions or disability become available for more 'social purposes"? How will our responses to these possibilities be shaped by religious, cultural and philosophical traditions?

Many of the papers reviewed for this report are quite generic, primarily concerned to alert readers to the issues. Only a few progress the discussions beyond a general overview, or offer sophisticated arguments that place the issues within a wider cultural and intellectual tradition. It is notable that the conversations are appearing in only a few bioethics journals, and these conversations appear to be driven by the writing of a few authors. It is also clear that several of the authors leading the conversations are not primarily bioethicists, but come from neuroscience or sociology.

Early indications are that the conversations about neuroethics will involve a fresh convergence between the relatively new discipline of bioethics, and more established disciplines of philosophy and sociology. Philosophy has a long tradition of thought about some of the central issues raised by neuroscience, but has only begun to link that to biological understandings of the brain – there remains quite a lot of work to be done to bring the worlds of philosophy and brain science together. Sociology on the other hand reminds bioethics (and philosophy) of the need to ground reflection in the lived practices of various communities of people, to describe the patterns of behaviour and interpretation that are adopted as technological possibilities open up. Bioethics is able to bring to the conversations the fruit of reflection on the ethical dimensions of other biotechnologies, such as genetics, which have already raised some similar issues.

In addition, there are new communities of scientists who have not necessarily seen their work as socially contentious, or raising ethical issues. They too are being drawn into the conversations about neuroscience, and will need to be engaged not only to ensure the public are well informed, but also to ensure they are alerted to the ethical dimensions of their own work. Conversations with scientists will also be critical if neuroethics is to be responding to the actual science, and not some abstracted or inadequate understanding about what the science is making possible. Stories about the exciting developments in neuroscience are now frequently occurring in general media. It will be interesting to see how the less academic conversations about neuroscience and its ethical implications play out, and to what extent the technological possibilities are integrated into social practices with little fanfare or discussion.

3

Impact of Genetic Technology on Prenatal Management

INTRODUCTION

Sir Victor Windeyer once commented that the law was "marching with medicine but in the rear and limping a little." As biotechnology, particularly genetic technology, has advanced even more rapidly in the two decades since this observation was made, care should be taken that the law is not left behind completely.

It has been observed that rapid changes in social conditions and medical science demand clear rules of law to govern the new fields of advancement. In order to accomplish this goal it is suggested that "... the law must build a framework that will recognise the complex moral and ethical issues surrounding research ..." With this in mind, it is proposed to examine bioethics and the law as they apply to the issues of prenatal diagnosis and abortion on genetic grounds. Specifically, attention will focus on the impact of genetic technology in these areas.

The purpose of this paper is to determine the extent to which existing law and legal policy is consistent with bioethical principles, and the extent to which it is adequately equipped to deal with emergent genetic technologies and the prenatal issues they raise. It should be noted that the parameters set by the topic of this paper require a comparative analysis of bioethics and the law. It therefore falls outside the scope of this paper to undertake a detailed analysis of feminist thought in the area of research. However, given the centrality of women to the issue of childbirth and pregnancy, it is submitted that one is (bio)ethically compelled to consider the interests of women in these areas. Thus, whilst not comprehensive, nor intended to be representative of all women's views, some of the most common criticisms and concerns encountered in feminist literature will be examined in the course of discussion. This will be done particularly with respect to the maternal/foetal relationship, and in the arguments against genetic testing based on the eugenic fear. Similarly, some of the most commonly expressed concerns regarding genetic testing raised by the disabled community will be addressed. In view of the technical nature of some aspects of this paper, a glossary of medical terms is provided. Discussion will begin, in Part 1, with an outline of some of the most important current advances in genetic technology. The Human Genome Project represents one of the most ambitious and influential projects in biotechnology, introducing with it a range of technological advances that will influence both the type and scope of genetic knowledge. A brief outline of this project's achievements and ultimate goals will therefore be undertaken to illustrate its importance to, and anticipated impact upon, the genetic technology applied before birth. Since the law and legal policy will be examined in light of bioethical thought, the first part will include an overview of the core bioethical principles which will facilitate analysis in subsequent sections.

It is proposed to begin the subsequent analysis with an outline of the current legal context in which the debated issues arise, followed by an examination of the bioethical and philosophical considerations those issues entail. Each section will conclude with an analysis of whether the law and legal policy, in light of current technology, are consist with bioethical principles, and their ability to cope with the issues arising from genetic advances.

By way of conclusion, a summation of the arguments, and an outline of the submissions, made in the paper will be given. Some issues requiring consideration which were raised by this research, but which fell outside the scope of this paper, are suggested for future research.

GENETIC AND BIOETHICAL BACKGROUND

The Human Genome Project

In order to predict the effects that genetic technology will have upon pregnancy management, it is necessary to consider the most recent research undertaken in the field of genetics. An examination of this type should concentrate not only on the findings of such research, but also upon the methods, technologies and resultant testing and therapeutic capabilities it embraces. By far the most recent, ongoing and ambitious research being undertaken in the genetic arena is that involved in the Human Genome Project (HGP), which has been described as "a coordinated effort to characterise the entire human genome." Technical advances made in the 1970s and 1980s introduced the possibility of a large human genetics research project. The impetus for the project took the form of a "radical" proposal that there should be a massive injection of funds to enable a systematic and international effort to analyse the human genome. To this end, international funding in the amount of an estimated $5 billion has been allocated for the 15-year duration of the programme.

Genetic research and testing are by no means new to the field of medicine. For example, genetic screening was mandated in the 1970s in some US states for the hereditary disorder sickle cell anaemia in black children. However, the size and structure of the HGP have required the formulation of specific goals and the organisation of resources required to attain those goals. The magnitude of the HGP has been described as "biology's equivalent to putting a man on the moon" and has therefore attracted vigorous debate regarding its legal, ethical and economic implications. Thus, whilst some issues are not unique to the HGP, "[w]hat the ... project has done is to intensify the debate and bring it into the public domain." In order to appreciate these issues, however, the project itself will need to be examined. Genetic Background Every human has traits developed from a combination of genetic characters inherited from each parent. Human heredity is based upon genes passed on in genetic material originating in equal proportions from the parental gametes. Each gene encodes information specifying a single gene product. These gene products, either singularly (in so-called Mendelian inheritance) or in combination with other gene products, determine a specific inherited trait. These genes are arranged in linear sequences along chromosomes located in the nucleus of each cell.

The human genome includes 23 pairs of chromosomes in each non-reproductive cell in the form of DNA (the molecular basis for the genetic code). Genes are composed of unique segments of genetic code (that is, a unique sequence of nucleotides) along a given chromosome. It is the individual assemblage of our genes and the proteins derived from them that make us unique. Thus, if the location of each gene on our chromosomes is known, and its code can be determined, much information may be extracted about the functioning and make-up of our bodies. The difficulty of the location of specific genes is highlighted by the fact that: "[l]ess than 10% of the human genome is estimated to contain coding regions associated with genes. An important part of the Human Genome Project ... is the location of the 50,000-100,000 genes buried within the human genome." Despite this inherent difficulty, technological advances associated with the HGP - including automated cloning equipment, techniques such as the polymerase chain reaction (PCR) and rough computerised maps of regions of DNA - have enabled extraordinary progress since the project's inception in 1991. Scientists are currently locating human genes at a rate of one or more per day and over the past year have, amongst others, specified genes associated with Huntington's disease, adrenoleukodystrophy (a major form of ataxia) and, significantly, the first breast cancer gene.

Goals for the HGP

A set of specific goals for the 15-year HGP had, by 1990, been formulated and were presented to Congress in the USA. These long term objectives include the mapping of all the 50,000-100,000 genes and the determination of the complete sequence of the human genetic code. Further, more specific goals have been set for the first five years of the project to guide the shorter term progress of the initiative. Areas of goal-setting include genetic mapping, physical mapping and DNA sequencing, informatics, technology development and ethical considerations. These areas are closely interrelated as may be illustrated by the ultimate goal of the project, to produce the ultimate physical map by determining the entire DNA sequence of the human genome.

This goal will only be realised if the project overcomes the concern of the scientific community namely, whether the project is cost-effective in terms of the value of scientific information gained compared with the money and effort invested to obtain it. Utilising today's best available equipment, an approximate 50,000-100,000 nucleotides can be sequenced annually at a cost of around $1-2 per nucleotide. This would result in an unacceptable 30,000 work-years and at least $3 billion to complete the task. In order to improve cost and efficiency, two approaches are being taken: the enhancement of current sequencing techniques, and the formulation of novel strategies for large-scale sequencing projects. The resultant technologies must be largely automated and capable of high through-put. It is worth noting that a significant portion of the allocated budget for the HGP has been dedicated to the goal of developing programmes to address ethical, legal and social considerations arising from medical advances resulting from the project. Prenatal diagnosis represents one of the most obvious and contentious areas in which these advances will take effect.

As the HGP assists with earlier, more comprehensive and more accurate diagnosis of genetic diseases, it helps to increase the available management options, including those of pregnancy termination and the possibility of genetic therapies. From a regulatory point of view, the legal position should be examined in order to assess the availability of these management options under current Australian law. However, the application of genetic testing to these ends will also inevitably involve considerations concerning the moral and ethical implications of pregnancy management. Therefore, the core bioethical principles, which will facilitate discussion in subsequent parts, are outlined below.

Bioethical Principles

Human development may be viewed in a number of ways, ranging from clinical approaches (for instance biology and chemistry) to disciplines incapable of scientific analysis (such as theology and philosophy). However, medicine arguably falls somewhere between, being concerned both with the systematic study of the unique workings of the individual and the total context in which that individual lives. As such, it is appropriate that medical ethics be based not only on strong philosophical grounds, but that physiological, psychological and other relevant perspectives also be taken into account. Developed from these considerations (and first extrapolated in the Hippocratic Oath) are six fundamental principles which are central to any discussion regarding ethical concerns in a medical context. These principles underlie bioethical decision making and strongly influence the scope and practices in that body of ethical guidance. Any detailed examination of these principles would involve extensive discussion and is hence precluded by the constraints of this study. However, a summarised table of these tenets of medical ethics is produced to facilitate discussion of the ethical issues arising in subsequent parts.

The principle of proportionality, or the "utilitarian" principle, is also often included in examinations of medical ethics. This standard refers to the duty, when taking actions that involve risks of harm, to so balance risks and benefits that action s have the greatest chance to result in the least harm and the most benefit to those involved. Strongly related to this concept is the theory of common good in medical ethics. This theory requires that medical institutions give explicit consideration to the relationship and possible clash between social and individual values. Accordingly, interests other than those of the individuals directly involved may validly be taken into account in decision making. The weight accorded to those external interests will, however, seldom be determinative and will necessarily depend on the circumstances of each case. The concept of justice embraces two dimensions: horizontal and vertical equity. The former refers to the obligation to treat equals equally. The latter refers to the obligation to treat unequals unequally in proportion to their morally relevant inequalities. A thorough discussion of these principles and their application has not been attempted in this section. Rather, it is intended to refer to, and apply, them in subsequent discussions concerning the issues arising out of genetic technology prenatally.

THE CURRENT LEGAL CONTEXT

Since the stated purposes of this paper are to analyse the law for its consistency with bioethical principles and its ability to cope with genetic advances, it is necessary to undertake an examination of current law. This will be done in the context of prenatal care, focussing on the body of law applicable to the post-implantation embryo/foetus.

Post-Implantation - The Legal Position

Existing law regarding the legal status of the foetus tends to revolve around the issue of abortion, although legal attitudes towards the unborn are also reflected in child destruction and homicide law.

Regulation of abortion dates back to the non-legal prohibition against providing a woman with the means of procuring an abortion in the Hippocratic Oath. Present day regulation reflects a State interest in the matter with statutory provisions criminalising abortion. Australian abortion laws fall into three categories of jurisdiction: common law jurisdictions, Code jurisdictions and "statutory reform" jurisdictions. Between these different types of jurisdiction, variation exists with each Australian State or Territory using different criteria to determine the legality of an abortion. For the sake of discussion therefore, it is proposed to concentrate primarily on the Code jurisdictions of Western Australia ("WA") and Queensland. The Criminal Codes in those States make it unlawful to attempt to procure an abortion or to supply drugs or instruments to facilitate an abortion. The prohibition in these sections must however be read in light of the case law concerning abortion. In order for the abortion to be unlawful, it must be shown that the procedure was not performed "for the preservation of the mother's life" and was not reasonable having regard to the patient's state at the time and all other circumstances of the case. There is a noticeable absence of case law regarding these phrases in WA, however, limited judicial consideration has been given to them in Queensland, which has virtually identical Criminal Code provisions to those in WA. The phrase "the preservation of the mother's life" was held in the Queensland cases of K v T37 and Re Bayliss to have the same meaning as that given in Re Bourne and expanded in R v Davidson.

In Re Bourne it was held that if a doctor reasonably found that pregnancy would result in a woman becoming "a physical or mental wreck" then this may justify a finding that an abortion is performed for the purpose of preserving the life of the woman. Liberalising the meaning of "unlawful" even further, Menhennitt J in R v Davidson applied the general defence of necessity to abortion. In deciding what is "necessary" and "proportionate," serious danger to a woman's physical or mental health may be considered, and the abortion should not in the circumstances be out of proportion to the danger being averted. The case of R v Bayliss and Cullen confirmed the adoption of this approach in Code jurisdictions. It should be noted that in the common law jurisdiction of New South Wales, the case of R v Wald adopted the R v Davidson approach, then expanded it by holding that it would be for the jury to decide whether there existed in the case of each woman any economic, social or medical ground or reason which in their view could constitute reasonable grounds upon which an accused could honestly and reasonably believe there would result a serious danger to her physical or mental health.

This approach represents significant gains for women's reproductive rights by inserting economic and social factors into t he necessary and proportionate tests adopted in R v Davidson. R v Wald was applied in New South Wales in K v Minister for Youth and Community Services but has received no comment in the Code jurisdictions. Whilst R v Davidson has been adopted in these latter jurisdictions, the case law has been silent as to the adoption, or the extent of adoption, of the approach in R v Wald.

Despite the existence and legal consideration of abortion laws in Australia, there remains in practice a significant gap between the letter and the practice of the law. On the one hand, the effect of medical developments tends to strengthen the status of the foetus legally, with ever more premature babies being able to be kept alive, therefore decreasing the age of viability and hence increasing the application of the term "a child capable of being born alive" under child destruction law (which overlaps with the statutory prohibition of unlawful abortion). On the other hand it may be argued that, the availability of, and lack of prosecution for, abortion seriously undermines the legal position of the foetus. It is notable that British and Australian courts have consistently refused to recognise both foetal rights prior to birth and the legal personality (or personhood) of a foetus. In the Australian case of K v T it was held that a foetus lacks such independent legal personality and rights until it is born.

This approach has found approval in A-G (ex rel Kerr) v T and, most recently, the re has been a denial of any right to protection against abortion being vested in the foetus. Whilst in R v Wald it was argued that society has an interest in the preservation of the human species, and in particular the life and welfare of its members, the focus upon maternal rather than foetal health in the abortion cases cited, together with the reference in R v Wald to socioeconomic factors, suggests that society's interest in the foetus may be subsumed to the interests of the mother. This lack of legal rights is also reflected in the law relating to unlawful killing. Under Australian law, a foetus in utero cannot be a victim of homicide, regardless of its gestational age. It is therefore unprotected by the most serious offences designed to protect the sanctity of human life. As the previous discussion illustrates, there is a significant gap between the law regarding abortion as it stands and its enforcement.

A number of reasons may account for this phenomenon, for instance, "[t]here is a disparity between situations where according to the law an abortion would (or probably would) be lawful, and situations where such an abortion is actually available to a woman...". The situation is further explained by the unlikelihood of successful prosecution under current law. The tests in R v Davidson and R v Wald cast a heavy burden of proof upon the prosecution.

Non-enforcement of the criminal law regarding abortion is illustrated by the fact that prosecutions for unlawful abortion effectively ceased in Australia in the early 1970s. Although this and, where cases are brought, the wide interpretation of the risk to maternal health are thought to be liberalising factors, the existence and inconsistency of abortion law is still a significant factor in a discussion of prenatal diagnosis and pregnancy termination. This is so because current and proposed laws concerning abortion can have a profound effect on the decision to abort. Issues affecting prenatal decision making are said to relate to the timing of the diagnosis, the nature of the genetic condition (type and severity,) the religious and moral convictions of the mother (or both prospective parents) and societal pressures. For a number of people, their moral stance is greatly influenced by the law (what is illegal is taught to individuals to represent what is "wrong" morally). Further, legal sanctions form an important source of societal pressure and may be seen to represent standards that are socially acceptable (this is not surprising given the democratic nature of our society where legislating is the role of Parliament who in turn are elected by, and are technically the representatives of, "the people"). Thus the decision to terminate a pregnancy following prenatal diagnosis may, at least obliquely, be influenced by the legality of abortion.

As outlined above, the focus in determining the lawfulness of abortion has been upon maternal rather than foetal health. However, in the "statutory reform jurisdictions" of South Australia and the Northern Territory, legislative reform has introduced to statutory exceptions to unlawful abortion a "foetal ground" to abort. As such, grounds to abort exist where there is a risk to a pregnant woman's physical or mental health or where there is a substantial risk that the child would be seriously physically or mentally handicapped if the child were born.[62] In all other states, abortion remains criminally unlawful subject to it being necessary to preserve the mother's life or health. Although this provision, especially when interpreted widely as in R v Davidson and R v Wald, would be likely to sanction abortion where severe genetic defects are diagnosed, the law still remains ambiguous and undefined in this area. As such, the perception of abortion as a criminal act by most women is likely to make the already difficult decision to terminate a pregnancy after abnormal genetic results, even more burdensome.

This then calls into question the ethics of a community, or a powerful part thereof, taking a moral stance against abortion and, accordingly, promulgating binding laws to that effect. The issue becomes whether abortion should remain under legislative control, or be left to private conscience (and, in the latter case, whether private conscience should be limited under certain conditions). As illustrated above, abortion law in Australia is inconsistent, uncertain and unenforced. It does not adequately deal with medical technology [and] ... [i]t does not address the social and ethical problems posed by abortion.

Abortion laws had their origin in the protection of maternal health. However, as medical technology has progressed, protecting the mother's life by prohibiting abortion becomes nonsensical (particularly in the first trimester). The lack of reform in this area has been explained by political cautiousness, given the electorally sensitive nature of abortion. Although politically expedient to avoid the issue, such political manoeuvring prevents the law from reflecting social attitudes, particularly a s there is an overwhelming consensus that abortion should be legal, inter alia, in the case of birth defects. In opposition to strict legal regulation of abortion, and in the interests of developing a flexibility that would allow new evidence and new technical (and social) developments to affect the communal ethos, it has been argued that: "[e]nforcement of such matters legitimately belongs within the social sanction of specific groups or belief systems. The community that enforces such belief systems in legal form arguably disrupts its own peace." Given the lack of enforcement of the law in this matter and the "proper" place for decisions regarding abortion being in the ethical arena, it is appropriate to turn to an examination of the moral and ethical considerations that will affect prenatal management options.

BIOETHICAL AND PHILOSOPHICAL CONSIDERATIONS

The Status of the Post-Implantation Embryo/Foetus

The discussion in Part 2 on the legal status of the embryo/foetus revolved primarily around the "foetal rights" debate, particularly in the context of abortion. Consideration of the status of the embryo/foetus, however, goes beyond the issue of "rights" and involves a number of ethical as well as legal considerations that interact against a backdrop of evolving technologies and social values. "One critical set of values undergoing re-evaluation centers on the relationship between the mother and the foetus." This has largely been due to rapid advances in foetal medicine that allow the foetus to be seen, operated on and even "created". These advances are altering the societal and scientific understanding and perception of the foetus. The emergent trend has increasingly been to consider the foetus as an individual separate from its mother. It is important therefore to evaluate the current status, both bioethically and philosophically.

This part will begin with an outline of some of the broader philosophical approaches to the conceptual treatment of the embryo/foetus. These approaches range from the recognition and treatment of post-conception ova as being "fully human," deserving of the same moral standing as a "life in being", to that of the unborn being "subhuman" with no moral status. The bioethical principles outlined in Part 1 will then be considered in determining the most appropriate model. It will be argued that an intermediate approach is the most realistic model for bioethical decision-making, given current medical knowledge and contemporary social values.

As alluded to above, the interests of the foetus are inextricably linked to those of the mother. Where these interests conflict, it is necessary to consider the ethical implications of balancing the interests of the two parties. It is therefore useful to consider the maternal/foetal relationship from a philosophical viewpoint in order to establish a bioethical framework for making such decisions. The resultant model will necessarily rely heavily on the conclusions reached regarding the moral standing of the foetus.

Philosophical Models of the Status of the Foetus

The "Conservative"/"Fully Human" Approach

Considered to be the most extreme "anti-abortion" or "pro-life" position, this view holds that once fertilised, a human ovum has the same moral standing as any other human being. In the course of the ethical debate surrounding embryonic and foetal standing, the "fully human" view has received its earliest support from religious traditions. However, although significant in their own right, and for the impact they have had on the development of contemporary moral and ethical stances, religious arguments will, for the present purposes, be excluded from discussion.

The conservative approach is supported by two arguments: scientific/genetic and social. The scientific/genetic argument relies on the fact that the foetus is indisputably genetically human. From the moment of conception, all genetic information is present and all the physical characteristics for life are contained in that newly developed code - no new genetic information is added during the life of that individual. Thus fertilisation is said to mark the spatiotemporal beginning of a new human being.

Hence, "[a]n argument that the foetus is not human life biologically does not hold water. The chromosome count is correct, and a sufficient number of other criteria for both "life" and "human" are met to leave no doubt as to this." This approach does not accept the distinction between a newly formed embryo and a viable foetus. Unlike the legal trend of attaching ever greater significance to the foetus as it approaches viability, proponents of the conservative view argue that it is a mistake to confuse independence with separateness. Despite its dependence on the mother, a non-viable foetus is still a separate entity, with its own genetic code and, Steinbock argues, its own moral worth.

Whilst the scientific argument emphasises the significance of the fact that an embryo/foetus is genetically human, the second of the supporting arguments for the conservative view attaches moral weight to this humanity from the time of conception. This social perspective is founded on a number of considerations, the notion of potentiality being an important component. It is this "potentiality" argument that will be addressed here.

It is said that since the embryo/foetus is potentially, just like us, so we cannot deny it any rights or other forms of protection that we accord ourselves. The fact that a fertilised ovum is not yet "just like us", it is said, is simply a temporal constraint and it would therefore be morally wrong to kill or otherwise prevent it reaching its potential. In its strongest form, this view maintains that a potential human subject should be accorded the moral standing of an actual human subject. The standard objection to the potentiality argument is that it involves a logical mistake: that of equating a "potential person" to an "actual person" and, on this basis, ascribing to the former the same rights as the latter. The logical position is that a potential bearer of the characteristics to which the rights attach, should only potentially bear those rights.

It is submitted that the defence offered by Steinbock, that the argument makes only a normative proposal (that potential persons ought to have the same rights as actual persons) does not wholly overcome this logical objection. In the absence of a strong moral reason for this normative approach, the potentiality argument remains flawed.

Further, it has been suggested that an early embryo has no greater difference in potential than that possessed by a sperm and egg when separate, but considered jointly. From a statistical viewpoint, three ova placed in a test tube containing sperm, but which have yet to be fertilised, have a greater potential to produce human life than one early embryo in a test tube. Taken to its logical conclusion, the "potential argument" would accord greater moral worth to sperm and a number of unfertilised ova than to a smaller number of early embryos.

Given the criticisms outlined above, it is contended that the "potentiality" argument provides strongest support, not for the conservative view, but for the more moderate stances which fall between the two extremes. On this basis, as the embryo develops into a foetus and increasingly acquires the characteristics of a person, so its moral worth and incumbent rights attach. The continuity of human life is another argument raised in support of the conservative view (and may be offered as a moral basis for the normative ascription of rights to fertilised ova under the potentiality approach). It is said that human life is an uninterrupted flow, with new individual life appearing at conception. The life at that point is argued to be every bit as human as its parents, otherwise human life would have a discontinuous break between conception and birth. The social voice of the conservative view, reflecting the continuum of life approach, is apparent in the following declaration of Dr A. Liley, the so-called "father of modern foetology":

"Not all of us will live to be old, but we were each once a foetus ... surely if any of us counts for anything now, we counted for something before we were born."

However, the mere fact that there is no genetic or physical discontinuity does not seem to support the necessary conclusion that there is no moral change in the status accorded to the embryo and foetus. Further, this same continuity argument has also been used to detract from the view that conception marks the beginning of human life and the attraction of moral worth. An evolutionist may view the beginning of human life as the accumulation of chemicals which first produced life forms, a Theologian may ascribe its beginning to God, whilst the psychologist or philosopher could attribute the origins of human life to the intent of a couple to procreate. Accordingly, it is argued that the only certainty in defining the beginning of human life is the difficulty of how best to define the beginning. Like all life, human life is a gradual and continuously evolving process. It begins when and where you want it to. This depends on your approach and perspective.

Various other arguments have been levelled at this conservative approach, the most prominent of which will be outlined in the course of explaining the alternative philosophical models examined below.

The "Personhood"/ "Subhuman" Approach

Predictably, the most strenuous objections to the "fully human" approach are raised by proponents of the opposite view, the so-called "subhuman" argument. This position is the most extreme "pro-choice" stance, expounding the belief that an unborn human l acks moral relevance. Under this model, no woman should ever be forced to have a child against her will, irrespective of the condition or gestational age of the foetus Joseph Fletcher maintains that "no unwanted and unintended baby should ever be born."

In direct contradiction to the significance placed on genetic humanity by the conservatives, supporters of the "personhood" view espouse the irrelevance of genetic make-up. These proponents, like Mary Anne Warren, argue that it is not genetic human beings that have any special moral status or right to life, but persons. Implicit in this view is the capacity to become a moral agent - to have not only moral rights, but moral obligations to others. It is the possession of certain characteristics that defines personhood: consciousness, self-consciousness, rationality and language.

Since no foetus is self-conscious, this would support the treatment of the unborn as subhuman - on this basis Warren concludes it is not seriously wrong to kill a foetus or embryo (and goes so far as to say that abortion is "morally neutral", comparable to having one's hair cut). This latter view of Warren's alludes to another argument for the absence of moral worth in the embryo/foetus: that the unborn (at least until viability) is no more than an extension of the mother's body. Clearly, medical science would contradict such an assertion in that an embryo has, from the moment of conception, its own sex and genetic blueprint. Whilst the gestational embryo depends on the mother's body, it remains a distinct entity (medically speaking).

Returning to the central theme of the "personhood" theory, a primary objection to the use of the "personhood" criteria to ascribe moral worth is that this approach would treat infants as well as the unborn as morally irrelevant. Since babies do not differ significantly from late term foetuses in terms of "person-making characteristics", and do not develop self-consciousness within about the first year and a half of life, infanticide in this view would also be treated as "morally neutral". Of course, the fact that a conclusion is counter- intuitive does not prove the argument wrong.

Indeed, Michael Tooley argues that the objection to infanticide is not based on rational principles, but rather on a non-rational taboo resulting from the distressing effect to our sensibilities. Given that bioethics must operate in, and be contextually relevant to, the communities it serves, strong and widespread social opposition must be more persuasive than it would be in pure philosophy. However, a philosophical objection to the "person view" is also offered by Steinbock who claims that Warren fails to explain the moral significance of the psychological and cognitive capacities that attract the rights of "persons". In the absence of such explanation, the person view is seen to be as arbitrary as the genetic-humanity criterion. From the above discussion, it is contended that neither extreme view provides a satisfactory approach to the determination of the ethical standing of an embryo/foetus. An examination and evaluation of more moderate stances is therefore warranted.

The "Moderate" Views

The Interest View As we have seen, Steinbock criticises Warren's "personhood" view on the basis that no moral significance attaches to the stated "personhood" criteria. In response to this criticism, Steinbock therefore posits an alternative theory, which states that all, and only, beings who have interests have moral status. This idea of interests hinges on the notion of caring about what is done to one:

"[i]t is this notion of mattering that is the key to moral status. ... Whatever reasons we may have for preserving non-sentient beings, these reasons do not refer to their own interests.

For without conscious awareness, beings cannot have interests. Without interests, they cannot have a welfare of their own."

It is argued that without welfare, nothing can be done for that being's sake, and hence, that it lacks moral standing or status. In this way, Steinbock links the "personhood" characteristic of sentience with that of interests and thus, moral significance. Steinbock is, however, mindful that the concept of interests does not overcome an objection to the "person view", namely that foetuses and embryos are rendered morally irrelevant by this reasoning. In response to this, she calls on the concept of potentiality to augment her interests argument.

Potentiality Revisited

The ability of the embryo/foetus to have interests raises both factual and conceptual difficulties. Since non-sentient creatures are assumed incapable of having interests, the factual concern is raised of when a conscious mental state can be said to emerge in human development. Precisely when foetuses attain conscious awareness is controversial, although it is likely that some sensations begin to be experienced during the third trimester of pregnancy. However, Steinbock argues that this does not mean that earlier life forms are morally neutral.

She says that as potential persons, embryos and foetuses have a symbolic value that precludes using them in unnecessary experiments or for purely commercial activities. However, this symbolic value is "less important than the actual interests of born human beings in life and health." The appeal to potentiality under this view can be seen to have both medical and ethical support. First, it is medically evident that human development is interconnected with physical development.

Not all bodily organs and functions peculiar to humans are apparent at conception, rather they develop gradually through the prenatal period. Further, there is a connection between psychological and physical development. As the central nervous system (CNS) develops and the brain stem emerges, so too does the capacity for thought and sentient experience. On this basis, it may be argued that human personhood develops along with the human body.[104] Similarly, human personality develops over time through a gradual process of development. Conception does not mark the beginning of self-identity. It is argued that one becomes a person as personality develops through relations with others and that prior to this, we are only potentially or emergently human persons. It seems then that Steinbock uses potentiality to justify the symbolic moral value of the pre-sentient embryo/foetus. Recognition is given to the fact that parents and society may value the developing child for its anticipated role in, and contribution to, its family and society. A foetus may also have important symbolic value to those who see it as representing and extending their own existence and/or relationships. From an interest perspective, this recognises, and gives moral weight to, the interests that others may have in the welfare of the unborn. A similar approach is found in the primary/secondary moral worth theory.

Primary/Secondary Moral Worth

In expounding the concept of primary or secondary moral worth, Loewy embraces the notion of "interests" (as opposed to "rights") in an examination of foetal status. Arguing against the "subhuman" position, Loewy appeals to biological evidence that satisfies both "human" and "life" criteria to describe the embryo/foetus. This, however, he says is insufficient in itself to endow the unborn with moral worth. Instead, he argues that what we hold as having prima facie rights against wanton destruction are entities endowed with either primary worth (those of value now or in the future again to themselves) or of secondary or symbolic worth (those of value to another in themselves or as representative of something held to be of value). Loewy refutes the conservative argument on the basis of potential, maintaining that a developing entity has the potential to become many things, which are unknowable.

Whilst the foetus undoubtedly has the potential for being of primary moral worth (and this carries more moral weight than does the lack of that potential), a zygote also has the potential for being spontaneously aborted, being malformed or becoming a villain. Glover supports this view by maintaining that under the "potential" approach, what is valued is not the embryo itself, but the person it is expected to become. Thus, whilst the potential for possible primary worth is of some significance, the question becomes the extent to which moral weight should be accorded on this basis. Of more certain and existent value at the prenatal stage is the secondary worth of the human embryo/foetus which is derived from its symbolic value both to the family and to society. This latter notion provides a moral basis for legal intervention in the area o f prenatal care. However, the moral weight that this interest is accorded should be balanced against other relevant interests in determining the appropriate role of the legal system in this respect.

The "Social Persons" Perspective

A final "moderate view" is expressed by Engelhardt who tackled the problem of assigning moral significance to the embryo/foetus by developing the notion of "social persons". This phrase may be said to describe human beings who are "treated by society as persons even though they are not." An entity's moral standing is expressed in terms of the social sense of its "personhood" by identifying the place of that being in a social relationship with persons possessing full moral status. In the case of the embryo/foetus, it may be treated as a family member and be accorded moral standing in this respect.

Engelhardt sees considerable value in protecting anything that could reasonably play the role person and thus strengthen the social position of persons generally. According to this view, "social persons" have rights but no duties, meaning that they are not morally responsible agents, but are accorded the respect associated with them. The "moderate views" outlined above resemble each other in two important respects. First, they all recognise the notion of developing moral status (with neither a complete absence nor full assignation of moral status accorded to the fertilised ovum). Hence, as an embryo develops, so its social and symbolic significance is enhanced, together with its incumbent moral standing.

Second, these views all consider the interests of others in determining the status of the embryo/foetus. In each case, the moral significance attached to an entity may, to some degree, be determined by that being's significance to other human beings possessed of moral standing. This second aspect contemplates the importance of the maternal-foetal relationship as a determinant of the "rights" assigned to the implanted embryo.

On the basis of the ethical principles outlined in Part 1, it is contended that, from a bioethical perspective, the "moderate views" concerning the moral status of the foetus are to be preferred. This is so given the recognition those perspectives give to the interests of others, thereby embodying the principles of justice, respect for persons and the notion of proportionality. Further, these views acknowledge the biological development of an embryo as an important consideration when assigning it moral status. In this way, philosophical, physiological and social perspectives are incorporated into the determination of the bioethical standing of the developing human. This is particularly important in light of the rate at which genetic technology as it applies to prenatal care is advancing. The flexibility facilitated by a "moderate" approach would allow new evidence and new technological developments to affect the communal ethos from which, after all, such judgments emerge.

THE MATERNAL/FOETAL RELATIONSHIP

Clearly the perceived status and physical well being of the foetus are inextricably linked to those of its mother. Rapid advances in prenatal diagnosis and therapy are joined with new reproductive-aiding technologies such as in vitro fertilisation and more precise genetic tests. Combined with the burgeoning knowledge of foetal development and the causes of congenital illness, these technologies are altering our perception of the foetus and prevailing values are being challenged by the new biology.

Overall observes that the capacity to place the foetus "in full public view" carries with it the ability to affect our moral attitudes towards the embryo/foetus. Genetic technologies have enhanced our capacity to "create", observe, diagnose and treat the embryo/foetus as an individual entity. These technologies have the embryo/foetus as their focus and objective, thereby encouraging the developing child to be viewed as a patient (if secondary) in it s own right. Medical recognition of the embryo/ foetus as an entity separate from the mother has led to some concern about the way this will impact upon the mother. It is therefore imperative in any discussion concerning the status of the foetus to consider the impact that this perceived moral status will have upon the interests of the mother. The models used to explain the maternal/foetal relationship are closely related to those addressing the moral and philosophical standing of the foetus.

In a recent report commissioned by the Australian Medical Association (AMA), Seymour[122] outlines three models of the maternal/foetal relationship. The first model views the foetus as part of the woman's body, a view consistent with the "subhuman/personhood" approach to the foetus outlined in the previous section. As a framework for legal policy, this model is inappropriate as it is inconsistent with current medical knowledge. As this paper seeks to examine the law for its consistency and ability to deal with current medical technology, it must reject the "body part" approach to the foetus as being biologically inaccurate. The foetus, inclusive of its supportive placenta, is not a biological part of the mother. It is both physiologically and genetically a distinct organism, having its own physiological integrity, genetic code etc. At the opposite end of the scale, the "separate entity" model relies on the biological distinction between mother and child in endowing the foetus with full moral standing. This view, in accordance with the "fully human" approach previously discussed, views the pregnant woman and foetus as two beings, each having a full complement of rights (despite both being in a single body).

It has thus been noted by Seymour that the use of the language of rights is an unavoidable consequence of the adoption of the separate entities model.The adoption of a rights discourse with respect to the maternal/foetal relationship has been widely criticised, most vociferously by feminist commentators. The argument against reference to foetal "rights" in the context of the maternal/foetal relationship is that it simultaneously generates conflict, devalues the woman, and subjects her to control. Further, both the "separate entities" model and the "body part" view may be criticised as not reflecting women's perceptions of pregnancy. Specifically, some feminist theorists argue that male and female conceptual frameworks differ, the former ascribing to notions of individualism and rights, whilst the latter relies on concepts of connection. A rights discourse, which by its nature focuses on the potentially conflicting rights of the mother and foetus, is therefore inconsistent with the notions of connectedness and interdependence. Bennett observes that the foetal rights debate can easily ignore the experiences of women and their centrality to the issues. Thus,

"[t]o underline the importance of connectedness and interdependence is to underline the importance of w omen's perceptions of pregnancy".

It is therefore argued that both of these "extreme" views should be rejected on the grounds that they distort and over-simplify the complex relationship between mother and foetus. Further, they pay insufficient attention to the views of women. A final criticism of the "separate entities" and "body part" models is that they fail to differentiate between the relationship that the foetus has with the mother, and that which it has with other members of society.

If one were to ascribe no rights to the foetus, then it would have no moral (or subsequent legal) claim against third parties who inflict harm on it prenatally. Since third parties have no compelling interest to morally justify the infliction of "harm" to the foetus (such as the threat to their bodily integrity), it is submitted that such a distinction is ethically indicated. Similarly, ascription of full rights to the foetus would not distinguish any act of the mother's resulting in harm to the foetus from acts of third parties, notwithstanding her unique interests in respect of the pregnancy. It is submitted that the principles of justice and autonomy require that the mother be permitted to exercise far greater control with respect to determining foetal welfare, given her necessary and compelling interest in the pregnancy.

Given the very geography of pregnancy, questions as to the status [and welfare] of the foetus must follow, not precede, an examination of the rights of the woman within whose body and life the foetus exists. Flowing from the criticism of the above two models, we see the basis for the third model, described by Seymour as the "indivisibly linked" view. The key feature of this model is that it centres on the shared needs and interdependence of the mother and foetus. "Connectedness, mutuality and reciprocity" therefore constitute the crucial tenets of the model.

Seymour cites Ruddick and Wilcox's description of this model: Mother-and-child is a complex, both bodily and morally: just as we cannot easily say whether pregnancy involves two bodies or only one (in a special expanding state), just so we cannot easily say whether pregnancy involves two sets of overlapping interests or only one set (in a special expanding state). If we allow that there are two sets, then we must recognise that they are mutually dependent to an unusual degree. The "indivisibly linked" model is consistent with the "moderate" views of the status of the embryo/foetus in that it allows for the recognition of the interests or needs of the foetus, without these being absolute. It also enables a flexible approach to be adopted with respect to the differing relationship the foetus has with its mother, as compared to that which it has with the rest of society. Shifting the focus away from rights and onto interests allows a middle ground to be adopted, where the connectedness of the mother to the infant is recognised by the moral weight given to their respective interests. The moral weight of foetal interests will differ when viewed in the context of parties other than the mother. Such an approach is consistent with the principle of justice, particularly the principle of vertical equity, which imposes an obligation to "treat unequals unequally in proportion to the morally relevant inequalities." It may be seen that a mother's special connection to her foetus, and the direct emotional and bodily impact which it has on her, constitute morally relevant considerations. These considerations justify a moral and legal distinction to be drawn between the maternal/foetal relationship and the relationship which a foetus has with the rest of society.

It is therefore submitted that, as a basis for legal policy, the "indivisibly linked" model is the most appropriate, being a more refined conceptual and analytical tool than the two more extreme models. This moderate model allows for a legal policy reflective of the philosophical and bioethical principles concerning pregnancy and, in addition, enables greater flexibility in coping with the challenges that advancing genetic technology will create concerning our values and perceptions in respect of the foetus and its mother. Importantly, it transcends the contractarian policy models which focus on rights and duties and which have been criticised by feminist theorists as being particularly inappropriate in respect of reproductive issues.

LAW & LEGAL POLICY

It was concluded in the previous part that legal policy should reflect the more moderate views concerning the embryo/foetus (both in terms of its intrinsic moral standing, and of its relationship with the mother). It now becomes necessary to examine the law in light of current medical technology to determine the adequacy with which it deals with the issues raised by this technology, and to analyse its underlying policy for consistency with the bioethical models suggested.

Current Technology

Foetal medicine has been characterised by rapid development in recent years, with a tendency to apply rapidly new technology and to put the most recent laboratory and diagnostic methods into medical practice. In order to appreciate the impact the HGP will have upon prenatal diagnosis, one should begin with a basic review of the current and prospective technologies in this area.

Noninvasive Screening Tests

The earliest and most traditional methods of prenatal diagnosis involved noninvasive measures such as palpation and auscultation. However, developments in radiology and the advent of ultrasound technologies and particularly realtime sonography have greatly increased our ability to detect foetal malformation, growth retardation and multiple births noninvasively. Radiography enables the foetus to be studied directly to detect any skeletal abnormalities, with amniography and foetography enabling the detection of soft tissue abnormalities. These methods however are only of proven value in later pregnancy, which limits the management options resulting from such diagnosis. Ultrasound facilitates the location of the foetus and placenta and the detection of gross structural abnormalities in the foetus. This process appears, after 25 years of diagnostic use, to be safe and has enjoyed increasing popularity among pregnant women, including those in low risk categories for foetal abnormalities. The diagnostic value of this procedure has been in rapid karyotyping, where amniocentesis is undertaken after suggestive ultrasound findings. Thus ultrasound may suggest the possibility of genetic defects and indicate the use of more invasive diagnostic measures to confirm this.

Isolation of Foetal Cells from Maternal Circulation

With the advent of PCR, this particular non-invasive prenatal testing technique has significant diagnostic potential. PCR technology enables the generation of large amounts of genetic material from initially minute quantities. It therefore has the potential to increase the range and accuracy of diagnoses made from isolated foetal cells. The diagnostic potential of this method of testing justifies the separate consideration of it.

The test involves the isolation from maternal blood of foetal cells such as trophoblasts which may cross the placenta into the mother's circulation. Because all invasive procedures carry a small but appreciable risk, this technique would be favoured. However, until recently, foetal cells could not be sufficiently isolated to be of use. Although recent techniques have improved the accuracy of the procedure, the specificity and sensitivity of this new test need to be established before it can be decided whether it provides a truly diagnostic or screening test. Should the technique be approved however, current results indicate that it could be applied during the first trimester. Timing is significant because the earlier the diagnosis, the broader the spectrum of management options. The least invasive techniques are bioethically favoured as they involve the least interference with the mother's bodily integrity and the least risk to both mother and foetus. It may therefore be seen that as genetic technology improves to allow increasingly accurate procedures, so the number of prenatal care options requiring less interference with, or risk to, the mother increases.

Invasive Techniques

It has been characteristic of the field of prenatal diagnosis that many alternative techniques ... have been developed over the years that offer a more adequate selection, taking gestational age, speed and other factors into account. This is beneficial, but the safety of every new procedure has to be evaluated against the background of the more established techniques.

The concerns about safety are particularly acute when considering invasive diagnostic procedures, which include foetoscopy, amniocentesis and chorionic villus sampling (CVS).Foetoscopy is a method which may prove useful in the antenatal diagnosis of congenital malformations. It utilises fibre optics to allow visualisation of the foetus; however, the significant risks it involves indic ate that its use should be limited to high risk pregnant women who have already produced a baby with severe congenital defects. In terms of genetic testing, the most widely used invasive diagnostic procedure is that of amniocentesis.

The foetus is enveloped in a membranous sac called the amnion which is filled with amniotic fluid. This fluid, similar in content to extracellular fluid, contains excreted foetal enzymes, amino acids and, importantly, foetal cells derived primarily from the skin and amnion. Using ultrasound guidance, amniotic fluid can be extracted easily after 14 weeks of pregnancy. The advantages of the procedure include its accessibility to patients in many regions of the world (because amniotic fluid can be mailed to specialised laboratories) and a relatively low risk rate of foetal loss (estimated to be 1% or less) or maternal cell contamination. The procedure was also found to potentially encourage women in high risk categories to have another pregnancy by offering greater pregnancy management options, and hence greater reproductive choice, to these women.

The major disadvantages of amniocentesis include the need to produce amniotic fluid cell cultures and, importantly, the late results in second trimester pregnancy, when most centres would no longer terminate the pregnancy. Induced abortion at this late stage involves not only considerable medical risks, but also a severe emotional impact on the mother (particularly after the experience of quickening). In response to the risks associated with amniocentesis, the alternative invasive procedure of CVS was introduced. Given that this procedure involves sampling from the larger chorionic cavity, CVS allows for first trimester testing. Although recent trials have indicated that the number of repeat procedures required was significantly higher, and that mosaicism is observed more frequently in CVS, the procedure does have distinct advantages. The significant factors in CVS's favour include earlier and more rapid diagnosis, more privacy in reproductive decision making and earlier reassurance (or an earlier abortion if that is indicated).

The HGP's Impact on Prenatal Diagnosis It may be seen from the preceding discussion that the confrontation of foetal maldevelopments by parents and physicians is not new, but because of the better technology, it is more frequent and more precise. The gene mapping component of the HGP is the first step in developing DNA probes that can be used in prenatal diagnosis. The project offers the possibility that the mapping and sequencing of disease genes will accelerate and that diagnostic procedures will become ever cheaper, quicker and more sensitive. As a consequence, it may become feasible to extend testing from high risk pregnancies to the population at large, and to offer prenatal testing for a whole spectrum of conditions. As the HGP assists the earlier, more comprehensive and more accurate diagnosis of genetic diseases, it helps to increase the available management options, including that of pregnancy termination. However, it also involves technologies and raises issues that have not (or may not have) been contemplated by the law. It is therefore incumbent on legislators and policy-makers to consider the implications of the HGP not only for medical practice, but for the regulation thereof.

Molecular genetic techniques are widely used to analyse DNA in prenatal diagnosis, allowing early diagnosis from undifferentiated tissues (such as trophoblasts which may become available via foetal cell isolation from maternal blood). As the project continues, an ever-increasing number of conditions may be tested for in this way, thereby replacing considerably more invasive techniques (for example, foetoscopy and foetal liver or muscle biopsy by CVS). Further, technical advances such as PCR have made possible the earliest form of prenatal genetic testing, namely, pre-implantation diagnosis from a trophoblast before embryo transplant. This technique is available where in vitro fertilisation (IVF) is undertaken and may represent a significantly beneficial option for those requiring IVF and for those opposed to terminations of pregnancy (even in the first trimester) but who would undergo assisted reproduction. Various professional, political, and policy stances can influence the degree to which the introduction of more genetic markers [and technologies] into normal prenatal care is accepted, or indeed, encouraged. The question is, then, Will such [technologies] actually improve the quality of prenatal care, and at what cost? This paper aims to address a number of the issues arising from the information and technologies emerging from the HGP from a bioethical and legal viewpoint. This is done to highlight policy considerations that should underpin the legal review made necessary by the HGP and advances in genetic technology generally.

Prenatal Genetic Testing:- Ethics and Policy

In the course of foetal prenatal diagnosis, cells from a foetus are screened as early as possible in pregnancy and, if found to carry a deleterious gene, parents are often given the option to terminate. Dianne Nicol points out that the "application of such procedures will inevitably feed into the ongoing debate over the ethics of abortion". Many objections have been raised against the practice of prenatal genetic testing, a number of which are addressed below. The Hippocratic Oath, as one of the earliest records of the value placed on potential human life, included a pledge given by doctors not to give a woman the means to procure an abortion. It has been argued that this "sanctity of (potential) life" approach forms "the nucleus of all medical ethics" and on this basis, is put forward as a reason to prohibit abortion today. There are, however, convincing reasons why this approach should no longer be adhered to. Moral and ethical standards are necessarily a reflection of societal standards and conditions. The fact that it appears that the status of the foetus was placed so highly as to subordinate the autonomy and self determination of the mother some 400 years before the birth of Christ in ancient Greece, does not make a convincing case for the same status to be accorded to the foetus in a modern day context. Rather, the interests of the mother must play a vital role, thereby reflecting the status of women in present day society.

Now these women, the daughters of Eve, scarcely had any rights until the 20th century. The emancipation of women and the rise of feminism gave primacy to the woman's choice...It has now become legal and ethical to terminate pregnancies, often under conditions that are very loosely defined. However, it is important at this stage of the discussion that recognition be given to the fundamental distinction between the ethics of pregnancy termination following prenatal diagnosis and those of abortion for unrelated reasons. This distinction rests largely on the fact that:

> *"[m]ost pregnancies that proceed as far as prenatal diagnosis are wanted, even if not originally planned or intended, by the time the procedure is performed. Abortion of a wanted pregnancy differs in a psychological and ... moral quality from abortion of an unwanted pregnancy."*

Further, "[u]nlike pregnancies aborted for "social" reasons, the abortion for genetic indications generally occurs later in the pregnancy, often after recognition of foetal movement, and requires a physically more demanding procedure." Thus it is submitted that the moral and ethical dilemmas raised by the topic of pregnancy termination should be viewed in the context of the special considerations involved in prenatal diagnosis. The following discussion will therefore examine the ethics relevant to, and arguments concerning, antenatal genetic testing itself. It will also explore inevitable moral and ethical conundrums involved in abortion on genetic grounds.

Arguments Against Prenatal Testing

Of interest is the observation that the choices made based on prenatal diagnosis are not so much new in character as they are in timing. Wertz and Fletcher point out that historically, parents have always made choices (often negative) about non-healthy children. For centuries, disabled newborns were exposed or left to die, the Catholic Church having made no effort to eradicate this custom. However, the advent of modern medicine, legal and hospital regulations and perinatologists' quest to save life has precluded such practices. This is so even where the extent of medical technology available cannot cure, or even effectively alleviate, the infant's ailment. Hence it is observed that

"[f]or most parents, choices are now limited to the preconceptional or prebirth period. Having foreclosed choices that once existed postnatally, medicine now offers new choices prenatally."

Prenatal diagnosis is now one of the most frequently used procedures in prenatal care and, as it becomes more common and more effective, the significant ethical dimensions involved need to be addressed. The detection of any defect, particularly of genetic origin, is of considerable consequence for the affected individual. However, it should be recognised that it may also be equally consequential for society and for all who deal with that person (particularly family) throughout life. Ethical debate surrounding prenatal diagnosis, has seen a number of criticisms levelled at the practice, the earliest opposition arising from religious traditions. However, as has previously been explained, religious objections will, for the present purposes, be excluded from discussion. Of the more contemporary arguments against prenatal diagnosis, some significant objections of the previously "hidden voices" of the feminist and disabled communities will be addressed. Firstly however, two fairly common philosophical arguments against genetic testing will be evaluated.

Aborting Beethoven

The first and most common philosophical objection is raised by the possibility of denying the birth of potential genius on the basis of a genetic defect. The hypothetical is put that a pregnant woman is tested and found to be carrying a foetus inflicted with inherited syphilis who will, in all probability, develop an associated meningeal deafness.

On the basis of this diagnosis, the question of whether to recommend an abortion to the mother is put and, if answered in the affirmative, the response given is that "You have just aborted Ludwig Van Beethoven." With respect to this argument, Harris points out that aborting Beethoven can only seem a good thing to do if we, or the world, or his family, or perhaps even Beethoven himself would have been better off without him. And since this seems an unlikely possibility we seem to be forced to the conclusion that Beethoven should not have been aborted and so neither should other foetuses in related circumstances.

Whilst superficially appealing, the argument falls down on a number of bases. One proponent of the approach, George Steiner used it to argue that "what in many cases is a hideous disease, a handicap can also be profoundly creative. Without the kind of [meningeal] deafness which comes from inherited syphilis ... you and I would be sitting here without Ludwig Van Beethoven." Most striking about Steiner's reasoning is that he fails to account for the effect of "nurture", as opposed to "nature". It may certainly be argued that despite disability, or perhaps even because of the upbringing arising out of their handicaps, people have not been precluded from leading creative and productive lives.

This is however fundamentally different from asserting that it is the same genetic defect giving rise to a disability that also determines a person's creativity or genius. It certainly cannot be asserted that all genius is solely or even principally drawn from that part of the community suffering from genetic disorders. Further, a decision to abort a foetus is not necessarily consistent with a view that the world would be better off without that individual. As outlined in the previous part, an argument from potentiality can be made in favour of a foetus, but this potential refers only to the potential for human life. Nothing more can be assumed from this stance.

In all cases what we are aborting is an actual foetus and the rights or wrongs of that are determined by a consideration of the moral status of the foetus. The foetus we abort will never become anything, and it is nothing but a foetus at the time it is aborted. It is as senseless to bemoan its loss as the loss of a Beethoven as it is to celebrate its loss as the pre-emption of a Hitler. Another ground upon which the argument falters is that of selfish biases. The argument seems to assume that because artistic culture or society as a whole is better off with these individuals' contributions, we are morally justified in requiring their birth. Here, the principles of nonmaleficence/beneficence, autonomy and the theory of common good come into play. Whilst social interests may certainly be taken into account, proportionality dictates that the good to society must be so convincing that it outweighs the risk of harm to individuals directly involved.

Where the parents are inclined towards abortion base d on considerations not only of the potential child's quality of life, but also upon their own, the ethical weight of potential benefit to society would be scant in light of the uncertainty of the child's ability to contribute, let alone the value of any contribution. This final point raises the last glaring weakness of the "Beethoven" approach: that it neglects to distinguish between the types and severity of genetic disorders. Quality of life considerations are unavoidably tied to decisions made on the basis of information regarding these sorts of disorders.

Certainly, deafness may not warrant abortion and in fact clinical studies indicate a marked disinclination to abort for such mild abnormalities. However, where diagnoses reveal severe disorders, particularly mental ones, the potential for valuable societal contribution (or even interaction) is substantially lessened. Thus, at least to the extent that it applies to severe genetic defects, prenatal diagnosis should not be excluded on the basis of this argument.

Advantageous Disadvantages

This philosophical argument is closely related to the preceding one. Germaine Greer offered the opinion that there may be a positive side to pain and suffering which would justify our declining to eradicate it when given the chance. Her argument follows that if a trait is totally maladaptive, then it would not survive. Thus, if a trait has survived, there must be a positive reason for it which we have just never found. Greer believes that humankind should have the advantage of the disadvantages of particular people. Even assuming that this reasoning holds true, at what cost should we wait to discover the benefits society might reap from genetic disorders? Again, the principle of nonmaleficence seems to contra-indicate this approach in the face of severely debilitating, painful and incurable disorders. Like the previous argument, this approach also fails to differentiate between the various types of genetic defects.

Further, Greer seems to base her reasoning on the evolutionary theory of natural selection. On this foundation she rests her assumption that the continued existence of a genetic trait indicates its (at least partially) positive nature. However, evolution of a species, particularly more advanced species such as humans, takes place not over decades, but over huge periods of time. Even a completely maladaptive trait would takes hundreds of years to disappear from the human genetic pool. Even accepting that there may, from an evolutionary viewpoint, be positive aspects to a trait, this does not always translate into a positive aspect for the particular species involved. Nature has in-built mechanisms to limit the numeracy and longevity of a species. It may be that very severe deformities are an expression of this restriction since, certainly in the absence of modern medicine, most of the inflicted individuals would die. From a purely evolutionary stance, this is in fact a positive aspect since it prevents the over population of an environment. Abortion then does not alter this particular "positive" aspect; rather, it achieves the same result whilst preventing the unnecessary suffering of the child and its family. The principle of nonmaleficence would strongly sup port this option in the case of terminal conditions being prenatally diagnosed. Harris opines that, before adopting Greer's stance, one would need to be very confident firstly that there is indeed a positive side to the specific disorder in question, secondly that such a positive side is sufficiently important to justify the human suffering required to preserve it, and finally that such positive effects could not be, or are unlikely to be, achievable by other means.

In the absence of such confidence I hope that no sane, let alone moral, being would think it worth preserving disability and disease on the off-chance that some good might come of it at some unspecified and unpredictable point in the future. The Eugenic Fear (Some perspectives from Feminist and Disabled Theorists) It has been argued that current bioethical constructs fail to take into account the views and opinions of those groups of society who are most directly associated with prenatal diagnosis and decisions regarding pregnancy termination on the basis of genetic abnormality: women and the disabled community. It is said that

"[i]n sum, it appears that ethical and theological, as well as economic arguments have been treated as legitimate and important contributions to the debate, and the views of certain participants ... have been taken seriously, but that critiques based on feminist perspectives have been treated as marginal."

Similarly, Newell argues that scientific and ethical discourse has yet to recognise adequately the social construction of disability. Newell further postulates that prenatal diagnosis and pregnancy termination is inherently a technology of oppression and control which serves to devalue the lives of those identified as having disabilities. This latter argument is strikingly similar to those espoused by many feminist critics of genetic testing, who argue that these technologies serve to increase the scope of control exercised over pregnant women's lives and bodies. In essence, the major (but certainly not the only) criticism commonly levelled by these groups at the practice of prenatal diagnosis and genetic manipulation is that its effect is eugenic. Kaplan cites as the most frequently given reason for antenatal testing, that of preventing or ameliorating medical or disabling conditions that are genetically based. Feminist criticism has included the objection that this perceived diagnostic goal contradicts policies for the empowerment of people with disabilities with the selective abortion of foetuses with disabilities. These theorists warn that social constructs that influence people's choices (such as to eliminate those with lives "not worth living") may constitute a eugenic programme.

In answer to those who opine that a eugenics programme reminiscent of the Nazi era would not occur in this day and age, the example of China is offered. In December 1993, the Chinese government announced a programme of abortions, forced sterilisation and marriage bans to "avoid new births of inferior quality and heighten the standards" of the country. Feminists have further argued that women may be placed under social pressure to have prenatal diagnosis in a technologic culture in which it is felt to be an "imperative" to undergo prenatal testing, simply because it exists (this is particularly so as testing develops and becomes more routinely used in prenatal care). Moreover, it is argued that given the social construct of disability and the economic burdens that our institutional structure allows to fall on the carer of a disabled child, many women may find the choice of raising a handicapped child so unattractive that it appears tantamount to there being no choice at all regarding abortion. Since these individual "choices" have social consequences, they are therefore said to be eugenic.

Additionally, the disabled sector has argued that although the majority approach in bioethical and scientific literature accepts disability as a given, based on dominant socially constructed information. It is upon this basis that a decision may be made to abort. These theorists argue that the better approach is to treat disability as a social construct and to seek management options which reflect this view. The underlying concern from the disabled perspective is the belief that, implicit in the practice of abortion based on genetic characteristics, is the message that it is better not to exist than to have a disability. Whilst something may be said for the social policy points raised in this context, an examination of genetic testing as a prenatal care procedure does not support the view that it is eugenic in effect. Of all abortions performed in Australia, only an estimated 1% occur after prenatal diagnosis. Further, in 95% of pregnancies at increased risk for foetal abnormalities, testing offers reassurance of foetal health.

An additional observation has been made that an intention to pursue testing does not necessarily correlate with an intention to terminate in the event of an abnormality. It may therefore be seen that these datainvalidate the notion of prenatal diagnosis as a "seek and destroy mission" and support the [position] that such testing provides information to patients ... which they view as profoundly valuable and which they very much want to have. It appears, therefore, that the bioethical notions of autonomy and veracity would strongly support the practice of antenatal testing. Moving away from responses to eugenic concerns on an empirical basis, trends in genetic counselling a lso strongly contra-indicate prenatal diagnosis being used as a eugenic practice. As the HGP reveals more information about our genetic code, and as the availability and precision of testing for various disorders increases, genetic counselling has been t he focus of increasing attention.

Addressing this issue, the Council for Science and Society have said that it must be made clear that the aim of testing is not a eugenic one, but rather to enhance the range of choice and quality of life for individuals and families. Most, if not all, genetic counselling strives to be non-directive, helping individuals understand their options and the present state of medical technology so that they can make informed decisions regarding pregnancy management. The current approach is reflected by the following discourse on genetic counselling:

"Patients should be told of the advantages and disadvantages and the various options. ... Termination of pregnancy is one possible outcome and must be discussed, but it should not be made a condition of having a test ... and neither should women be pressurised into having a termination if the foetus is found to be affected. The delivery and birth of an affected child after prenatal testing is not a failure at all; indeed it is a triumph, because here is a child that is, after all, wanted despite its abnormality." According to this view, prenatal testing is designed to facilitate informed reproductive decision making and to offer the widest possible scope of management options to patients. A more rational approach to making difficult choices is possible, with the opportunity to adequately prepare and to provide appropriate medical measures where an affected foetus is kept. Wertz and Fletcher opine that not only the non-directiveness, but also the individual family focus of contemporary genetic coun selling p laces the practice outside the definition of eugenics. It has been argued that there is no other field of medicine in which the need for accuracy is so high, because the consequences of a test may result in pregnancy termination." Where results are ambiguous, decision making becomes even more difficult. The question of "what is too high a risk to take" is a very personal one, based on social, family, emotional and moral considerations.

In terms of bioethics, there may, in such situations be s ome beneficence based obligations to the foetus, but those to the mother and to family, as well as the autonomy based obligations to the mother, could be stronger and they might well favour termination of pregnancy. Thus it seems that, at the level of actual decision-making, the choice to abort following abnormal diagnostic results is based on factors other than those intended to improve the gene pool, hence taking the practice outside the meaning of eugenics. Finally, it has been said that to argu e for the inevitability of eugenic regimes of allowing the discovery and use of genetic information, is to rely too heavily on the slippery slope argument. Holtug argues that both logical and empirical arguments fail to support the slippery slope vi ew that eugenic abuses will necessarily occur from the application of genetic technologies. However, in rejecting the slippery slope argument, Holtug is careful to note that this should not suggest a carte blanche approach towards gene therapy (or, it is submitted, towards genetic testing).

There are dangers lurking if we are not careful. In order to avoid such dangers, it is necessary to decide on reasonable moral limits for the kind of society we want. It is this last point concerning moral limits for society upon which Hughes centres his response to the eugenic fear. He argues that nothing a democratic society does to forbid itself of genetic technology will have any impact on future or contemporary fascist regimes. Rather,

"... the way to stop fascist uses of genetics is to prevent the rise of fascism, not to restrict the emergence of genetic technology."

It is contended that this view seems correct. It is not the genetic technology that is inherently objectionable, from a eugenic point of view, but rather its application for the purposes of eugenic practices. These practices may be carried out in the absence of genetic technology, and it is the social constructs which enable this to occur that must be addressed. Applications of genetic technology may include the positive elements of increasing the range of obstetric and perinatal options for women and families faced with the issue of genetic disease. Respect for maternal autonomy and the obligation to avoid harm strongly support these applications of the emerging biotechnology and provide a rationale for continued research such as that conducted by the HGP. Educative responses and regulatory policies should be concerned with eliminating eugenic practi ces and it is in this process that the previously "hidden voices" of feminist theorists and minority views (including those of the disabled community) should be heard.

The Ethics of Economic Considerations

Closely linked to the issue of eugenics is the concern over placing either too much or too little importance on the economic aspects of prenatal diagnosis and abortion. On the one hand, it has been argued that there is a social interest in limiting avoid able health care expenses. Ethically, arguments from this perspective find support in the utilitarian principle of seeking a result that will yield the greatest good or welfare for the greatest number of people. Figures used to support this include the observation that the costs involved in diagnosing one handicapped foetus are estimated to be less than one twelfth of the cost of maintaining a resulting disabled child in a public institution for ten years, and that the Australian community spends $2.5 billion each year on caring for people with genetic diseases.

However, these figures do not take important intangible costs and benefits into account. Arguments have been made that in the interests of benefiting society, or avoiding harm to others, affected foetuses should be aborted. On the other hand, strong criticism of this approach may be made by the argument that the harm, or risk of harm, involved in some interventions may be of such a nature that those interventions may be absolutely unacceptable no matter how much benefit they promise. The better approach seems to fall somewhere in between these two extremes. Economic evaluation claims neutrality with respect to ethical issues. Other ethical and moral considerations must be taken into account and value attached to economic factors based on the personal belief structure of the patient. This approach should place significant emphasis on respect for autonomy and self determination. From an institutional, as opposed to a patient point of view, economic considerations should only be determinative in the unlikely event that all other ethical criteria are equally balanced. Bioethics recognise the importance of the common good approach, but a doctor's duty lies first with the individual patient. As such, the economic societal interest should be subsumed to the patient's interests, all other things being equal.

Having examined the ethical aspects of prenatal testing, it is submitted that the law in respect of embryo biopsy in WA, and of pregnancy termination in Australia, is inadequate to deal with the issues raised by current and emergent genetic technologies. This is particularly so with respect to the inconsistency between the law in the books and the law as it is practiced concerning abortion. Current laws prohibiting abortion reflect a policy that is inconsistent with the law as it is applied. The body of case law concerning abortion has developed in a piecemeal fashion, yielding judgments that seem increasingly willing to extend the scope of the law beyond its intended boundaries. Such inconsistencies in the law and its application are unacceptable frm a policy point of view. It was concluded by Seymour in his report to the AMA that "[t]here is no place for legal intervention designed to impose controls on the behaviour of a pregnant woman when this behaviour is potentially harmful to the foetus. ... At best, the invocation of the law is ineffective and at worst counter-productive."

Whilst bioethical principles indicate that it is morally incumbent on a woman to consider the interests of the foetus in making choices concerning prenatal care, this is very different from imposing a legal restriction upon her reproductive choices or from enforcing legally sanctioned interference with her bodily integrity. It is submitted that the law as it stands does not adequately reflect the importance of maternal autonomy, nor does it recognise the unique relationship between mother and foetus (in contrast to the morally different relationship between the foetus and the rest of society). It is therefore submitted that legislative reform is essential in this area, so as to accord adequate recognition to the interests of women in making reproductive choices, and to achieve consistency between the letter of the law and its application. It is suggested that bioethical principles should guide the development of legal policy in the reform process.

CONCLUSION

This paper has examined genetic technology, bioethics and the law in respect of prenatal care, involving the related issues of prenatal diagnosis and pregnancy termination for genetic indications. These issues raise, quite literally, matters of life and death.

It has been seen that the law in these areas is wholly inappropriate and fundamentally underdeveloped in Australia. Significant differences exist between the letter of the law and its practical application. To leave the situation in these areas as it stands is clearly bad legal policy. It has been postulated that the options are either to enforce the law as it stands, or to make appropriate legislative reforms. Bioethics and medical practice would seem to favour the latter option. Current law regarding abortion is not adequately equipped to deal with the emergent issues arising out of advances in genetic technology. It has been left to courts to apply the law in an ad hoc manner (at least on the few occasions, given the lack of prosecutorial action, that it has been given any judicial consideration). From a policy point of view, this situation is undesirable as it renders the law arbitrary and uncertain. Although absolute certainty cannot realistically be achieved, legislators should seek to maximise certainty within the pragmatic limits required to achieve the flexibility needed for the law to deal with the variety of situations arising reproductively.

Further, it is submitted that an undue burden is being placed on the judiciary, who are supposed to apply legal policy and not to develop it in the absence of legislative or political consideration. The "sanctity of life" doctrine reflected in these areas of law has been shown to be inappropriate, particularly given the advances made in prognostic capabilities by genetic technology. However, given the contentious and politically volatile nature of the topics involved, legislative reform has been avoided by politicians, despite the clear and articulated need for review. It is submitted that, in the face of significant contextual change, maintaining a legislative status quo is as value-laden as re form. Lack of legislative review is not morally neutral; it involves a positive decision not to change despite an alteration in the medical and social context in which the law operates. It is therefore unacceptable that policy-makers remain intransigent in the face of the critical changes that have taken place (both with respect to medical technology and to the status and recognition accorded to women) over recent decades. It is imperative that the law in respect of pregnancy termination be reviewed/reformed so as to reflect a consistent, socially acceptable, and ethically supportable legal policy. Regarding the reform process itself, it is vital that the views of women be recognised in accordance with their peculiar interest in, and centrality to, the issues of pregnancy and childbirth. Any resulting policy should be reflective of these interests.

It is also critical that the reform process should involve public debate, expert advice and ethical consideration in order to produce a regulatory framework that will adequately deal with the medical and social issues it covers. A number of issues have arisen in the course of this research which, given the constraints of the paper, have not been addressed, but which require further consideration. These include: the human rights issues arising in respect of genetic technology as it is applied in obstetric and perinatal care; a comprehensive critical analysis of feminist theory as it applies to these areas; and the regulation of the application of genetic technologies emerging from the HGP on an international basis. This paper has sought to highlight areas of inconsistency between bioethics and current Australian law/legal policy, and to indicate where the law is inadequate to deal with the new issues arising out of advances in genetic technology prenatally. However, further attention needs to be given to the appropriate role of law in society and to the appropriate regulatory mechanisms to achieve reform in these areas.

Debate over the relationship of law and bioethics is growing—what the relationship has been and what it should be in the future. While George Annas has praised law and rights-talk for creating modern bioethics, Carl Schneider has instead blamed law for hijacking bioethics and stunting moral reflection. Indeed, as modern bioethics approaches the 40-year mark, historians of bioethics are presenting divergent accounts. In one account, typified by Albert Jonsen, bioethics largely grew out of philosophy and theology, not law. In another account, law has deeply shaped bioethics from the start, forging its central commitment to the rights of patients and research subjects and the field's imposition of broad fiduciary responsibilities on health cam professionals and researchers.

In addition to debating how to properly describe law's historical relationship to bioethics, commentators have argued over whether law's influence in bioethics is now good or bad. Daniel Callahan and others have complained that law too often reduces bioethics to questions of process and regulation, stunting reflection on substantive questions of what constitutes the good. Yet Alexander Capron and others point to prominent arenas, such as the definition of death, in which law has sharpened thinking, helped define the stakes, and ultimately allowed a practical (if still debatable) solution. Though some despair about whether bioethics has had impact or, to put it another way, stopped anything, it is hard to think of an arena in which bioethics has tried to have an effect without using law. The field's efforts to prevent future atrocities in human research have relied heavily on federal regulation. Attempts to empower patients and families at the end of life have involved legislative recognition of advance directives, thousands of judicial decisions, recourse to the U.S. Supreme Court, and recently battle in Florida's Schiavo case over the proper role of the executive and legislative branches of government. Efforts to prevent human reproductive cloning have revolved around federal law and regulation, state law, the laws of other countries, and international agreements. Few in bioethics would now agree to jettison law from the toolkit.

Finally, some scholars have begun to write about what the future relationship should be between law and bioethics. Focusing on health law, Einer Elhauge argues that the crucial reform is for law to engage in a disciplined comparison among four reigning paradigms (market, professional, moral, and political) rather than using them inconsistently to create a "pathological" hodgepodge. Mark Hall suggests that recognizing the importance of patients' trust in their physicians valuably organizes health law, in keeping with work in the mental health field to develop therapeutic jurisprudence. Gregg Bloche finds many branches of health law striving to maximize welfare and social utility, in keeping with writing on law and economics, though Bloche decries this as obscuring the more varied aims of health care. I and others have argued that the role of law is best understood in terms of pragmatism, striving in a practical way to protect the interests of those most vulnerable in biomedicine—patients, research subjects, and those without access to care.

This ferment over what the relationship between law and bioethics has been in the past, is now, and should be in the future could be mistaken for mere in-fighting, the lawyers and the non-lawyers in bioethics jostling for control. Like sparring marriage partners we fight about who is responsible for what, who gets the blame and who the credit. But we have worked together so long and produced so much together that, like marriage partners, it begins to seem that we are really fighting about something else, something deeper.

The thesis of this article is that what we are actually fighting about is indeed something deeper. At a time of tremendous upheaval after 9/11 and a political shift to the right in our own country, we are fighting over fundamentals: whom our field will serve, with what use of law's force and power, and with what accountability. As Jonathan Moreno has written, "the strength of the rights orientation has waxed and waned, depending partly on perceptions of external threats." Post 9/11, external threats loom large. Bioethics is questioning its commitment to protecting individual rights and seeing no obvious limits on the use of legal force and power. Bioethicists are even running from legal accountability and constraints on our own practice. Rights of all sorts are on the wane.

4

The Past—The Marriage of Bioethics and Law

We should debunk from the start the notion that law and bioethics are two entirely distinct fields, two armies approaching each other across a plain. The relationship has long been far more intimate. Science studies scholars offer a useful term here, "co-production." Though the term has been used by Sheila Jasanoff and others to describe the complex process by which science and society interrelate to influence each other and develop together, its suggestion of mutual dependence and co-evolution could aptly be applied to the relationship of law and bioethics. The field that we call "bioethics" is clearly the collaborative production of lawyers and non-lawyers working with a set of tools, some legal and some nonlegal. Look at practically any roster of bioethicists from the inception of the field, be it those who collaborated on the first National Commission on bioethics or those who gravitated to the early think tanks, and you will find lawyers cheek-by-jowl with non-lawyers. If anything, the mix is even greater today, as witnessed by the leadership of the field's professional society, (20) the editorial boards of bioethics-oriented journals, and the personnel of countless IRBs and ethics committees.

Similarly, the response to practically every big issue in bioethics over the last 35 years has been a mix of law and ethics. The granddaddy of examples is end-of-life issues. The U.S. courts have secured a right to refuse treatment by articulating a common law right to be free of unwanted bodily invasion and a constitutional right of liberty, while our legislatures have codified entitlement to use advance directives. More recently, state legislators, federal and state regulators, state disciplinary authorities, and the courts have labored to clear barriers to pain relieving drugs and palliative care. Most controversially, the Supreme Court has rejected a constitutional right to physician-assisted suicide, leaving state legislatures free to maintain legal prohibitions or, like Oregon, legalize the practice. Yet for all the law—and there are undoubtedly more court decisions and more legal pronouncements in this domain of bioethics than in any other—the ethics debate has flourished. We continue to debate when to trump patient choice on grounds of futility, whether to urge or merely allow patients to exercise their autonomy and make treatment decisions, and when to override even written directives on grounds that the patient is no longer the same "self" who wrote the directive. The well-known Philosophers' Brief in the Supreme Court litigation on physician-assisted suicide is even an example of arguing ethics and philosophy to alter law.

Protecting human research subjects (or "participants"), another major project of bioethics, has provoked a different admixture of legal and ethics tools, but again an intimate mix. Here, common law and the Constitution have played little role until recently. Instead, the big legal tool has been federal regulation, with state legislation playing a secondary role as well. Thus, what has come to be the Common Rule (together with additional federal regulation, primarily from the Food and Drug Administration (FDA), plus recent enforcement actions from the Office for Human Research Protections (OHRP) and others) has organized a massive system of Institutional Review Boards (IRBs) and research approval requirements. Yet IRBs are a perfect example of a body conceived to do both law and ethics. They are required to apply the federal regulations, which are law, but those regulations are so open-textured and the overriding mission of IRBs is so clearly to protect human subjects, that IRBs must do ethics too. In reality, IRBs may have too little time, resources, and even expertise to do either well, but they are conceived to do both. And the existence of federal regulations in this area has provoked, not thwarted vigorous debate. Each federal bioethics commission leading up to the present one has examined ethical issues in human subjects protection and the question of how to use law and regulation to protect human subjects from harm. The literature abounds with continuing debate over nonbeneficial research on those who cannot consent, the need for clinical equipoise, the wisdom of group consent, standards for international research, and a host of issues in pediatric research, to name only a few areas.

The field of reproductive technologies has again prompted a mixture of ethics and law. The mix is different than in the prior two areas; federal legislation has played a relatively minor role given the traditional dominion of the states over family matters. A federal statute does assign responsibility to the Centers for Disease Control (CDC) for making publicly available success rates for in vitro fertilization programs, but that remains the most prominent piece of federal regulation. The debate over reproductive cloning has provoked numerous proposals for more federal legislation and the President's Bioethics Council has raised the question of whether an array of procedures in reproductive medicine, from preimplantation genetic diagnosis (PGD) to reproductive cloning, should prompt creation of a federal regulatory and oversight body.

But as yet, the bulk of law in this area is state law. Indeed, state law on assisted reproduction and family relationships is so copious that there have been at least two attempts to systematize that law by offering the states model legislation. That said, federal constitutional law has loomed much larger than federal statutes. John Robertson has been among those arguing that the U.S. Constitution protects a right to procreative liberty, limiting state interference. The backdrop to this, of course, is Supreme Court jurisprudence on rights to privacy and liberty, much of that from the abortion cases starting with Roe in 1973. Yet for all of the law in this area, some of it necessitated by the fear of seeing children caught in legal limbo, the ethics debates have been vigorous. Prominent state and federal bioethics commissions, including the New York State Task Force on Life and the Law, have issued important ethics analyses, invariably taking account of the law as well. Indeed, the related debate over maternal-fetal relations has yielded what remains a classic examination of the different but interrelated roles of law and ethics.

A final example, the many issues raised by genetic mapping, testing, and manipulation, again shows law and ethics in intimate relationship. Unlike the federal role in assisted reproduction, largely laissez-faire and deferential to the states, federal regulators have been aggressive in asserting control over genetic advances. This is largely due to the fact that the federal government has been a major funder of genetic research, but decades ago severely limited funding for research on assisted reproduction. Funding for genetic research has meant that federal regulation of human subjects research has applied, as well as added regulation on some genetic research such as required review by the Recombinant DNA Advisory Committee (RAC), at least until the requirement of RAC review was changed. Other large swaths of federal law have applied to genetics as well including patent law, federal disability law, HIPAA, and FDA regulation, though the FDA has asserted limited jurisdiction over genetic tests, for example. The brouhaha over reproductive and therapeutic cloning as well as embryo stem cell research has involved calls for federal law in each of those areas, each debate relating in part to genetics. A number of states have legislated in these areas as well. Yet certainly the legal action in this domain has in no way squelched the ethics debate. Ethics discussions routinely integrate attention to the legal history and proposals, but seem unbounded by them. Clearly, law and bioethics have married. But it would be wrong to say they have merged. When judges have mistaken ethics for law, as in some litigation over the right to refuse life-sustaining treatment, for example, scholars have leapt in to restore the distinction. And conversely, when calls to ban cloning through law have been mistaken for ethics argumentation, commentators have reminded us of the need to argue the ethics.

BIOETHICS AND PATENT LAW

Animals are called "transgenic" when DNA from other species has been artificially introduced into their genome.

Transgenic animals have been developed for potentially beneficial applications, such as medical research, enhanced food production, and the production of proteins or organs. But the genetic manipulation of animals, particularly mammals, also raises a host of ethical issues that can be highly controversial.

Such issues are much wider than the questions relating to patentability. And governments may of course at any stage of research and development directly outlaw any technology deemed inherently unacceptable. But it is notable that some controversial new technologies only surface publicly when they reach the patent office. So what has happened when inventors have sought to patent transgenic animals?

HARVARD'S ONCOMOUSE

Among the first transgenic animals to be produced was the *oncomouse*. Researchers at Harvard Medical School in the early 1980s produced a genetically modified mouse that was highly susceptible to cancer, by introducing an oncogene that can trigger the growth of tumors. The *oncomouse* (from the Greek word for tumor) was conceived as a valuable means of furthering cancer research. Harvard College sought patent protection in the United States and several other countries.

The case raised general ethical issues regarding transgenic technology in itself. But it also raised two key issues for the patent system:

- should patents be granted at all for animals or animal varieties, particularly for higher-order animals such as mammals, even if they do otherwise meet patentablility criteria (novelty, industrial applicability/usefulness, inventive step etc.)?
- how should moral implications be addressed in relation to specific cases, e.g. the question of suffering caused to the transgenic animal?

These issues have been resolved differently by the patent authorities of different countries, as the following examples illustrate.

United States - Patent Granted

The United States Patent Office in 1988 granted a patent no. 4,736,866 to Harvard College claiming "a transgenic non-human mammal whose germ cells and somatic cells contain a recombinant activated oncogene sequence introduced into said mammal..." The claim explicitly excluded humans, apparently reflecting moral and legal concerns about patents on human beings, and about modification of the human genome.

EPO - Applying the Utilitarian Test

The European Patent Office (EPO) considered the *oncomouse* case at length and at several levels. It was only resolved in 2004 *, and we touch here on only two aspects of a very complex case. The EPO applies the patent standards of the European Patent Convention, which contains two key relevant provisions: Article 53(a) excludes patents for inventions "the publication or exploitation of which would be contrary to *ordre public* or morality". And Article 53(b) excludes patents on "animal varieties or essentially biological processes for the production of...animals."

The EPO decided that the exclusion on patenting animal varieties did not constitute a ban on patenting animals as such. It concluded further that the *oncomouse* was not an animal variety, and so did not fall within that exclusion.

In order to address the *ordre public* or morality exception, the EPO developed a utilitarian balancing test. This aimed to assess the potential benefits of a claimed invention against negative aspects, in this case weighing the suffering of the *oncomice* against the expected medical benefits to humanity. Other considerations could also be taken into account in the balancing test, such as environmental risks (neutral in this case), or public unease (there was no evidence in European culture for moral disapproval of the use of mice in cancer research i.e. no moral disapproval of the proposed exploitation of the invention in this case). The EPO concluded that the usefulness of the *oncomouse* in furthering cancer research satisfied the likelihood of substantial medical benefit, and outweighed moral concerns about suffering caused to the animal.

In the original application, the claims referred to animals in general, but in the course of the proceedings, the patent was amended and finally maintained with claims limited to mice.

The Upjohn Mouse - same Approach, Different Outcome

The same utilitarian approach to the morality issue was applied by the EPO in the Upjohn case in 1992, but with a different outcome. The patent in question, filed by the Upjohn pharmaceutical company, was on a transgenic mouse, into which a gene had been introduced such that the mouse would lose its hair. The objective was to test products to treat human baldness and wool production techniques. The EPO again weighed up benefits (usefulness in research to cure hair loss) and harm (suffered by the mice), but concluded that in this case the latter outweighed the former, such that the exploitation of the invention was contrary to morality and therefore not patentable.

Canada - Patent Rejected

In Canada, the patent examiner initially rejected claims to transgenic animals on the basis that they were not included in the definition of an invention, but allowed claims on the process for obtaining the *oncomouse*.

The Supreme Court of Canada finally ruled in 2002 that higher life forms were not patentable because they were not a "manufacture or composition of matter within the meaning of invention" of the Patent Act **. Manufacture was interpreted as a non-living mechanistic product or process. "Composition of matter" was understood as ingredients or substances that had been combined or mixed together by a person. So while microorganisms, or an oncogene-injected egg capable of maturing into an *oncomouse,* may be a mixture of ingredients and thus patentable under Canadian Law, the body of a mouse was not. Moreover, the drafters of the Patent Act (1869) had not had mammals in mind and so the Act did not address higher life forms. It was recommended that, as the patentability of such life forms was contentious, the Parliament should engage in public debate to address the complex social and moral issues and close the legislative gap.

The dissenting justices, however, questioned the justification for distinguishing between lower life forms, seen as a composition of living matter, and higher life forms, which were not deemed to be compositions of matter. They held that the scientific achievement of altering the genetic material of which an animal - which does not exist in nature in this altered form - is composed, was itself an inventive "composition of matter" within the meaning of the Patent Act.

Different Approches

Transgenic animals pose questions for bioethics in general, and specific ethical questions in the context of the patent system. The *oncomouse* case highlights how different jurisdictions have dealt with the basic question of whether a transgenic animal -provided it complies with the patentability requirements - should be considered patentable subject matter; and how they have then weighed the ethical dimension of this particular technology.

Genetic Engineering is the heritable, directed alteration of an organism. A heritable alteration is a change that can be carried from one generation to the next. Genetic engineering is performed by modifying an organism's own DNA or introducing new DNA to perform desired functions.

Biotechnology is a broader term than genetic engineering and includes non-genetic techniques to modify organisms. Genetic engineering is the most powerful and least understood tool for biotechnology.. Many of the same principles used in genetic engineering are involved in biotechnology

Genetic Engineering involves DNA modifications

DNA is the genetic material in all known forms of life. DNA contains genes (just as a recipe book contains recipes) that give us many of our physical characteristics. However, we are not simply gene-based machines - the environment we are in also determines our traits. One of the challenges of genetic engineering is to determine how genes influence our traits and how to modify DNA to alter these traits. Genes affecting disorders such as alcoholism provide only a predisposition.

Having the gene for alcoholism may make one more prone to alcoholism but does not guarantee that one will become alcoholic, nor does not having the gene mean one is immune.

An important distinction in genetic engineering is between germline and non-germline cells. In most organisms, there are cells set aside just for reproduction. These are the eggs and sperm in humans. Non-germline cells are all the other cells in the body - muscle cells, skin cells, liver, etc. If a genetic modification does not alter germline cells, it should not have any effect on the genetic makeup of future generations (there are some possible exceptions to this). Thus, if one were to introduce the gene for purple hair into mouse hair cells, the offspring would not have purple hair, but the parent would. If the gene for purple hair were introduced into the parental germline cells, then the children could carry the purple hair gene.

This is complicated in plants because while many plants have germline cells, they can also be propagated asexually by taking cuttings. Additionally, it is possible to clone animals from single cells. Thus it is possible to clone a mouse from even non-germline cells. So even though introducing the purple hair gene into hair cells isn't a strictly heritable alteration, it is still possible to grow a whole mouse from a single hair cell (note: a hair cell, not a strand of hair).

Non-germline alterations are not carried to the next generation. Only half of our genes are given to our offspring, diluting any germline genetic modifications over time. DNA carries the instructions as genes, proteins perform the actions. Regulation is as important as gene function. Foreign DNA may be rejected.

While the human genome project may give us the entire sequence of our DNA, scientists must still determine how all the encoded proteins work.

Agriculture Concerns

Is the modification of seeds, plants and animals making up the foods we eat causing these foods to be unsafe? Will the selling and use of genetically-engineered seeds, plants and animals cause food production costs to increase to the point where small farmers are forced out of the market? Will the use of genetically-engineered seeds turn farmers into economic dependencies on seed companies? Are the regulations of the United Stated Department of Agriculture and Food and Drug Administration sufficient to keep people from contamination? Why are Europeans, Asians and Canadians refusing to eat these foods?

The production of transgenic animals and transgenic plants seem to have much to offer to the productivity and quality of farm products. However, small family farmers fear that allowing patents on transgenic animals will push them out of the market. Because generally altered animals, plants and seeds may be more expensive, small farmers fear that small number of large corporations will corner the market on genetically engineered animals, etc., and thereby deprive the small family farms of their livelihood. In addition, the small family farmers fear that the initial acquisition price of genetically altered plants, seeds and animals as well as subsequent royalties will increase rather than decrease the costs for farmers and consumers. On the other hand, transgenic farm capital assets could be stronger and more disease resistant and might balance the cost of the initial investment.

Another concern of the American farming community is the intense resistance to "altered" (artificially-engineered) food and animal products by European and Asian consumers. This resistance has forced European and Canadian governments to ban foods having any transgenic components. Since transgenic seeds have been known to "jump" from a transgenically-planted field to a non-transgenic planted field, farmers can not ensure that the food they harvest will pass European food inspectors. Recently, millions of dollars in lost harvests hurt farmers who had planted corn using the "StarLink" Monsanto seed. This transgenic seed jumped to other plantings of corn; thereby rendering them unacceptable for export or for use as the ingredients in other food products. In addition, some farmers did not realize the need to separate corn planted with the "StarLink" seed from non-altered corn. This resulted in all of their harvests being banned by food millers who could not afford to mix transgenic corn with unaltered corn.

A related issue concerns the level of review of transgenic food products by the federal Food and Drug Agency and the United States Department of Agriculture. Until recently, the USDA was under a mandate to assume that genetically-altered foods were safe unless proven to be otherwise. The Clinton Administration changed the operating assumption to be that these foods were not safe unless proven to be so.

Biosafety and Environmental Concerns

What harm if any is caused to the rivers, lakes, land and forests by the release of genetically-engineered organisms? Are sufficient regulatory controls in place to ensure that our environment is safe? What do you think the answers are?

Some environmental groups are concerned with what effect the release of transgenic organisms would have on the environment. The National Wildlife Foundation opposes patenting for transgenic animals because of the lack of legislation in the area concerning their release into the wild. The National Wildlife Foundation fears that allowing patents will cause a greater number of transgenic animals to be created, thus increasing the risk to the environment.

There is little experience with environmental introductions of GMOs on which to base an assessment of their potential risks and benefits to biodiversity. For example, in Canada, there is growing information from small-scale field studies with genetically modified crop plants, but comparable information for microorganisms and animals is lacking. GMOs could pose risks to biodiversity if novel traits enabled the organisms to become more invasive of natural habitats. GMOs could also pose risks through gene transfer to other organisms, such that a novel gene could persist in the environment even after the GMO is no longer present. The introduction of GMOs could also provide benefits for biodiversity. Genetically modified microorganisms could be used to treat industrial wastewater and air emissions and to degrade toxic chemicals at contaminated waste sites, restoring habitat for other species.

At this point, however, many of these risks and benefits to biodiversity remain uncertain, and yet a wide variety of GMOs is expected to enter the Canadian marketplace in the coming years.

Some environmentalists in the United States also speculate that such a release might be possibly harmful to human and environmental health. (See The Evaluation of Federal Programs in Agriculture Research, Education and Extension: Hearings Before the Subcomm. on Resource Conservation, Research, and Forestry of the House Comm. on Agric., 104th Cong. 250 (1996)). The uncertain nature of the environmental effects is certainly a plausible argument for regulating the release of transgenic animals into the wild. Should the Environmental Protection Agency have stricter regulatory review of release of GMOs into the environment?

Animal Rights Concerns

Is it reasonable to inject genes of other species or genes containing human viruses into animals in order to more efficiently learn how diseases work and, ultimately, how to cure them? Or, is this just another way that humans justify cruelty to other species? These are concerns about which some people think we should change.

It is customary in all Western societies to breed animals in order to study the effects of human illnesses on them in order to prevent or cure these illnesses. It is unpleasant to consider the experimental conditions that these animals must endure. Now, with the ability of science to place disease-carrying genes within an animal's genetic code, a sharp increase in the number of disease-carrying animals exists. The "engineered" animals are bred to suffer from diseases such as AIDS, sickle cell anemia, cystic fibrosis, and cancer. Some members of the public argue that it is inhumane and unethical to raise animals that will suffer as a result of genetic tampering.

On the other hand, it is quite possible that transgenic animals will actually limit the amount of animal suffering endured by research subjects and animals in general. For instance, using transgenic animals requires the use of fewer animals because the animals are created for the particular study purpose and are more responsive to the experimentation. However, there is no denying that some animals do suffer with transgenic research. Perhaps Congress should regulate the types of research performed. Legislation already exists that limits animal research and transgenic research is not among the varieties limited.

In addition, the goal of producing transgenics in agriculture is to create healthier animals and food products. Therefore, transgenic animals that do not improve market value and provide healthy foods will not be produced.

Some opponents of transgenic engineering belief that the sanctity of life is not well served by allowing the creation of transgenic animals. The argument then suggests that patenting animal life exacerbates that problem because it increases the economic value of the patented animal. It is true that patent law reflects what activities a society believes should be encouraged. However, the responsibility for making this decision seems to rest with the American public and Congress, not with the Patent Office.

ETHICS OF HUMAN CLONING. REPRODUCTION AND STEM CELL

Should testing and research be done on fetal tissue in order to learn how to repair and heal human disease? Is it moral/ethical to abort "extra" or "dying" fetuses and then use their tissue to study genetics? Should the government fund research that may enable us to clone babies and solve infertility in a world where there are already too many people to feed? If the government doesn't fund the research and chooses not to prohibit it elsewhere, will cloning and artificial reproduction cause a de-valuing of people in general? These are some of the current issues in reproductive law involving genetics.

On October 3, 1995, President Clinton established the National Bioethics Advisory Commission (Exec. Order 12,975, 3 C.F.R. 409(1996)). (See http://bioethics.gov/general.html) One requirement of the Commission is to review the appropriateness and implications of human gene patenting. On December 19,

2000, the Commission submitted a draft of its findings for public comment. The draft, entitled Ethical and Policy Issues In Research Involving Human Participants, contains the following conclusions and recommendations:

The Commission concludes that at this time it is morally unacceptable for anyone in the public or private sector, whether in a research or clinical setting, to attempt to create a child using somatic cell nuclear transfer cloning. The Commission reached a consensus on this point because current scientific information indicates that this technique is not safe to use in humans at this point. Indeed, the Commission believes it would violate important ethical obligations were clinicians or researchers to attempt to create a child using these particular technologies, which are likely to involve unacceptable risks to the fetus and/or potential child. Moreover, in addition to safety concerns, many other serious ethical concerns have been identified, which require much more widespread and careful public deliberation before this technology may be used.

The Commission, therefore, recommends the following for immediate action:

- A continuation of the current moratorium on the use of federal funding in support of any attempt to create a child by somatic cell nuclear transfer.
- An immediate request to all firms, clinicians, investigators, and professional societies in the private and non-federally funded sectors to comply voluntarily with the intent of the federal moratorium. Professional and scientific societies should make clear that any attempt to create a child by somatic cell nuclear transfer and implantation into a woman's body would at this time be an irresponsible, unethical, and unprofessional act.

The Commission further recommends that:

Federal legislation should be enacted to prohibit anyone from attempting, whether in a research or clinical setting, to create a child through somatic cell nuclear transfer cloning. It is critical, however, that such legislation include a sunset clause to ensure that Congress will review the issue after a specified time period (three to five years) in order to decide whether the prohibition continues to be needed. If state legislation is enacted, it should also contain such a sunset provision. Any such legislation or associated regulation also ought to require that at some point prior to the expiration of the sunset period, an appropriate oversight body will evaluate and report on the current status of somatic cell nuclear transfer technology and on the ethical and social issues that its potential use to create human beings would raise in light of public understandings at that time.

The Commission also concludes that:

Any regulatory or legislative actions undertaken to effect the foregoing prohibition on creating a child by somatic cell nuclear transfer should be carefully written so as not to interfere with other important areas of scientific research. In particular, no new regulations are required regarding the cloning of human DNA sequences and cell lines, since neither activity raises the scientific and ethical issues that arise from the attempt to create children through somatic cell nuclear transfer, and these fields of research have already provided important scientific and biomedical advances. Likewise, research on cloning animals by somatic cell nuclear transfer does not raise the issues implicated in attempting to use this technique for human cloning, and its continuation should only be subject to existing regulations regarding the humane use of animals and review by institution-based animal protection committees.

If a legislative ban is not enacted, or if a legislative ban is ever lifted, clinical use of somatic cell nuclear transfer techniques to create a child should be preceded by research trials that are governed by the twin protections of independent review and informed consent, consistent with existing norms of human subjects protection.

The United States Government should cooperate with other nations and international organizations to enforce any common aspects of their respective policies on the cloning of human beings.

The Commission also concludes that different ethical and religious perspectives and traditions are divided on many of the important moral issues that surround any attempt to create a child using somatic cell nuclear transfer techniques. Therefore, the Commission recommends that:

The federal government, and all interested and concerned parties, encourage widespread and continuing deliberation on these issues in order to further our understanding of the ethical and social implications of this technology and to enable society to produce appropriate long-term policies regarding this technology should the time come when present concerns about safety have been addressed.

Finally, because scientific knowledge is essential for all citizens to participate in a full and informed fashion in the governance of our complex society, the Commission recommends that:

Federal departments and agencies concerned with science should cooperate in seeking out and supporting opportunities to provide information and education to the public in the area of genetics, and on other developments in the biomedical sciences, especially where these affect important cultural practices, values, and beliefs.

Note: The Commission also observes that the use of any other technique to create a child genetically identical to an existing (or previously existing) individual would raise many, if not all, of the same non-safety-related ethical concerns raised by the creation of a child by somatic cell nuclear transfer.

But efforts to clone human beings continue by private agencies and physicians. (See Richard Seed (People in Biotechnology News). For example, in October of 2000, leaders of a Canadian group said that for a six-figure fee they will help infertile or homosexual couples have cloned children. The group is led by a former race-car driver called Rael who claims knowledge of extraterrestrials. Surprisingly, the group has (acc. to the Washington Post) connected with a wealth American couple willing to finance the cloning of their 1-month-old daughter who died in a medial accident.

In January 2001, another human cloning project was announced when two fertility experts said that they have lined up 10 infertile patients who want to be cloned. An international team of scientists will plan the project with the goal of producing a baby within two years, said the project's leaders, Italian doctor Severino Antinori and Panos Savos. (from Minneapolis Star Tribune, Feb. 18,2001).

NIH PROPOSES NEW RULES GOVERNING HUMAN GENE TRANSFER STUDIES

The NIH published a proposed notice changing the NIH guidelines for research involving recombinant DNA molecules in regards to the reporting and analysis of serious adverse events in human gene transfer studies in the Federal Register on December 12, 2000.

The proposed changes involve four main issues:

- the scope and timing of serious adverse event reporting
- public access to information about serious adverse events
- protection of individually identifiable patient information as it relates to serious adverse event reporting
- a new mechanism for the review and assessment of data on serious adverse events and other relevant safety information.

(S.2015 *Stem Cell Research Act of 2000 (Introduced in the Senate)*) is one part of the federal government's efforts to amend a 1995 congressional ban on embryo research, which specifies that federal taxpayer money cannot be spent on biomedical research involving embryos outside the womb. Last December, the National Institutes of Health issued preliminary guidelines that would allow government-funded researchers to use stem cells from already destroyed embryos. If passed, S 2015 would allow researchers to use and destroy embryos under specific circumstances.

Copyrights and Patents of Indigenous Cultures' Artifacts and Native Knowledge

The United States Department of Agriculture and the National Institutes of Health list over 200 different plants found on American Objiway land that contain medicinal or food properties? Should the Objiway Indians receive royalties for these plants or should the "inventor" (who discovered the genetic code, filed the applications and paid for the legal work) receive royalties for the plants? What about the fabric designer who developed textile fabrics based on Australian aboriginal designs found in a book? The Western concept of "inventor" and "invented" is today being challenged by the United Nations and many tribal (non-governmental) groups who say that traditional information about their environment, their customs and their art are exploited by non-indigenous people while the tribes receive nothing in return.

Biotechnology has created the ability to realize create new wealth from the genetic code of plants, seeds, animals into the billions of dollars. However the search for these genes and the raw products they are contained in has caused a clash between peoples, countries and cultures on a scale never seen before. Instead of isolated contacts between tribes and Western biotech companies, today there are numerous forays into aboriginal and isolated tribal communities in search for the new genetic product. But many indigenous people have been poorly equipped to negotiate value for their knowledge and information.

For example, in Costa Rica, a nongovernmental organization named INBio, which maintains close links to the government, was given rights to commercialize biogenetic resources for Merck Pharmaceuticals. The agreement entitled them to collect samples on national lands, including those of eight indigenous peoples. No one ever consulted with any of the tribes about the collections, and none of the tribes was named as a beneficiary in the original agreement between Merck and INBio, which was signed in 1991.

Biodiversity prospectors assume that organisms and ecosystems are wild and therefore part of the public domain. Thus, even when indigenous peoples provide leads or processed materials, the company takes credit for the legally protectable "discovery." But the circumstances surrounding some of these discoveries raise doubts about the equity of this position.

The discoveries made from human blood samples provide a compelling example. The Human Genome Organization (HUGO), founded in 1988, and one of its subsidiary projects, the Human Genome Diversity Project, coordinates the collection of blood samples from isolated communities threatened with extinction. The goal of this ongoing blood collection project is to reveal evolutionary links and identify genetic sequences for gene therapies to improve human health. This effort, dubbed the "human vampire project" by indigenous peoples, has discredited much scientific research. Collections were made without the prior informed consent of the sampled groups, and the data and blood cells were made available for commercial exploitation after they were collected.

To date, at least three patent applications have been made for cell lines developed from this blood. The U.S. Department of Commerce holds the patent on one of these applications. The patent lists as inventors the government scientists involved in the project and the anthropologist who introduced the research team to the Papua New Guinea tribe from whom the blood was collected. To date, the government of Papua New Guinea has not lodged an official protest about this situation, and it is unlikely that it will ever do so. Is this a flaw in the intellectual property rights' laws?. While intellectual property rights laws are understood and accepted in most Western European nations, they remain an inappropriate mechanism for securing indigenous peoples' rights for a number of reasons.

First among these is the fact that the law is designed to protect information resulting from a specific individual act of discovery. However, indigenous knowledge is transgenerational and communally shared. It may come from ancestor spirits, vision quests, or lineage groups that transmit it orally but not necessarily from a specific individual act of discovery.

Once knowledge is in the public domain, it becomes impossible to establish the quality of uniqueness required for a patent application. Moreover, because of the difficulties involved in documenting inventions and identifying individual inventors, patents are ultimately of little use to most indigenous peoples. Even if they could satisfy the technical requirements, the costs of filing, maintaining, monitoring, legally implementing, and enforcing patents would be prohibitive. The same difficulties arise when indigenous peoples attempt to qualify for plant breeders' rights.

In 1961, the International Convention for the Protection of New Varieties of Plants created plant breeders' rights to protect the economic interests of plant breeders, people who breed, discover, or develop crop varieties. To be eligible for protection under the convention's 1991 revised guidelines, a plant variety must be "distinct, stable, uniform, and novel." A distinct variety is "distinguishable by one or more characteristics from any other variety whose existence is a matter of common knowledge." To qualify as stable, a variety must "remain true to its description after repeated reproduction or propagation."

A uniform variety remains "homogenous with regard to the particular feature of its sexual reproduction or vegetative propagation," while a novel variety must not have been offered for sale or marketed, with the agreement of the breeder or his successor in title, in the country of petition, or for longer than four years in any other country. While indigenous farmers can in principle meet these requirements, they would have to invest in considerable laboratory research, necessitating both time and money. Even then, the protection afforded them by going through such a process is limited at best: The convention only has force in its 20 member countries.

The laws governing trade secrets and know-how (information that may give a person or a company a competitive advantage yet fail to fulfill the criteria of patentability) could potentially have greater applicability to indigenous peoples' situation. But they too entail specialized legal advice and corresponding expenses. To claim protection for a trade secret, for instance, an effort must be made to prevent its disclosure. Agreements to respect the confidential nature of the information (such as strictly enforced access restrictions) would have to be made between indigenous peoples and others.

Relatively speaking, appellation of origin and trademarks are the most accessible IPR mechanisms at indigenous peoples' disposal, and they can be effectively applied to products coming from indigenous lands or produced under indigenous auspices or licensing agreements. For instance, certifications of authentic indigenous art could be issued and medicinal plants and products could be affixed with a label indicating where they were produced. This would make it impossible for someone to claim to be using a genuine indigenous product if it were not affixed with the official (legally recognized) stamp.

Copyright is also easily obtained and can help protect written texts, works of art, and databases. But as with all the other IPR law mechanisms, enforcement and monitoring can be difficult, time-consuming, and costly. Nevertheless, some countries are attempting to put copyright-like mechanisms in place. Local communities that are compiling their own community inventories of indigenous knowledge are being offered a choice about whether to publish the information.

Publishing puts the inventory (referred to as a registry when it is compiled for the purposes of legal protection) into the public domain. Some people argue that information in the public domain should not be patentable. Thus they feel that publishing can help impede patent applications. This defensive publication strategy is risky, however.

The problem is that biodiversity prospectors find leads to useful products or to sources of new products in publications. While the material (the inventory or the registry) that provides the lead to the original product or compound may not be patentable, the product or compound itself is, particularly since most patents are actually on processes of extraction, purification, or synthesis. In this way, publication may actually facilitate commercial exploitation of knowledge and resources.

Take, for example, the case of tiki uba, an anticoagulant used by the Amazonian Urueu-Wau-Wau tribe that was described in a well-known magazine. Based on the published information, Merck Pharmaceuticals "discovered" that the plant extract was indeed effective and might be useful in heart surgery.

Merck were ahead and began trying in 1988 to develop a new pharmaceutical product based on this compound without any consideration for the Urueu-Wau-Wau, who were by then threatened with extinction. To date, Merck has not announced what progress (if any) it has made. The pitfalls of expense and expertise aside, the ultimate flaw in IPR law is that it grants exclusive rights to "natural" and "juridical" persons or "creative individuals," not to collective entities such as indigenous peoples. In other words, contemporary intellectual property law is constructed around the notion of the author as an individual solitary and original creator, and it is for this figure that its protections are reserved. Those who do not fit this model - custodians of tribal culture and medical knowledge, collectives practicing traditional artistic and musical forms, or peasant cultivators of valuable seed varieties, for example - are denied intellectual property protection.

But for Indigenous peoples, knowledge and determination of the use of resources are collective and inter-generational. No Indigenous population, whether of individuals or communities, nor the government, can sell or transfer ownership of resources which are the property of the people and which each generation has an obligation to safeguard for the next. Given the divergence between indigenous peoples' views of intellectual property rights and the law itself, how can the inequities of situations like INBio's collection on indigenous lands be resolved? As the Coordinating Body of Indigenous Organizations of the Amazon Basin (COICA) sees it, indigenous peoples need "a system of protection and recognition of our resources and knowledge which is in conformity with our world view and contains formulas that will prevent appropriation of our resources and knowledge." This alternative system, based on rights and not economics, is known as traditional resource rights.

Traditional Resource Rights Traditional resource rights (TRR) reflect the awareness that maintaining control over knowledge and traditional resources (including tangible and intangible cultural, scientific, and intellectual resources) is a central part of indigenous peoples' struggle for self-determination. A statement on intellectual property rights and biodiversity issued by COICA and the United Nations Development Programme (UNDP) in 1994 embodies this stance. It states that all aspects of the issue of intellectual property (determination of access to natural resources, control of the knowledge or cultural heritage of peoples, control of the use of their resources and regulation of the terms of exploitation) are aspects of self-determination. For Indigenous peoples, accordingly, the ultimate decision on this issue is dependent on self-determination.

TRR amasses bundles of rights that are already widely recognized. These include basic human rights to development, environmental integrity, religious freedom, land and territory, privacy, prior informed consent, and full disclosure as well as farmers' rights, intellectual property rights, neighboring rights (which are similar to performance rights wherein the performance of something is protected and not the thing itself), cultural property rights, cultural heritage recognition, and the rights of customary law and practice.

These rights are found in a variety of legally binding and non-legally binding agreements Because they exist on such different political footings, however, these rights are still inadequate and need to be unified.

Contracts are legal agreements consisting of negotiated promises. Drawing them up requires only limited legal assistance, and indigenous peoples can find them useful for ensuring that any transfer of knowledge and resources is fairly compensated. Contracts typically provide the following benefits: up-front payments, training, technology transfer, royalties, and other financial and nonmonetary forms of benefit sharing.

Covenants establish principles that can lead to legally binding agreements, but they also contain ethical and moral commitments that go beyond mere commercial agreements. The Global Coalition for Bio-Cultural Diversity developed a model Covenant on Intellectual Cultural and Scientific Property that has been used to ensure equitable relationships between the Body Shop, International (a cosmetics corporation) and various indigenous groups. This covenant includes provisions for immediate benefits, including a trust fund for legal assistance, consultation, negotiation, and possible litigation, and an independent monitor to effect a yearly socio-environmental audit of the agreement. Provisions for compensation and profit sharing in the case of commercialized products are also included.

Benefits may be in the form of up-front benefits, a trust fund, or future royalties. In exchange, MTAs usually grant the recipient of the material the right to apply for patents if the material turns out to have commercial potential. The patent holder is then free to commercialize a product based on the material.

Information transfer agreements (ITAs) are adaptations of material transfer agreements. They are negotiated between indigenous groups and outside organizations interested in using traditional ecological knowledge in a commercial way. Because biogenetic resources are often modified by human action, these agreements recognize the traditional processes, medicinal formulas and other mixtures, and conservation practices that afford the germplasm improvements. Copatenting agreements be-between researchers and indigenous communities would be extensions of ITAs.

In India, local communities have developed community registers documenting all the known plant and animal species in an area and the details of their use as a means of securing control over their traditional ecological knowledge. Members of the community can exercise practical control by unilaterally refusing access to the register or by setting conditions under which access is allowed.

From a legal standpoint, community registers serve as evidence of local people's intimate knowledge of their environment and thus support their claims to legal title of the land and territory. Ultimately, these community registers could become part of regional and national registers provided the local communities agree.

Other indigenous peoples have taken a slightly different approach to documentation. For instance, the Canadian Inuit of Nunavik and another Canadian people, the Dene, have established electronic databases. Other communities, including the Kuna of Panama and the Inuit Tapirisat of Canada, are instead trying to control the research conducted with their information.

The Kuna and Inuit Tapirisat insist that only community-controlled research be carried out within their territories. This strategy allows them to decide what the research objectives and methodologies will be. The Proyecto de Estudio para el Manejo de Areas Silvestres de Kuna Yala and the Asociacion de Empleados Kunas of Panama put together an information manual outlining the principles of scientific monitoring and cooperation they wish researchers to uphold. The guidelines summarize the Kuna's objectives with regard to forest management, the conservation of biological and cultural wealth, scientific collaboration, and research priorities. The tribe encourages collaboration with Western scientists for basic ecological research, botanical and faunal inventories, and the study and recording of Kuna traditions and culture. All such research is, of course, designed to provide the Kuna with information useful to them that remains under their control.

The CBD and related UNCED agreements call for access to, protection of, and benefit sharing from the use and wider application of traditional technologies. However, neither a general consensus about what to enforce nor any enforcement mechanisms are close to appearing on the international scene. The fundamental question of what should be legally required versus what should be moral and ethical responsibilities portends many difficulties for all stakeholders. There are, however, efforts underway to grapple with this and other pressing questions. At a workshop held at the Green College Centre for Environmental Policy and Understanding at Oxford University in June 1995, participants from around the world drafted several findings and formulated a number of recommendations. Those recommendations included (among others) a call for NGOs and governmental organizations to follow the principles already established in legal documents dealing with indigenous rights and to disseminate and integrate these principles into their guidelines for policy and operations.

The participants recommended that a consortium of institutions be formed to establish codes of conduct, identify gaps between policies and practices and correct the deficiencies, and make sure that scientists, government officials, and NGOs are properly informed of indigenous peoples' rights and views. To address concerns about biosafety, they suggested that local communities be included in monitoring and evaluating genetically modified organisms; that institutions exercise the precautionary principle; and that the creation of life patent-free zones be investigated. In addition to fostering the development of traditional resource rights, stakeholders were encouraged to explore other legal systems and other ways of protecting intellectual and cultural resources, including customary practice. Until adequate and effective mechanisms for protection and compensation have been established, participants suggested that a moratorium on biodiversity prospecting be observed.

Some governments have recognized these new kinds of rights based on the concept of traditional resource rights. In 1997, the government of Brazil established the Brazilian Programme of Molecular Ecology for Sustainable Use of Biodiversity (PROBEM). It is aimed at making the Amazon region a source of high value-added products and advanced scientific know-how, especially through the use of biotechnology.

The need to conserve natural wealth and develop eco-tourism was late in gaining recognition in Brazil. Its Amazon region is home to as many as half of all the world's insect species and over one- fifth of plant species. This programme is aimed at changing the current model of economic growth in the region, which is based on the extraction of wood and minerals, ranching and one-crop farming - activities that destroy the forests.

In addition, indigenous people and other long-time residents of the region will also benefit through remuneration for their contributions to the development of new products, such as their traditional knowledge of the medicinal properties, food value and cosmetic and aromatic uses of native plant or animal species. The knowledge held by forest-dwellers helps local and foreign investigators reach their discoveries much earlier. PROBEM was endowed with a financial mechanism enabling its implementation: a fund for financing biotechnology projects and for paying royalties to local residents. The organization was inspired in the Permanent Alaska Fund created by the United States in 1977 for the payment of royalties from oil in exchange for environmental conservation and the payment of indemnification and dividends to Eskimos/Innuit. That successful experiment had already accumulated 27 billion dollars by 1998.

Any companies or institutions interested in developing products based on substances found in the Amazon will have to associate themselves with Bioamazonia, a mixed organization set up by the Brazilian government in conjunction with the scientific community and representatives of civil society to administer PROBEM. Bioamazonia has been equipped with the Amazonian Biotechnology Centre, as well as a financial instrument, the Permanent Fund for the Conservation and Sustainable Use of the Biodiversity in Amazonia (FPBA).

To set up the FPBA fund, Bioamazonia turned to the Axial bank, a unique financial institution specializing in investments in the environment, especially biodiversity. The Axial bank obtained one million dollars in aid from the United Nations conference on Trade and Development and the Inter-American Development Bank to get the FPBA off the ground.

Companies interested in biological material and data obtained by Bioamazonia will pay a fee that will go into the fund. As in prospecting for oil, companies doing research on biological substances found in the region will be subject to bidding and paying for concessions and to paying royalties from the products developed and marketed, he added.

PROBEM still requires the passage of a law regulating access to Brazil's genetic resources in order for it to control genetic and biological material from the Amazon. Given that legal vacuum, the UN Convention on Biological Diversity, which makes authorization by the State in question necessary for the removal of any genetic material, applies. Without government authorization, the removal of any biological substances by foreigners is illegal, the Environment Minister pointed out. The key to a successful program is removing activities damaging to the environment, conserving biological diversity, all the while converting the natural wealth of the Amazon into business profits.

Data Privacy of Citizens' Health and Genetic Medical Histories

Insurance Companies closely measure risk factors in order to earn profits from employers' health insurance programs. Therefore, it is not fair for employers and their health insurers to demand access to predictive genetic tests for employees from their doctor? Scientists and medical researchers predict that such genetic tests will be available no later than one decade from now. Use of such tests could result in certain people being refused jobs based on their tendency to inherit disease or refusal of health insurance coverage. The Americans With Disabilities Act prohibit employers from asking or seeing such information before hiring. However, no legislation currently prohibits such information subsequent to the hire.

What about the state and federal government? Do they have a right to inspect your health and genetic records as part of a review for state-paid health insurance, welfare benefits, imprisonment, etc? If so, is it likely that non-government parties can receive the same information under a Freedom of Information Act?

Each time a patient sees a doctor, is admitted to a hospital, goes to a pharmacist or sends a claim to a health plan, a record is made of their confidential health information. For many years, the confidentiality of those records was maintained by our family doctors, who kept our records sealed away in file cabinets and refused to reveal them to anyone else. Today, the use and disclosure of this information is protected by a patchwork of state laws, leaving large gaps in the protection of patients' privacy and confidentiality. There is a pressing need for national standards to control the flow of sensitive patient information and to establish real penalties for the misuse or disclosure of this information.

President Clinton and Congress recognized the need for national patient record privacy standards in 1996 when they enacted the Health Insurance Portability and Accountability Act of 1996 (HIPAA). That law gave Congress until August 21, 1999, to pass comprehensive health privacy legislation. After three years of discussion in Congress without passage of such a law, HIPAA provided HHS with the authority to craft such privacy protections by regulation. Thee President drafted regulations to guarantee patients new rights and protections against the misuse or disclosure of their health records and the President and Secretary Donna E. Shalala released them in October of last year. This final rule provides the first comprehensive federal protection for the privacy of health information. However, because of the limitations of the HIPAA statute, these protections do not fully achieve the Clinton Administration's goal of a seamless system of privacy protection for all health information. Members of both parties in Congress will need to pass meaningful, comprehensive privacy protection for American patients that would extend the reach of the standards being finalized today to all entities that hold personal health information.

Covered Entities

As required by HIPAA, the final regulation covers health plans, health care clearinghouses, and those health care providers who conduct certain financial and administrative transactions (e.g., electronic billing and funds transfers) electronically.

Information Protected

All medical records and other individually identifiable health information held or disclosed by a covered entity in any form, whether communicated electronically, on paper, or orally, is covered by the final regulation.

New Requirements: The new standards would require that health-care providers obtain written consent form patients for the use or disclosure of information in their medical records. The new regulations will also:

- Allow all Americans to review and copy their medical records, and change them if they find errors.
- Require health-care providers to state their privacy policies in writing. Patients will also have to consent to any disclosure of information related to treatment, payment and health-care operations.
- Allow patients to request that their health-care information not be disclosed. Doctors may choose to override the request if they have compelling reasons.
- Prevent employers from receiving medical information that could be used in employment decisions.

Congress is also readying more legislation to help protect Americans' privacy with regard to medical genetic information. In February 2001, Congressmen Louise Slaughter (D-NY) and Senator Tom Daschle (D-So.Dak.) introduced a bill that would bar health insurers from using predictive genetic information to deny, cancel or change the rates and conditions of insurance coverage. Employers would be prohibited from using the information in hiring, firing, promoting, and other employment-related decisions. The bill had 171 cosponsors.

On Feb. 17, 2001, Slaughter addressed scientists at the conference of the American Association for the Advancement of Science. She said, "The science is not fully understood," and conclusions that insurers or employers could draw at this point would be "so inaccurate as to be almost useless." For example, when a genetic mutation underlying breast cancer was discovered, scientists initially claimed that women who carried the mutation faced a 80 percent risk of getting the cancer. but within two years, the risk was lowered to 50 percent.

Slaughter also stressed that genetic discrimination shouldn't be allowed to happen because everyone has genetic defects of one kind or another and people with genes increasing the risk for a certain disease don't always get the disease.

Within 10 years, doctors will be equipped with genetic tests that can predict a patient's risk for at least a dozen major diseases, including heart disorders, diabetes and some cancers, said Dr. Francis Collins, director of the National Center for

Human Genome Research. J. Craig Venter, president of Maryland-based Celera Genomics, called genetic discrimination one of the "key issues" raised by the genome project. but efforts to pass a genetic privacy bill have failed five times, he said. "We hope we will have a much better outcome this time."

The bill is opposed by groups representing several different industries. The Health Insurance Association of America argues taht insurers are not using genetic test results in coverage decisions and therefore the legislation isn't needed. "There is no discrimination by health insurers and no plans for it." said the association's spokesman.

The pharmaceutical industry also has weighed in against the bill, said Slaughter, because of provisions that would keep genetic information about individuals private and therefore off limits to companies that want it for research or marketing reasons.

Lawsuit Filed to Protect Workers' Genetic Information

In late February 2001, a lawsuit was filed by a group of employees of the Burlington Railroad objecting to their privacy and worker's compensation rights that they say were violated by the company's demand for genetic screening tests. Several employees had filed health insurance and worker's compensation benefit requests based on disability caused by carpal tunnel syndrome. As part of the worker compensation benefit process, the insurance company doctor requested extra vials of blood be drawn from each worker. The purpose of the blood was to run a test for "genetic screening" to see if the workers had a genetic propensity for carpal tunnel syndrome. The employees objected to this procedure and filed a lawsuit. The railroad agreed in court not to run the test. Outcome of the lawsuit is still pending.

CONFLICTS WITH FOREIGN GOVERNMENTS OVER INTELLECTUAL PROPERTY RIGHTS

Should the United States change its patent and copyright laws in accordance with other countries? Should the United States' government require pharmaceutical companies receiving government research money or government inventions to lower the cost of drugs in areas of the world suffering from health epidemics? Must United States' citizens bear the cost for drug companies providing needed drugs at a lower price for other people? Should the United States quit trying to impose its economic priorities on other countries? Are patents issued in the country so broad as to hamper future medical research? These are the current issues in intellectual property law.

Many countries realize that their intellectual property rights' laws can be used to reflect their particular cultural values and maximize the economic value of the products of that country. The United States, in the last 15 years, has pushed other regimes to harmonize their IPR (intellectual property rights) with those of the United States - or at least, with the Berne and Paris Conventions. In the context of rapidly changing technologies, international markets, and inadequate international regimes (WIPO, WTO, TRIPS, GATT), national policymakers try to decide how to adjust domestic and international policies in a manner that appropriately accommodates the new technologies at home and encourages similar accommodation abroad, preferably without undermining the otherwise useful international IPR regimes.

A coercive approach to international IPR reform can undermine foreign support for the particular policy goals and perhaps damage the prospects for international cooperation in other areas. The international patent and copyright regimes may move slowly, but they do provide a sure and predictable method of coordinating domestic and foreign IPR rules, which facilitates investment in information-intensive technologies (such as biotechnology). In addition, the international agreements help to disseminate new technology globally by reducing the transaction costs of obtaining and enforcing exclusive rights in different countries. Bilateral understandings, on the other hand, may introduce policy inconsistencies, interpretive difficulties for domestic businesses, increase administrative complexity, and raise the transaction costs of obtaining IPR abroad. If the United States circumvents the IPR regimes of other countries, it could lose it ability to influence how other nations and the international regimes accommodate the new technologies and protect U.S. intellectual property products in general.

The serious economic consequences of IPR reform have increased major cleavages in the world economy, cleavages that set rich countries against poor as well as rich countries against each other. Many countries do not even share the basic definitional underpinnings of western IPR concepts. For example, copying in traditional Korean society is an expression of honor, to an infringement of an inherent ownership right. Other countries object to U.S.-style IPR protection on economic grounds. Brazil has long denied IPR protection for U.S. pharmaceutical products on the dual grounds that doing so would lock Brazil into technological dependency and would create an enormous public health problem by making much needed pharmaceutical products prohibitively expensive.

The most cooperative strategy is to facilitate other country's harmonization process through international conferences, cross-national policy reform discussions, and so forth—as has primarily been the case with regard to biotechnology patent rules. Coercive tactics are somewhat broader in range—the United States can encourage foreign adherence to regime rules through "carrot and stick" tactics such as the reciprocity provocation of the Semi Conductor Protection Act, or it can use even more forceful tactics such as the threat of trade retaliation (as has been the case in software).

Although most of the advanced industrial states have PR regimes with similar normative underpinnings, there are nonetheless substantial conflicts between them over the proper scope and terms of IPR protection. For example, members of the European Patent Office (EPO) only recently (9/99) agreed to allow the patenting of human cells as well as transgenic plants and animals. Compare this with the decision by the USPTO to allow the patenting of transgenic animals and life forms since Diamond v. Chakrabarty in 1980.

Biotechnology is an industry that commands higher and higher R&D outlays at the same time that relatively inexpensive copying technologies are available. Because biotechnology is so complex and unusual, and because the industry that deploys them is largely international in scope, the politics of adjusting domestic IPR rules invariably coexists with political pressure for foreign IPR reform. This duality suggests that external IPR negotiations are influenced by international competitive pressures as well as by domestic political bargaining concerning the creation and regulation of biotechnology products and processes.

In terms of market structure, the biotechnology industry is relatively new and based on rapidly changing, information-intensive technology. In addition, the market for biotechnology is global in the sense that products are developed, produced and sold on an international scale. However, neither condition is uniform. Technology varies in terms of its level of development and markets vary in terms of the product cycle. Because of this variability, IPR reform should vary across different technological and market circumstances. In a new market involving developing technologies (like biotechnology) IPR reform has more long-term implications for economic competitiveness. IPR reforms primarily affect the potential for developing new products and markets. Consequently, IPR reform does not provoke immediate trade conflicts.

IPR policy in Biotechnology reflects the industry's relatively low level of commercialization and generally cooperative intra-industry relations. although biotechnology is highly international in terms of R&D and marketing requirements, it is still a developing technology and consequently confers a relatively low degree of trade leverage. Because international markets are underdeveloped and expanding, IPR disputes have not provoked trade tensions except in the secondary markets of pharmaceutical sales. In drug sales, countries having lower economic standards of living are pressured to either allow for sales of "generic" copies that replace the more expensive foreign (mostly U.S.) patented drugs or negotiate (either singly or through an international organization) for markedly lower prices from the drug companies for these much needed drugs.

Biotechnology is characterized by a symbiotic and generally cooperative relationship between small, highly innovative R&D firms and large multinational enterprises, both of which stand of gain from stronger patent protection for biotechnology products. Their ability to pursue IPR reform has been aided by the lack of a contrary industry coalition, either from the biotechnology field or form unrelated holders of industrial patent rights. The primary resistance to increased IPR protection for biotechnology products has come from consumer advocates and some public sector agencies who are wary of both the ethical implications of patenting life and the uncertain health and safety ;implications of new biotechnology. In addition, although the Human Genome Project (to identify all the genetic composition of the human body) has been funded and undertaken as an international research project by various governments, several well-financed private commercial companies have competed to identify and patent gene sequences. Public concern with potential restriction to these gene forms and their potential for medicines has caused several well-known biotechnology researchers to speak out against patenting of these markers.

Another concern of public policy is whether patents granted to biotechnology companies cover too broad a subject area and ultimately stifle further research instead of providing motivation in pursuing research. Broad patents may also reinforce social protests against the patenting of life forms. For example, In 1992 a patent was granted to the North American biotechnology company *Agracetus on all* genetically engineered cotton plants. Two years later, the same company obtained a similar patent on *all* transgenic soya bean plants in Europe. At least five other companies have obtained similar broad patents on plant species, among them *Coffea arabica*, the most important commercial coffee species, and the entire *Brassica* family. In January 1995, *Mycogen Corporation*, California, obtained a patent on a method to design synthetic genes probably covering all plants containing these genes. And in March 1995, also in the USA, a patent was issued to the *National Institutes of Health on all ex vivo* gene therapies

There is an advantage of some broad patents. One example is Bell laboratories' patent on the transistor. The holders of such patents have a good prospect of royalty income and a strategic position in negotiations with other firms. However, for most firms, such an early position in a technology cannot be realized. Instead, they rely on alternative methods. One such method is to claim an invention in an early phase, too early to indicate the precise function of what has been invented. This process was followed by he US national Institutes of Health when the organization filed for r a patent on several thousands of partial human DNA sequences it had identified. This patent would ensure NIH a strategic position at the time a commercial product would come out of their work.

A second option for pursuing a strategic position in he biotechnology research is broadening the scope of the patent. This can be achieved by claiming an area in which the invention can be applied on the basis of limited exemplification. In this case the inventor extrapolates the effect of his invention in the "model system" to a number of other organisms without providing proof for that. For example, in 1988, Harvard University claimed that their invention on transgenic mice would work with every other non-human mammal, even though the working examples included only mice.

In the case of Agracetus and its modification of the genome of cotton and soya bean with Agrobacterium tumefaciens, it claimed patent coverage for all possible transgenic plants of these species, regardless of the techniques and genes used for the transformation. In contrast, patents in the chemical and pharmaceutical industry cover both the process and the product obtained by that process as described in a chemical formula (my emphasis). Agracetus's claims covered possible transformations of cotton and soya beans that had no connection with its techniques.

Research that is conducted with a non-commercial objective is usually not hampered by a patent even though formal authorization is required from the patent holder. But, every commercially-oriented type of research in a wide technological field will be effected. Researchers can be sued because they are using the same or similar process or transgenic. As an alternative, when researchers find out that a patent covers their research, they have to negotiate for a license with the patent holder in order to continue their work. The patent holder may grant non-exclusive licenses against conditions which are considered to be reasonably or the patentee may ask for payments that are too high for smaller companies. Agracetus reportedly asked $1 million dollars for a license. In addition, the patentee may restrict the exploitation by the licensee.

These patent rights can extend far beyond the United and Europe. Argacetus filed for patents on transgenic cotton in the main other cotton producing countries, such as India, Brazil and China. In India, a broad cotton patent was initially granted in 1991, but subsequently revoked in October 1994 because the government decided that the objective of the patent was to deny opportunity to biotechnologists in India to develop pest-resistant cotton plants by recombinant DNA techniques. Most government retain the right to prevent patents from frustrating innovation if they determine that the patent grant would impair public safety, health, or "morals". However, governments are pressured not to invoke these sanctions unless absolutely necessary. (However, compulsory licensing and parallel imports are both being considered by the governments of poor nations in the grip of medical crisis' now)

The attempt by the NIH to patent thousands of DNA fragments was eventually rejected by the United States Patent and Trademark Office. NIH did not appeal the decision and decided to abandon its policy to seek patent protection for DNA sequences. In early 2001, the USPTO adopted new guidelines for its patent claim examiners, requiring that specific use for transgenic materials be adequately shown in the patent application to satisfy the utility requirement of the Patent Act. (See United States Patent and Trademark Office Final Computer-Related Patent Examination Guidelines). Under the new guidelines expected to take effect in the next few months, gene fragments (ESTs) will probably not qualify for patents. However, fully characterized genes whose functions are known will continue to be patentable. This action will alleviate some of the concerns the American public as to the reach of genetic patents by forcing companies to narrow their scope of claims and to justify the public good of the patent grant.

PATENTABILITY OF HUMAN GENE SEQUENCES UNDER AMERICAN LAW

Human gene sequences occur naturally. The current policy of the U.S. Patent Office is to treat human gene sequences like naturally occurring substances and chemicals. Naturally occurring substances and chemicals may be patented if they are extracted, isolated, and purified. However, the substances must have some greater value than previously existed in the naturally form. (See Merck & Co. v. Olin Mathieson Chem. Corp., (upholding a patent for a vitamin B concentrate which had been extracted from its natural form and purified) and Parke-Davis & Co. v. H.K. Mulford & Co., (upholding a patent for adrenaline isolated from animal suprarenal glands).

Gene sequences contain a great deal of extraneous information because they are composed of sections which code for proteins as well as sections that do not. When scientists clone sequences hey isolate only the protein-coding portions, thus isolating and purifying the gene sequences. Is it appropriate that isolated and purified gene sequences be awarded patent protection in accordance with the novelty standard?

Patents have sometimes failed for lack of utility. It is generally known that gene sequences produce human protein but not what the actual function of the protein is . In these cases, the patent applicants try to show that the gene sequences function as different types of markers, probes and primers for various genetic research. If the applicants are capable of showing that their sequence can be used for one of these purposes, they will have satisfied the utility requirement under 35 U.S.C. Sec. 101.

However, the guidelines for refusing a patent for human gene sequences require the examiner to clearly assert why an innovation is rejected for lack of utility. (50 Pat. Trademark & Copyright J. (BNA) 195, 304-05 (July 20,1995) (holding that human testing of pharmaceuticals not necessary to satisfy the utility requirement). In January of 2001, the PTO published Final Guidelines for Determining Utility of Gene-Related Inventions.

The utility Guidelines are applicable to all areas of technology. However, they are particularly relevant in areas of emerging technologies, such as gene-related technologies, where uses for new materials that have not been fully characterized are not readily apparent. The guidelines were issued because of concerns by the scientific community that gene sequences were being patented without any express or specific use for them. Ultimately, that situation would result in patents on many gene sequences for which a medical or scientific use would be found later. This meant that companies could "stockpile" gene sequences and prevent important research from being undertaken by reason of their patent. This Guideline is expected to require more specifics on the projected use; i.e., a justification why the patent should be given to the applicant (what useful public policy reason does it fulfill).

In re Deuel, the court relaxed the obvious standard by stating that general motivation to search for some gene that exists does not necessarily make obvious a specifically-defined gene that is subsequently obtained as a reusIt of that search. This case seems to allow patents to be granted for DNA molecules even if the method for finding the DNA was obvious. But note that the 1995 amendment to 35 U.S. C. Sec. 103 seems to require that both the process and the molecule be nonobvious to satisfy the nonobviousness requirement.)

On October 3, 1995, President Clinton established the National Bioethics Advisory Commission (Exec. Order 12,975, 3 C.F.R. 409(1996)). One requirement of the Commission is to review the appropriateness and implications of human gene patenting. Some experts have suggested that the NBAC identify and separate categories of biotechnology research that are appropriate (from a social standpoint) for patents from those that are not. such categories could include transgenic research animals, transgenic farm animals, and human gene sequences with unknown utility. Isolating separate categories of biotechnology will allow more narrow categories than limiting the discussion to the issue of biotechnology patenting as a whole. The NBAC should present these categories to Congress for adoption under Title 35. Creating categories and offering suggestions as to the appropriateness of patent protection for each category would give the PTO some guidance so that the PTO may continue to decide "novelty" rather than "morality". There is some guidance existing in the Constitution, current precedent, and formerly proposed legislation to aid in the creation of such guidelines.

In August of 1999, the U.S. Patent and Trademark Office rejected an application for a broad patent on the creation of human-animal chimeras. The patent was rejected because a chimera "includes within its scope a human being" and "people are not patentable', according to the patent agency. Stuart Newman and Jeremy Rifkin plan to appeal the ruling to the U.S. Supreme Court if necessary.

5

Annals of Bioethics

Bioethics cannot be thought of as a primarily North American and Western European academic discipline. Bioethics has become a truly international phenomenon, moving beyond academic discussions into politics, social policy, and law.

Regional Perspectives in Bioethics illustrates the ways in which the national and international political landscape compasses persons from diverse and often fragmented moral communities with widely varying moral intuitions, premises, evaluations, and commitments. It explores, documents, and critically assesses the moral, cultural, and religious viewpoints representing the various regions of the world, from mainland China and Hong Kong, Taiwan, Japan, India and East Asia more generally, to Europe, the Middle East, Australia and New Zealand, to South America and North America. It portrays the often widely varying bioethical perspectives reflected throughout the international community's regions, religions, laws and policies. Here one appreciates the significant plurality of fundamentally different, incompatible, and often mutually antagonistic moral visions and moral rationalities, within which complex bioethical issues are addressed.

A Case Study in Bioethics

Bioethical questions rarely have cut and dried answers. They include the scientific, legal and ethical considerations of a specific case. The case below asks these types of questions and will pique your curiosity to look into how such a case could affect you personally.

Since the Human Genome Project was announced in the 1990s, bioethicists have been arguing the many ethical and legal aspects of its future. Some have suggested that everything from eye color to genetic conditions would be controllable, and we would have the ultimate ability to change our own genes and those of our fetuses. But first we would have tests. Tests for all conditions and traits, tests that can determine both prenatally and postnatally what our children will be.

This case presents a scenario set in the future. It asks the question, who will be tested and for what and who will control this testing? There was a wonderful party going on. Representative Roland Smith had been to many parties since being elected Congressman from his state, but this was the best.

The party was given by Maxigene, a large pharmaceutical company that had just developed a test for the gene that causes a serious condition. The condition is rare, serious and had no treatment or cure.

Finally, by the end of the evening, Maxigene came to the point. They were suggesting a law to having every baby born in the US tested for this gene. The company's president, Dr. Irving Dahler, made a short presentation. He explained how much time and money was spent to develop the test. Part of the funding had come from the Orphan Drug Act, but the company had put up hours of research and development. Even though the condition is rare and probably only 1/10,000 people carry the gene that causes it, Dahler suggests that parents would want to know this information about their newborns, and eventually, their unborn fetuses.

Today, states test for many genetic diseases, as mandated by law. But in the future, companies will want to recoup the money they spend on research and development and one of the best ways is to lobby politicians to legislate a law to test all newborns and possibly test for carriers.

Dangers of Genetic Screening

The issue of genetic manipulation has certainly stirred up a big can of worms this past year or so. Readers may be aware of the movement in agriculture to create man-made versions of fruits and vegetables that are more resistant to frost, pests and disease. Attempts by environmentalists and consumers to have these foods labeled genetically- altered have met with limited success.

The July 1990 issue of *Consumer Reports* discusses another potentially serious ramification of this advance in science: genetic screening. As you may know, contained in every human cell are the genetic instructions that give each person's organs their specific form and ability to function. In the past twenty years, researchers have been able to identify some of the genes that determine whether a person is carrying the "marker" for many inherited diseases. So, for example, when a person is found to be carrying the marker for juvenile diabetes, their chances of developing that condition are much greater than if they were not carrying that marker.

In and of itself, this is a great advancement. Scientists have been able to make great strides in controlling many inherited diseases, especially ones that occur in specific cultural groups, such as Tay-Sachs disease (in Ashkenazi Jews), sickle-cell anemia (in African Americans), cystic fibrosis (in Caucasians), and various forms of a blood disorder called thalassemia (in Mediterraneans, Africans and Southeast Asians). The article notes that, "Widespread acceptance of genetic screening for Tay-Sachs disease has nearly wiped out that deadly disorder in high-risk groups. Among Jews in the U.S. and Canada, the incidence of the disease has dropped more than 90 percent since 1970."

Amniocentesis is now available for pregnant women who wish to determine if their unborn child is carrying the marker for Down syndrome, as well as other disabling or disfiguring conditions. Parents who discover that their child is likely to be born with such a problem have the option to terminate the pregnancy if they feel they are unable to cope with a "special" child. Because of these advancements, genetic testing is routinely done in hospitals and sperm banks. "Many parents are unaware that their newborns are screened for up to nine inherited disorders. (Such testing is required by law in most states.)"

What could be the problem in having such valuable information available to the person who wishes to know? Of course, the most obvious issue is a moral one: "Because most genetic disorders can be detected but not treated, prevention means avoiding the birth of an affected child. And that backs genetic screening into the jaws of the abortion debate."

Beyond this emotional issue, however, lies a more serious problem. As genetic screening becomes more advanced and refined, its potential for abuse becomes greater. There are already movements in certain sectors of society to use this information as a kind of "crystal ball" in order to make policy decisions. For example, one reason doctors are performing genetic screening of newborns is to avoid litigation charging failure to inform. Will the day come when an obstetrician refuses to assist a birth of a child determined to be carrying a disease that predisposes it to an early death or disfigurement for fear of being sued by the family?

Many employers and insurance companies are also utilizing this information in order to determine whether a particular applicant is a "good risk." The presence of a genetic marker does not guarantee that the carrier will develop the condition, nor can it determine the onset of the condition or the severity of it. Yet more organizations are looking at genetic screening as a sure-fire way to "beat the odds."

The article cites this frightening scenario: "When Harvard geneticist Paul Billings ran a medical-journal ad asking for reports of genetic discrimination, 29 respondents met study criteria. They'd been turned down for auto, life, health, mortgage, or disability insurance, turned away from adoption agencies, or denied employment, all on the basis of their genes. Yet most were neither disabled nor certain to become so. Some were excluded because their family history put them at risk, though their personal genetic status was unknown. Others were treated as if they were ill, despite therapy that kept them symptom-free."

Another way in which this information may be used harmfully is in the realm of social and medical policy. In the 1970's there were laws requiring all African Americans seeking a marriage licence or school attendance to be screened for sickle-cell anemia. Such laws have since been repealed, but the precedents have been set. It is not unthinkable that society may one day prohibit persons determined to be carriers of certain inherited diseases from participating fully in life.

Another disturbing development is discussed as follows: "...legal action may override a woman's rights in the interest of her child's health. Courts have ordered cesarean section when vaginal delivery would have threatened the baby's life; pregnant drug addicts have been imprisoned on charges of distributing cocaine to their unborn minors. As prenatal gene therapy or in utero surgery becomes possible, some law might require a woman to undergo treatment against her will. Another source of pressure may be subtle and more personal. Certain genetic tests require blood samples from family members, including those who might prefer to keep their genetic tea leaves unread." We've all heard about the "Mommy track" in the corporate realm, wherein women who seek to work and also have children are placed on a path of advancement with less potential opportunity then men or childless female co-workers. Will there also be a "defective track" in the work place, in schools, etc. for those known to be carrying the potential for an inherited disease? Will we, as a society, say to these people, "You're really not worth the attention or the effort, because you'll probably be dead in a few years anyway; or you'll be so dysfunctional that you'll only be a burden."

These are issues that should be discussed now, before the technology is so entrenched that there is no turning back. Science has given us great advancements and great opportunities for human development and potential. It's important to remember, however, that science should remain a tool of human society. Too often it is the other way around: humans are seen by science as the tools for testing every new advancement developed. Society should be in the position to determine the ethical use of technological developments such as genetic screening, and not let "the tail wag the dog." The availability of a new technology does not always guarantee that it is a proper tool to be utilized in human society.

GENETIC SCREENING

Genetic screening is the testing of variations in gene sequences in protein or DNA. Protein screening is easier, but DNA screening is more powerful. It is a 'physical screening for a protein or genetic abnormality that may allow detection of a disorder before there are physical signs of it, or even before a gene is expressed if it acts later in life.' (web). This is a technique that is used on nonhuman species such as plants and some animals and is not questioned. The real question is if we should use it on humans.

The procedure of genetic screening is the binding of a probe to a DNA molecule of the patient. Complementary DNA nucleotide sequences bind together, so the probe is single stranded DNA that binds to it's "mate" in the patient. Scientists try to use probes that are independent of family history, so there is no consent or samples needed from parents of the patient. The patients DNA is analyzed by Random Fragment Length Polymorphism, of RFLP. The DNA is cut by restriction endonucleases, separated and examined. The results are not always clear. Many diseases have mutations, so this makes screening even more difficult, and only the common mutations are screened for. There is also the problem of expressivity of the disease. It may be more or less severe in one patient than another because of age, progress speed, multiple gene activity, or ant number of environmental factors. Also, many diseases arise spontaneously and are not inherited from either parent and cannot be screened for.

There are many ethical concerns with genetic screening, just a few are social and physiological problems, the use by insurance companies, "ordering" a baby, selective abortions, more embryos made than implanted, and quality and reliability of services. These question may seem far fetched and not real concerns, but in the near future, any parent may be able to order a baby. This is not like the rich parents of today ordering babies that meet strict qualifications off the internet, this is genetically choosing the traits of an unborn child, and maybe disposing of embryos that are insufficient. Here also lies the problem that came with the abortion issue : when does life begin? Is it at the embryo stage, the third trimester of pregnancy, or at birth? Is disposing of embryonic tissue murder?

The social and physiological problems include the conscience of the parents about the results, the results themselves, and what they can do to the parents of unborn screened children. If all tests came back normal, it would alleviate worry by the parents and if there are problems that can be treated immediately, they can be taken care of. But some say let nature take its course. After a screening, there are many decisions to be made. These decisions used to be made after any pregnancy: keep, abort, or give the baby up for adoption. These decisions used to be made solely on the ability and want of the parents to take care of the child. Now there are a whole new set of rules. These parents may know the sex of the baby and what diseases it may be susceptible to. These are concerns of many new parents, but being able to select for these traits would be a dream come true, for some.

"Within a decade or two, it may be possible to screen kids almost before conception for an enormous range of attributes, such as how tall they're likely to be, what body type they will have, their hair and eye color, what sorts of illnesses they will be naturally resistant to , and even, conceivably, their IQ and personality type." (Lemonick). Parents may be able to insert genes and not only select against undesirable genes. Lemonick goes on to say that it will eventually be like buying a car and selecting options. This is a very scary thought. What would the world be like if all people were perfect and there were no faults? The birth of a baby is the most wonderful thing parents can go through, or it is supposed to be. Nature gives the gift of life and we as humans are never satisfied, we have to do better. We have to modify everything we see, even if it is our own children. What if the screening was wrong or there was a lab mix-up and they disposed of the wrong baby, would the baby that was born have the same love and affection from its parents or would it be "disposed of" like it should have been?

The use of this screening by insurance companies is a scare for many people. "Knowing you are susceptible to breast cancer or diabetes would be invaluable to an HMO looking for ways to screen out riskier candidates and thus keep costs down - and profits up." (Hallowell). But, thirty states have already passed laws prohibiting such screening for jobs and insurance. Thankfully, because "everyone is susceptible to one disease or another." (Hallowell). But will that statement ring true forever? If the babies are selected for healthiness, then there will be an elimination of some diseases, and maybe not everyone will be susceptible to something. Maybe no one will be susceptible to anything and we will live forever! I find that just as scary as "designer babies". "Five years ago, most Americans rejected the Clinton Administration's proposals for a larger government role in managing health insurance. But if genetic testing starts to have a real impact on their health-care coverage, they could have second thoughts, and may seek refuge in some form of nationalized health insurance. In that case, it will be up to the insurance industry to offer a free-market alternative that Americans find palatable." (Hallowell).

There is a large market for genetic screening in commercial and pharmaceutical business. The public needs to be educated on the reality of its use and ability. Like previously stated, the results are not always clear. It may be of great benefit for people to know what diseases they are susceptible to, to take the necessary precautions earlier in life. Presently, all babies born in hospitals are screened for PKU (phenylketonurea), because it is treatable disease if treated early and if left untreated causes severe mental retardation. The genetic screening process could be comparable to the vaccines children receive today. It may be "an extension of preventative medicine" (web).

In 1968, the World Health Organization (WHO) recommended criteria for a condition worthy of a screening program:

1. The condition sought should be an important health problem.
2. The natural history of the condition should be adequately understood.
3. There should be a recognizable latent or early symptomatic stage.

4. There should be a treatment.
5. There should be an agreed upon policy on whom to treat as patients.
6. Case finding should be a continuous process, not a once and for all project.
7. A suitable screening test should be available.
8. The teat should be acceptable to the population.
9. Facilities for diagnosis and treatment should be available.
10. The cost of case finding (diagnosis and treatment) should be economically balanced in relation to possible expenditure on medical care as a whole.

If there is to be a mass screening, it has to be voluntary, there has to be widespread education about possibilities, wide access to the population, quality assurance an screening and treatment, good public registers, and ethical and scientific training of screening personnel. (web). But even after these criteria are met, there is still the concern of geneticophobia, or the social discrimination. There is always a fear of the unknown, even if some of the people are educated, there will always be some that are not; and even if all people know the risks and benefits, they will never agree.

GENETIC TESTING LAW

On September 11, 1997, the Secretary of Health and Human Services submitted to Congress detailed guidelines on how to prepare federal legislation to protect the privacy of medical information. In June, 1997, the National Committee on Vital and Health Statistics issued its long awaited report on improving confidentiality in medical information and records. Two major privacy bills are pending in Congress. Clearly, forces of change are at work which require the formulation of new policies on privacy and confidentiality. While information systems are a major factor in any reassessment of how health information in managed, equally important is the type of information, for example the results of genetic testing, which can dramatically alter the way an individual is perceived.

The recent explosion of genetic testing and growing concern about how to manage genetic test results illustrates how privacy and clinical developments are straining existing laws. Interestingly, the federal government is behind the states in dealing with privacy and genetic information. Of course, some states, such as Pennsylvania, have not legislated at all specifically to control the use of genetic test results.

With the enactment of the Health Insurance Portability and Accountability Act (HIPAA), federal law for the first time undertook a broad range of insurance regulatory activities previously left to the states. Included among many other provisions is a brief provision which prohibits issuers of health benefits and health insurance from using "genetic information" in granting, denying, canceling and otherwise evaluating an individual's eligibility for health coverage. In Section 101 of HIPAA, Congress acted to alleviate growing concerns that the results of genetic research and biotechnology would be misapplied.

Over the past two years, breakthrough discoveries in genetic testing have suggested that the predictability or susceptibility of certain genetically related diseases would make available exquisitely sensitive information about individuals which heretofore did not exist. Thus, employers, insurers, law enforcement officials and a host of other interested persons might inquire or compel disclosure of information which could predict the onset of dread diseases or the increased likelihood of susceptibility to these diseases. Already a groundswell of state laws has sought to regulate the use or misuse of genetic testing information in the issuance of health and life insurance. However, the complexities of regulation of health insurance and health benefits made many of these protections inapplicable to many individuals who receive health benefits through certain employer sponsored plans. Section 101 of HIPAA began to bridge the gap between state and federal initiatives.

Genetic information is the end product of genetic testing. Genetic testing is not a novel clinical development and in some ways it has been practiced for many years. For example, some types of genetic information may be gathered from a focused medical history and physical examination. Likewise, for many years, states have required newborns to be tested for hereditary diseases such as phenylketonuria, a treatable metabolic disorder.

The current concerns stem from entirely new, dramatic studies in molecular science. Commencing in 1990, Congress authorized the National Institutes of Health (NIH) and the Department of Energy (DOE) to participate in a multinational effort to map the human genome. Literally hundreds of scientists have labored continuously since 1990 to complete the Human Genome Project (HGP). The HGP is intended to map the entire human genome, determine the sequence of genetic codes and ultimately to understand the function of genetic codes.

Notwithstanding the recent federal entrance into the regulation of genetic information, the states have played the most significant role in this type of regulation to date. At least sixteen states regulate how insurers use genetic information. In the aggregate, these statutes are of two types. A limited number of states have regulated insurers in the use of information relating to specific genetic traits such as sickle-cell trait or hemoglobin C trait. These disease-specific statutes were usually adopted in the 1970s in response to then permissible underwriting practices which permitted insurers to refuse to issue or renew a policy to the carrier of a trait disease. More recently, a dozen or more states have sought to respond to the complex issues presented by the rapid growth in genetic knowledge and technology. Within a range of predictable variation, recent state statutes on genetic information and insurance practices seek to:

- Define genetic information.
- Prohibit enumerated unfair insurance practices.
- Require certain consumer protections.
- In some but not all cases, provide for penalties for violations of these laws.

State statutes almost without exception articulate the scope of their genetic information laws by how they variously define what is meant by genetic information. Several southern states narrowly focus on sickle cell trait to define the scope of their laws on insurance discrimination based upon genetic information. Florida, for example, prohibits refusal to issue a disability insurance policy "solely because the person to be issued has the sickle cell trait." Maryland law prohibits insurance discrimination based "solely on sickle-trait, thalassemia minor trait, hemoglobin C trait, tay sachs trait or any genetic trait which is harmless within itself, unless there is an actuarial justification for it." Likewise, North Carolina keys its law to "the fact that the person to be insured possesses sickle cell trait or hemoglobin C trait."

In contrast, more recent state statutes which regulate the use of genetic information in insurance define genetic information without regard to a specific disease or genetic trait. State law in Montana focuses on a "genetic condition" meaning "a specific chromosomal or single-gene genetic condition." Ohio defines "genetic screening or testing" to mean a laboratory test of a person's genes or chromosomes for abnormalities, defects, deficiencies, including carrier status, that are linked to physical or mental disorders or impairments, or other disorders whether physical or mental, which test is a direct test for abnormalities, defects or deficiencies, and not an indirect manifestation of genetic disorders.

While the foregoing definitions are less narrowly drawn in terms of a specific genetic trait, these controlling definitions still confine themselves to sources or types of information which are restrictive. Although genetic information can be derived from many forms of inquiry, most state statutes restrict their definitions—and hence their applicability—to "genetic testing." The phrase "genetic testing" by its plain meaning suggests a process which is inherently narrow. Usually, the process involves a clinical laboratory test. Often, these types of definitions require that the test must be performed on human DNA material. These two elements of the typical state statutory definition of genetic testing limit the applicability of these laws to only the most sophisticated laboratory procedures on actual DNA. Pure laboratory based genetic testing is technologically complex and expensive. These underlying realities to what constitutes "genetic testing" tends to further narrow the applicability of state statutes predicated on these definitions. On balance, most state statutes that regulate the use of genetic information in insurance rely on definitions with three characteristics. First, the operative definitions include only limited activity (i.e., laboratory tests). Second, the controlling definitions require a specific purpose (i.e., determining the presence or absence of a gene abnormality). Finally, the definitions often exclude more commonplace sources of genetic information (i.e., a routine medical history).

Once state statutes on the use of genetic information in insurance establish the scope and type of genetic information to be regulated, they impose prohibitions on how insurers may or may not use the genetic information. These prohibitions are aimed at underwriting practices, policy issuance practices and differential rating practices. Prohibitions in current law will illustrate the range of practices that are regulated by current laws. California law prohibits discrimination in policy terms, discrimination in fees to brokers, refusal to accept an application, failure or refusal to issue an application, cancellation of a policy or charging a higher premium based on genetic characteristics. New Hampshire prohibits a health insurer from requiring or requesting a person to undergo genetic testing, or requiring them to reveal the results of genetic testing, or conditioning coverage or rates on whether someone has undergone genetic testing.

State legislators and regulators have constructed the prohibitions on insurers in the use of genetic information by relying on tools familiar to insurance regulators. In most states, the primary techniques for controlling the use of genetic information is to rely upon the state's existing laws on unfair insurance practices. These unfair insurance practice laws regulate an insurer's ability to classify risks by rationing the information that an insurer may include in the risk classification process. Finally, the prohibitions in state laws are intended to insure that coverage remains available to persons in the protected class by requiring initial and continued coverage on the same basis as risks that are not evaluated based on genetic information.

Although state insurance regulators typically rely upon unfair insurance discrimination laws to manage the abuse of genetic information, the state laws specific to genetic testing and insurance also provide additional controls on the conditions under which genetic information may be acquired and disclosed. Approximately one half of the states that regulate genetic testing and insurance provide for written informed consent to genetic testing and specific consents to disclosure of genetic information. Some examples will illustrate the range of protective provisions.

Most state laws that address the confidentiality aspects of genetic information rely on a combination of privilege, consent and limited permissible disclosures which must be authorized in writing. None of these statutes delves in great detail into the mechanics of confidentiality, but all of them articulate a public policy which recognizes the interests of the individual in maintaining the privacy of medical information.

State laws that regulate the use and abuse of genetic information in insurance provide a limited array of penalties and remedies in the event of a violation. California offers the greatest range of remedies with specified fines which increase in amount as the volition progresses from negligence to willful behavior. In addition to fines, California law states that actual damages are available to the injured party. Other states simply graft their genetic information laws onto existing systems for regulating unfair insurance practice. In these states, the remedies available to the individual may be very limited as a matter of state law, or non-existent under the preemptive effect of federal law.

To date, state legislatures have taken the lead in defining certain types of genetic test information and protecting against its inappropriate use in the insurance industry. These laws are motivated by a perception of the immutability of genetic information and the impact of that information in the hands of insurers. The problem of rapidly changing and significant clinical information requiring special use restrictions is not unprecedented. The advent of the AIDS epidemic triggered problems similar to the abuse of genetic tests results. Insurers viewed HIV positive individuals as a high risk minority and subjected them to canceled insurance, denied coverage and related underwriting practices which flowed from the perception of the immutability of a positive HIV finding. States responded with stringent laws designed to protect the confidentiality of HIV patient information. Strict federal laws were enacted also.

HUMAN GENES IN OTHER ORGANISMS: ETHICAL, SPIRITUAL AND CULTURAL DIMENSIONS

We in the Religious Society of Friends (Quakers) belong to a spiritual tradition which reflects and respects the experience of the individual, and places special importance on the sacredness of life. Thus we have been led into principled action in the world to promote integrity, peace, equality, social justice and a reverence for nature and the Earth. For us the spiritual is of central importance. Yet spiritual and ethical concerns are so closely interwoven that it is difficult to consider them separately.

Genetic Modification and the Web of Life

We perceive the universe as self-organising, self-healing, and with inherent creativity, intelligence and wisdom. We believe humanity emerged within this living and expanding system, and is only one species among the awesome diversity that Earth has produced. All life that has gone before the emergence of human beings is a prerequisite for our existence. We are connected to every tissue and fibre of the universe. We are an integral part of the whole web of life.

Our genes are the result of billions of years of evolution. The gene pool is a collective legacy and a collective responsibility. There is a need to reclaim a holistic view of the world, to act as if it were a sanctuary, to treat it with reverence, and to remember that we borrow the world from future generations.

There is a complex coherence in the genome of each individual species that is beyond our present understanding. Genetic modification intervenes in this greater complexity and may have unpredictable results. In spite of the bland assertion of some scientists that genes are largely 'the same' across the animal kingdom, it must be emphasised that the human gene is specific to human cells and tissue. The gene has a role integral to the whole. Taken out of the context of a whole human being, the human gene does not function as it has evolved. A human gene inserted into a mouse is dysfunctional; this 'new organism', so-called, is disorganised and stressed.

The Consequences of Gene Transfer

We do not know the full consequences of putting human genes into other organisms. Throughout the world scientists are experimenting with this. We do know the result of putting human growth hormone into pigs. They turned out to be arthritic, ulcerous, partially blind and impotent. The telos or nature and potential of the pig has been distorted. They can no longer function as healthy pigs. The same principle may apply to putting human genes into other organisms. This may cause distress and disease, and render the potential of that organism invalid. The milk of a genetically changed cow may no longer nourish her own calf.

Hopes were raised that sufferers of multiple sclerosis would be helped by the myelin in the milk produced by cows with human genes inserted. Yet after this cross-species transgression, which blurs the necessary distinctions of both organisms, it has now been confirmed that ingesting myelin does more harm than good. Shouldn't we be putting more effort into addressing the root causes of diseases such as multiple sclerosis and diabetes, thereby correcting the over-emphasis of treating symptoms without knowing the underlying cause? The aim should be to eradicate rather than alleviate.

We are concerned about the growing contempt of nature by some biotech scientists, who use creatures simply as tools. We wonder at the dehumanising of the researcher. Collectively we dehumanise ourselves if we acquiesce in these practices, demonstrating our insensitivity. We harm ourselves when we treat nature with disdain, as an objective entity, and we degrade its value. We degrade ourselves living in a degraded environment. What moral right do we have to interfere in the intrinsic genetic process of another organism for the supposed but unproven benefit to humans? Human genes in other organisms compromise the Hippocratic Oath ('Above all do no harm') and are unethical. Spiritually and ethically we should not tamper with the building blocks of our inheritance.

Our instincts are confirmed by scientists who say that species-crossing practices might well open the door for inventive and adaptive viruses to present a human-attacking variant of an animal disease, for which there are no human antibodies. Do we know that genetically engineered solutions will not eventually impact adversely on the wider population and on the environment? While we may have hope in technology which appears to hold promise of a brighter future, too often the proposed benefits are motivated by commercial expediency with scant regard for planetary health. We can't stop advancing technology, but we can change direction. Perhaps we need the courage to relinquish some of our aspirations.

Our world view influences our perception of genetic engineering. The view that was expounded by the mystics treated the Earth gently, with respect and reverence. Its wholeness and connectedness was appreciated. This was a holistic view, which saw the natural world as precious, sacred, a unity of many parts making up a unique whole. Humans learned to live in greater harmony with the natural world and thus prospered. This view has been suppressed. We need to reclaim this world view - a way of life that is joyful, compassionate, integrative and life sustaining. Our attitude towards other species changed only 400 or so years ago. We can continue in the illusion of our detachment, that all nature and other beings are *out there*, or recognise our inheritance as one with nature. We are not just a separate part of the web of life, but the *web of life itself*.

It is becoming vital that we recognise and give credence to the growing evidence of new and fundamental changes in scientific and philosophical thinking in the way we view our world. There is a growing shift from the reductionist, mechanistic paradigm of the last 400 years, towards a recognition and understanding of the inherent wisdom in nature, as evident in the ever-changing adaptability of sustainable communities of animals, plants and micro-organisms evolved over millennia. We need to face the evidence and begin to understand that our world is vastly more complex and inter-related than is allowed in the current view. Any cross-species research undertaken without the full recognition and acknowledgment of this web of life now faces the unprecedented risk of dangerous and unpredictable results, which may be irredeemable.

Dr Mae-Wan Ho, Reader in Biology at the Open University, UK, in her book *Genetic Engineering: Dream or Nightmare?* shows us the dangers of reductionist scientific thinking, which may be used to control and intimidate, to exploit and oppress. Genetic engineering threatens the health of the entire fragile ecosystem on which we all depend. Genes within a cell function as a complex network. Inserting engineered genes causes unpredictable effects. The risks of human genetic manipulation include:

- horizontal gene transfer, which threatens biodiversity
- recombination of vectors, producing new and potentially virulent diseases
- unplanned immune reactions
- the release of new pathogens.

Thus the ecological web is thrown dangerously out of balance.

Risk and Genetic Modification

Risk has taken on a new meaning. Prevailing risk-assessment models are being falsely applied to biotechnology. Progress has always involved risk. In conventional engineering a fault has limited consequences - faulty elements can be replaced or rebuilt. This type of risk is considered acceptable. However, with life's infinite propensity for change and adaptability there exists no way of halting a rogue product. The illusion persists that given sufficient research and knowledge we can be in rational control of creative, chaotic processes. We live in a society obsessed with speed, quantity and growth. Everything that is seen to threaten this approach must be eliminated. Even the idea that we should be *the stewards of the earth* is evidence of a dangerous hubris. The potential for disaster must be accepted to be an equal possibility as any intended benefit. We cannot risk damaging the balance of the ecological system. *Proceed with caution* must allow that it may not be prudent to proceed at all.

It is unacceptable that those who put us at risk should avoid liability. There is evidence that some vested corporate interests in bioengineering actively suppress evidence, including research that focuses on adverse outcomes or unacceptable risk-taking. This economic drive is reckless and dishonest, and means that no venture should be allowed which is not underwritten by a substantial insurance body. It is totally unjust to expect the community to take responsibility in this regard. There is little equity or fair play - two obvious signs of an ethical undertaking - where scientists are side-lined or discredited. Commercial self-interest has usurped the accepted process of scientific peer review and publication, which comprise the validation of scientific research.

Ethical Responsibility

The ethical voice has a huge responsibility. Ethics is not a peripheral or nuisance issue, but must be given greater prominence. Ethical concerns are frequently dismissed as negative or anti-progress. Ethical bodies need great courage, conviction, tenacity and articulation. We need to look at the impact of genetics on the values that inform human relationships like automony, kindness, dignity, truthfulness, justice and not causing harm.

We need to establish policies in which the ethical consideration is primary to the commercial drive, and supported by a well-informed and concerned citizenship.

Ethical considerations include:

- reverence for the planet as an entire, living, self-balancing system
- reverence and compassion for all life forms, including humans
- reverence for ecologic processes and systems

- respect and understanding of spiritual and cultural values, which enhance the quality of life
- a viable long-term vision, ensuring peace, justice, dignity, and equality.

We base our ethical, cultural and spiritual concerns about genetic modification on the ecological understanding that all life forms are interdependent and interconnected. What is needed now is a radical change in the way we relate to each other and to our living, natural environment, which nurtures and sustains us. Life is to be honoured. We need to recover the reverence for life and respect for other beings, and realise that putting human interests first becomes a pretext for safeguarding our own interests, with less and less regard for the sanctity of life in its full complexity of relationship.

We consider that genetic engineering is an inappropriate use of technology in that it violates the natural integrity of the host organism, by overcoming the evolved, intrinsic species-integrity-barrier of the host, and runs counter to universally recognised spiritual sensibilities. Sacredness has meaning. More than ever now we need to recognise that the whole is more than the sum of its parts.

The New Zealand Organisation of Rare Disorders (NZORD) exists to provide information, support and advocacy to people affected by rare disorders and assist their support groups to operate effectively. We support ethical research into human health solutions through the use of transgenic technology, and we believe approvals given for these experiments do comply with ethical standards and properly consider spiritual and cultural views. But to do this discussion justice we need to discuss the meaning of ethics. Ethics concerns what is morally right or morally wrong. People often say, *That's unethical* when they might mean something quite different, such as *I don't like that, It makes me queasy* or *That offends my spiritual beliefs or cultural view.* Further analysis is needed.

A Quick Overview

There are key traditional philosophical frameworks like utilitarianism and deontology which help determine if actions in many parts of life are ethical or not. But for most people with health or disability issues and their support groups, those frameworks can seem complex and remote. It can be difficult to apply them to the questions we are interested in are: What is ethical in this particular situation? How do we tell the difference? How are ethics applied in medicine and research? Getting there takes some explanation. Fortunately there are additional measuring tools to help the process.

My brief interpretation of ethics in medicine and research is this. Out of the broad philosophical concepts of ethics flow a number of specific concepts like justice, benefit, minimising harm, and promoting personal choice for others. When courses of action are considered in medicine and research, the proposal is measured against these ethical principles, to decide if the action should be taken or not. Benefits and harms are balanced, and the decision takes into account other factors including the circumstances in which the action is considered.

Balancing competing interests

In recent decades bioethics has become increasingly important in ensuring that medicine and research respect the people and animals that are being treated, or are the subjects of research. Ethical codes, and the ethics committees to oversee them, have been put in place for many reasons. These include our wish to have more control over matters of importance to us, social movements like human rights and animal welfare that influence social thinking, and the wish to prevent abuse. Changing knowledge and technology also reinforce the need for ethical controls. The ethical standards set the rules so that expectations are clear, treatment and research can be measured against them, and enforcement can be carried out, protecting us all in a neat, tidy and logical way - we hope.

One way of describing bioethics is to think of it as the point at which the technical capacity of science is influenced by the values of society. Guided by discussion and analysis, ethical controls manage the new possibilities. This has been described by some writers in phrases like *keeping values connected to science*, or *the crossroads where the possibilities of science meet the values of the community*. There is a connection taking place. In a nutshell, ethics in medicine and research determines what should be done, as opposed to what could be done. That sounds simple enough. But if only it were that simple.

For many people ethics is viewed as what is acceptable versus what is not, but that is not the same as what should or should not be done. Acceptable to the majority? Or acceptable to those directly involved? The presumption of majority interests may give one view, but the results may be different when considering benefits, harm minimisation and acceptability to the affected people.

The rights of individuals or groups to receive a benefit may prevail over community concerns where the benefit can meet the principles derived from ethical philosophy. In one sense this is a classic conflict of minority rights versus the power of a majority. This may get more complex to manage the more we analyse it - especially when support groups have a particular interest in controversial research. For example, there are situations where the benefit to an individual or group must be denied to them because there are risks, and the benefits would not outweigh that possible harm.

In the early 19th century there was community anxiety at the use of a vaccine derived from cow-pox virus, to vaccinate people against smallpox. An anti-vaccine society was formed. There were riots in the streets of London. The vaccine worked, millions of lives were saved, and smallpox was eliminated from human health concerns. The benefits to the whole population over-rode the vocal concerns of many in the community.

At the end of the 20th century experimental xenotransplantation placed genetically modified pig cells into six patients with diabetes. The experiments seemed successful as the patients were able to produce their own insulin, and therefore end drug treatment. However, the research was stopped when a risk of transmission of pig diseases to humans, was identified. The interests of a group were outweighed by the risks to the wider community. These examples relate to the situation of placing animal material into humans. Although the smallpox example was well before the formal discipline of bioethics was established, no doubt the debate was similar to the current debate about inserting human genes into animals. What these examples show is that putting ethics into practice is not simply a matter of looking up a list of approved or prohibited actions. It takes on the complexity of balancing competing interests, benefits and harms, in the context of the society we live in and the circumstances of the matter under consideration.

Adding Spiritual and Cultural Issues

Will the addition of spiritual and cultural issues to the mix make it even more difficult to work through the ethical decision-making, even before we take these complicated principles and interactions and contemplate inserting a human gene into a cow? Perhaps - but not necessarily. Ethical codes may not have explicitly taken spiritual and cultural issues into account, but it can be argued they have done so implicitly by taking society's values into account when balancing the benefits and the harms. Our values are strongly influenced by our spiritual beliefs and cultural norms. Mentioning spiritual and cultural factors as separate areas requiring consideration is probably not adding new matters to the list, but rather gives explicit acknowledgement to them as important factors in the ethical consideration. In the New Zealand context this may reflect social evolution, as in the Treaty of Waitangi increasingly being acknowledged in public policy and in case law.

The Specific Issue of Human Genes in Other Organisms

Let's now look specifically at the central issue of inserting human genes into other organisms. For this discussion I will focus exclusively on the insertion of human genes into cows, the very procedure that AgResearch has already carried out at Ruakura for its myelin basic protein project, and which it plans again in its next round of experiments. The specifics of these real projects probably provide a more useful discussion than a more general theoretical discussion. The consent application referred to here is the most recent application, GMD 02028.

Two main ethical issues were raised for consideration in the applications by AgResearch. The first concerned animal ethics. Not surprisingly, AgResearch as an experienced animal research institution was easily able to identify these issues and their management requirements. These potential problems were seen as manageable and not outweighing the potential advantages of the research. The Environmental Risk Management Authority (ERMA) noted that animal welfare risks were low, and also noted the animal welfare controls and oversight that were in place, when it granted its approval.

The second ethical issue raised by AgResearch was the risk of affront to spiritual beliefs and values of Ngâti Wairere, the local hapû. This matter had been the subject of previous hearings and a High Court review. Notably, there was support as well as opposition from Mâori to the research proposal, as there has been divided opinion among Mâori generally over uses of modern biotechnology. The discussion of these matters in the application, at the hearings and in the ERMA decision clearly shows how the spiritual and cultural aspects of ethics were thoroughly dealt with. ERMA's decision noted that spiritual issues were relevant considerations, that processes were in place to manage those concerns, and concluded that "the risks attributable to spiritual concerns is low".

Discussion in the ERMA decision about the principles of the Treaty of Waitangi demonstrates how important the spiritual and cultural aspects are considered to be, but of interest is ERMA's conclusion that taking those issues into account "does not extend to accepting those beliefs as the determinant of whether the research proposed by the applicant should be approved". In other words, there is no power of veto.

It was in the submissions of opponents to the research, and in public media comment by these submitters, that the claim of "unethical" research was frequently made. The opponents' submissions focused on:

- the ethics of animal use (as noted above)
- concern about the animals getting into the food chain (controls were established to prevent this)
- contravention of Biblical teachings (ERMA did not regard the research as necessarily unethical from a Christian point of view).

The ERMA decisions from a health and disability support group perspective: ERMA's decision on the AgResearch application took account of many spiritual, cultural and ethical issues and addressed them all, while still granting approval because of the potential benefits of the research. ERMA's position relating to Mâori concerns could perhaps be compared to earlier discussion about the 'acceptability' of practices or research to the community, and the influence such views might have, whichever social group they are held by and whether they constitute a majority or not. The outcome seems well balanced from a support group perspective. There was a very careful analysis of all the ethical, spiritual and cultural issues by AgResearch as the applicant, and by ERMA in its hearings and decision.

There is not one single view among support groups, or among those in a particular support group. We can be as diverse as the rest of society, but we usually have a close interest in the development of new treatments for our health and disability problems. As citizens and as members of communities we want those developments to be managed in a safe and ethical way. We would be most upset at a medicine or treatment option that was of benefit to us, but caused serious harm to others or to society. Remaining objective can come under some pressure when the issue gets close to home for a particular group, but I have yet to see any individual or group argue that risks or ethics should be ignored for their sake.

I feel sure that the thorough consideration of these issues - and the outcomes - would be welcomed by people affected by health and disability issues. A close scrutiny of the process shows that the right thing has been done, and has been *seen* to be done.

Public Comment on the Research Application

Perhaps the greatest volume of commentary on the ethical aspects of this research occurred in media reporting of opponents' views, outside of the hearing process. The Green Party, GE-Free NZ, Greenpeace, MadGE and others often made the bald claim that this research is unethical. At times they have received support from a small number of scientists who have made the same claim, including members of the Sustainability Council. This often-made claim needs examining.

Almost without exception such claims give little or no reasoning for why the research would be unethical. The statement is made and left hanging, unsupported. The implication is they are simply expressing personal or political views. If these claims are to be taken seriously in any decision-making process or in policy, there needs to be more rigorous analysis, which is why I began this article with a brief discussion on understanding ethics.

To give credit to the co-leader of the Greens, Jeanette Fitzsimons, she often stated why she thought it would be unethical, so an analysis of her statements may help in assessing the ethics of this research. To the Royal Commission on Genetic Modification, in oral evidence to support the official Green Party submission, Ms Fitzsimons stated, "It's ethically irresponsible to use sheep and cows as bio-reactors to [produce therapeutic proteins]... particularly when that manufacturing can be done with micro-organisms in a laboratory" [Transcript page 3231, lines 54 to 59.]. However, the Royal Commission noted the rebuttal evidence of Lysosomal Diseases New Zealand that "micro-organisms [are] not effective producers of the complex enzymes found in mammals", and concluded that it was "satisfied that it will not always be possible to use vats to produce the pharmaceuticals required". Of course an alternative source that is safe and effective may be preferable, but would that necessarily make a transgenic source unethical? What if the alternative had environmental impacts or limited effectiveness?

A press statement from the Greens stated: "In response to claims by the website of Professor Dick Wilkins that 'the medical claims made by AgResearch were largely a nonsense', Ms Fitzsimons said she was pleased the spin employed by AgResearch to try and make an ethically disturbing experiment acceptable to the public had been exposed." [Greens press statement, 6 May 2001.] The quoted page on the website was permanently removed more than a year ago. Subsequent pages from Professor Wilkins support the basic science, but note that medical applications may be some years away. No comments on the ethics of the experiment are included. In this context it needs to be remembered that the theoretical merits of a project have weight in deciding if an experiment meets ethical criteria; contrary opinion about the outcome of the experiment does not in itself make the experiment unethical.

Another Greens press statement reads: "Ms Fitzsimons said putting human genes into large mammals has raised more ethical concerns than any other genetic engineering experiments done in New Zealand so far"[Greens press statement, 13 August 2002.]. Although this type of assertion has been frequently made, we have yet to see any instance where such ethical issues have been discussed in a systematic, open and authentic fashion to support such statements. Here the phrase "ethical concerns" seems to be used loosely to support a political position rather than as a serious contribution to ethical debate.

Finally, in commenting on transgenic research in sheep, Ms Fitzsimmons is quoted as saying: "Sheep and cattle are put through intrusive and unethical procedures to cause them to produce a human protein in their milk before that protein has been tested to see if it has any medical use... The correct process would have been to first test the protein, which is already available from human sources." [New Zealand Herald, 23 June 2003.] However, there are serious safety issues with the use of post-mortem or placental tissue. The risk of transmitting diseases like Hepatitis, HIV and Creutzfeldt-Jakob disease is high. Human sources of medicine have been steadily replaced with genetically engineered proteins over recent years, for safety. The transgenic medicine projects proceed because of the potential value of reliable, standardised sources of these proteins, successful experimental treatments in animals, and the need for alternative production methods.

Safety issues and the development of cost-effective proteins are vital aspects of ethical considerations, justifying research into genetically modified proteins in animal cell lines, transgenic animals, transgenic plants and other sources. Experimental success with the protein in question seems a strong counter to

Ms Fitzsimons's claim. Her claims about correct procedures seem to confuse research purposes with research results.

Regrettably, these examples contribute little to the ethical debate. If we carefully analyse Jeanette Fitzsimons's statements we find they amount to little more than I don't like it, mixed with unsupported allegations of safety issues, confusion over research methodologies, and a barely disguised political agenda.

So are we any wiser for all this public comment? I believe the answer has to be, unfortunately, no. We see the words 'ethics' and 'unethical' used and abused in many ways to reinforce the various social and political agendas of opponents. There is little or no constructive dialogue about the objective ethical issues involved.

The Consultation Process: the Ethics of it All

Because public policy now includes detailed consultation processes, it is worth taking a moment to consider how well this process contributes to decision-making. Unfortunately, groups wanting to oppose innovations in science, especially in modern biotechnology, often act in ways that do little more than frustrate and impede the process, score political points and cause delays. Listening to opponents at hearings and reading their submissions exposes a serious absence of well-reasoned arguments that identify real or even potential problems with the science, risks to the environment, or matters of serious ethical concern. Many opponents are very poorly informed on the issues. A well-reasoned and challenging debate would be welcome.

The behaviour of these groups also raises a different question of ethics: in what sense do they embrace a community ethic of integrity, truth and fairness in terms of how they engage in the consultation process, and in the standards of behaviour they apply when they promote their concern or their political agenda?

CONCLUSIONS

In examining the nature of ethical decision-making and applying this framework to a specific example of inserting human genes into other organisms, there seems very clear evidence that all of the ethical, spiritual and cultural issues were thoroughly canvassed and given serious and meaningful consideration. The analysis was thorough, and the approval that was given signals to health and disability support groups that:

- innovation to find treatments for health and disability problems is supported
- the potential risks and benefits of research are thoroughly assessed
- the decisions carefully weigh the ethical, spiritual and cultural issues
- matters of potential risk are suitably dealt with, and potential harms do not outweigh the benefits of proceeding
- the approval to insert human genes into animals has been found to meet ethical criteria.

Some challenges will arise for the Bioethics Council out of these experiences, including finding ways to:

- encourage an environment in which the public become better informed about what ethics actually is, and how ethical decisions are made
- separate ethical considerations from a variety of social and political agendas that are often dressed up as ethics
- help an appreciation of ethics as a process of reconciliation of various concerns, not an opportunity for any group to have a power of veto because of their 'superior' issue.

THE MYSTERIOUS ETHICS OF SINGING SHEEP AND FEET POINTING BACKWARDS

There has been a deluge of articles, discussions, and even poetry written about genetic modification in recent years. The earnest if sometimes overly lawyerised words of the Royal Commission report have jostled with obtuse scientific articles and trendy T-shirt slogans or political posturing. Big business interests have collided with the concerns of parents, and organic farmers and environmentalists have fretted about the dangers it might pose to New Zealand's clean green image. At times the public must have felt rather like the Shakespearean character who struggled for understanding but was increasingly confused as he was "bethump'd with words".

However, for Mâori people the debate has been more frustrating than confusing. At one level, as so often happens, Mâori views and analyses have been regularly misrepresented as little more than a vaguely spiritual and quaint sub-text. Consultation on the issue has merely led to a feeling that the Mâori 'perspective' being sought was only a cultural explanation of something in which normality and truth had already been determined. Hohua Tutengaehe once noted that "Every time Mâori are asked to give a 'perspective' we are ... responding to something that's been decided or ... the main ideas are already set in concrete." [H. Tutengaehe, 'Submission to DSW Committee of Enquiry', Rehua Marae, September 1988.] In the whole genetic modification discourse the parameters seem predetermined by non-Mâori economic, scientific and political interests. In this context the serious concerns that Mâori have been raising have sometimes been acknowledged but then consigned to an addendum of cultural side issues, or diverted in a dubious consent process that has taken a terrible toll in terms of resources, time and damage done to deeply held and reasoned perceptions. Indeed, the costs exacted on the people of Tauranga and Pouakani by the now bankrupted transgenic experiments of PPL Pharmaceuticals and the ongoing struggle of Ngâti Wairere with the work of AgResearch on cows have been both unfair and unreasonable.

However, they also point to another more profound level at which Mâori are frustrated by the whole genetic modification discourse, because it has extended beyond the science involved to a more fundamental diminution of Mâori values. The Mohawk jurist Patricia Monture-Angus once stated that the Pâkehâ idea of an indigenous 'perspective' has always had this effect because it reduces complex cosmogonies and intellectual traditions to "something that is lesser," a mythology or a method of enquiry that is neither rigorous nor rational. Indeed the very idea of a perspective actually "diminishes and disappears the fact that each Aboriginal nation always had systems of knowledge and understanding, law and government." It denies the validity of other ways of seeing the world and effectively privileges the Western gaze above all others.

Such a stance has not necessarily been preordained by a particular bias in, say, the work of the Royal Commission, or even the too-often witnessed arrogance of individual scientists. Rather, it has been determined by a set of deeper social and cultural assumptions that have consistently denied or tried to minimise the validity of Mâori philosophical and scientific constructs. They indicate a stubbornly held certainty about the nature and history of the Western scientific method and an unwillingness to accept that like every other way of researching, testing and analysing facts or assertions it is culture bound. Like the English common law, which claims an inherent impartiality born of a unique tradition of customary and canon teachings blessed by the characters of God, or the idea of immutable market forces driven by an 'invisible hand', Western science is a product of a distinct cultural history. It was thought into being but has assumed unto itself a new kind of divinity.

In that sense the genetics debate, and the question of its ethics, has been and remains a contested cultural one in which science has been isolated from its own beginnings and accepted as simply the reality. However, as Irihapeti Ramsden once reminded us:

> Experience teaches the wary observer that ideas of truth ... are human in origin. Shaped to suit the times. Questions must therefore be asked. How have we arrived at these truths? Whose interests do they serve? What is real?

As we live in a post-moratorium New Zealand it is therefore necessary to seek answers to these questions and to pose new ones that more adequately recognise a different tradition, a different philosophical stance.

The Light of Isaac Newton and whare Wananga

Most historians agree that modern Western science developed out of the ferment of the European Enlightenment.

Inspired partly by the knowledge of earlier intellectual traditions and a discomfort with the restrictive teachings of the Christian church, it sought to know the world in a new way. It was in a sense a revolution against the centuries during which thinking had been an act of religious observance and there was no real distinction drawn between religion, ethics and science, since each contributed to the understanding of God's creation. The ability to be scientific or even philosophical depended upon the need to 'think God', because everything was determined by God's will.

Such a mind-set led to the notion of Christian dualism, which Ingrid Washinawatok has likened to a divinely inspired distinction between the man who had "dominion over ... every creeping thing that creepeth upon the earth," and the creeping things themselves. It was a closed system of enquiry in which:

> *... the universe was divided into distinct parts - the body and soul, good and evil, heaven and hell, reason and passion, civilised and uncivilised, Christian and heathen - and hierarchies were invented where everything that was different was also subordinate.*

In a sense, Europe thought itself into a sort of intellectual dualling opposites.

However, thought never develops in a vacuum and by the seventeenth century the political power of the church was declining and even many devout Christians were questioning whether the mysteries of the universe might be beyond the sight of heaven. It seemed instead that the world was knowable through the human contesting of ideas rather than just God's will. As a result there was a move away from the old thinking of the Church to a new scientific method. Religion and ethics were redefined as values-laden disciplines best suited to moral questions that were distinct from the observation, experimentation and neutrality needed to reach an ostensibly values-free conclusion. The need to think God was replaced with a man-centred reason in which the mind could listen to the reason within itself and produce a new objectivity that eventually replaced the old catch-cry of 'God said' with the aphorism 'I think, therefore I am'.

Yet science was assumed to be inherently objective in much the same way that the old God-willed reason had produced divine emanations and its conclusions were defined as "a truth from nowhere [that] claimed to be true for everywhere" [H. Waitere-Ang and P. Johnston, 'If all inclusion means in research is the addition of researchers that look different, have you really included me at all?', paper presented at the AARE-NZRE conference, The Challenge for Educational Research, Melbourne, 1999.]. It was "unbiased, and therefore applicable to all" because it was culturally constructed to be so, and it became an act of faith as certain as anything the Church had previously decreed. Alexander Pope even compared it to a new crusade in his tribute to Isaac Newton:

Nature, and Nature's Laws lay hid from sight:

God said, 'Let Newton be!' and all was light.

The 'reasonable man' was firmly European and he set the new universal standards by preserving the belief that he could know everything and had a right to do so. The scientific method itself became part of the dualling opposites, and although it would often admit to mistakes it was transformed into an acultural construct that could drag truth not just from faith but from error.

In other places and cultures knowledge and truth were sought through different methods that were equally bound by unique traditions and assumptions. Te Rarawa Kohere has described the Mâori intellectual tradition as being based in a "tûrangawaewae of thought" that has shaped and been shaped by a particular sense of place, and a whakapapa of learning which is rigorous in its application and imaginative in its approach to the meaning of life. It is also rooted firmly in a non-dualistic world that sees interrelationships rather than hierarchy, and positions the thinker as someone who is part of the world and not merely an elevated observer of it. It also contextualises spirituality and faith as parts of the same continuum of human experience as reason and logic. Indeed, to exclude the idea of a human longing for the mysteries of faith (as distinct from the strictures of an organised religion) or to compartmentalise ethics as something distinct from the scientific process would be regarded as both unreasonable and unreasoning.

This tradition nurtured a way of knowing that was tested against observation and experimentation and measured in philosophies that navigated esoteric and complex questions as easily as the ancestors navigated the Pacific Ocean. It was also debated in the realities of life as well as at whare wânanga that allowed each iwi and hapû to explore the many shared but different facets of what it was to be tangata whenua. At the site of one ancient whare wânanga, puna or springs of fresh water sometimes bubble to the surface and small vents of natural gas used to be lit whenever students were in class. Tohara Mohi once said that the lights burning there indicated not only:

> *... the maramatanga of knowledge being imparted but the light of learning itself and the realisation that there is power in knowledge ... it must be treated with respect not because it is unchallengeable but because it has a whakapapa ... an interconnectedness with everything and everyone that shines a light on who we are and how we relate with the universe. It is a search for what is tika. [Mohi, Tohara, personal communication, August 2, 1992.]*

In that context tikanga was fundamental to the knowing, but it was never just a vocabulary of discrete rituals or marae theatre as it is often regarded today, but part of the intellectual baseline from which important questions were raised and possible answers contemplated. On the island, knowledge and its pursuit was thus a process of enlightenment too, but it was one forged in a cultural tradition that saw no need to claim a universality of purpose nor impose a particular way of seeking knowledge because the universe like the spring water was always flowing in a state of constant flux.

The Mâori intellectual tradition therefore did not begin with an assumption that humans could know everything, but rather the certainty that to know anything one first had to ask 'Why do we need to know?' The question was never intended as a barrier to knowledge and enquiry. Rather it was a recognition that the ethics or potential risks in knowing had to be assessed before a task was undertaken. And in some cases there would simply be no need for any greater knowledge beyond the certainty that time and human existence have a cyclical reality that links the living with the dead and the mokopuna yet to be born. There is a continuity of whakapapa that is ever changing yet constant, a sense that while knowledge may shift in new circumstances the values that underpin its quest are like a mountain that does not move.

Thus the Mâori intellectual tradition has never been fussed with the idea of eternal youth and the strange fascination with botoxed beauty, nor with the fear of death that has led to the peculiar Western pseudo-science of cryogenics. Growing old and dying are simply part of whakapapa, and there is always a beauty in the wisdom of age that matches the vivacity of the young. People would ask how someone died, but the why of death was and is a question where the moral and ethical issues about needing to know have yet to be resolved. In some ways they even seem almost unnecessary because in the wisdom that can be gleaned from the whakapapa stories the wonderful dying of Maui between the thighs of Hine-nui-te-Po is explanation and lesson enough that some things are indeed immutable.

After 1840 the colonisers tried to destroy the ideas and values of that intellectual tradition with the same determination with which they sometimes destroyed the actual centres of learning. The possibility that Mâori might possess a unique let alone valid philosophical system was inconsistent with the aims of colonisation.

Mâtauranga Mâori was mocked or redefined in a deliberately imposed dumbing down, which included anthropologists filling Mâori skulls with millet seed to prove that smaller brains meant less intelligence, and bureaucrats and jurists contending that we did not have the reason or the capacity to be really sovereign or to make treaties. We could not really be rational or scientific because in the hierarchy of Western knowledge we were deemed to be irrational by our very nature.

Many of the old suppositions upon which nineteenth century colonisation was based are now debunked, but they linger in much social discourse as well as in the institutional assumptions about who has the right to rule. In the debate about genetic modification they have surfaced in a frequently unthinking re-run of the old dualism that has not only misunderstood the Mâori science of genetics but also the essentially colonising nature of the GM discourse itself.

A Discourse based in the Puna

When Mâori began the most recent engagement with the issues of genetic modification, the debates were intense and people were often concerned and bemused at the rapidity with which the new technology was accepted as inevitable by many Pâkehâ. At the first hui held in Tauranga to consider the attempts by PPL to insert human genes in sheep, many of the young people admitted their confusion about the project and the questions it raised. However, they were at least clear that something seemed not quite right, as if ancient fires were being lit and puzzling questions were being asked about 'Why do we need to know this?' One young man summed up this sense with the comment that he didn't want to hear sheep singing waiata on his way to work.

His comment was greeted with quiet laughter, but also a general awareness that in many areas of Pâkehâ society the ethics of the issue were being raised after the work had started and that the sort of questions that would have been asked within a Mâori intellectual framework about the rightness of mixing any genes and its impact on the totality of whakapapa were not being considered.

Instead, GM was simply accepted as an unchallengeable given and risk was being debated as something to be managed after the fact, rather than predicted with aforethought as an essential step in deciding whether the particular line of enquiry should even have been contemplated. The technological feasibility of inserting human genes in another species was accepted as the starting point of the discourse rather than the more fundamental querying of whether feasibility necessarily equated with wisdom. Western science had in fact set the parameters of the research as well as the meaning of the discourse.

Much has changed since the early 1990s, but the basic non-Mâori approach remains the same and bioethics has become a new and contradictory designer label that seeks to rationalise GM experimentation purely on the model of superior insight that evolved out of the Enlightenment. There is now even a hierarchy of genetic acceptability in which human genes are regarded as worthy of special consideration or regulation because they are somehow more valuable than those of other species. The genes of 'Man' have assumed dominion in a New Age dualism which sets them apart from all others. Even the oft-repeated question, 'He aha te mea nui, he tangata, he tangata?' has been redefined in a Biblical notion of human primacy instead of being read as part of a whakapapa of interrelationships with the Earth Mother.

In such a construct, ethics and moral restraint are narrowly defined concepts that seem to be too easily swayed by the hope of economic reward or the promise of medical breakthrough. The latter is understandable, especially for those suffering from diseases that currently seem incurable, but there are broader and more difficult questions that are not being addressed to do with whether in fact a cure might create something worse than the original illness in social, human and environmental terms. Instead the ethical issues are mere clip-ons, and GM itself is promoted with the same sort of confidence that once held that the people living on this side of the world had their feet turned backwards. They were the 'anti-podes', and sadly much of the GM discourse seems similarly misguided and back to front.

In quite profound ways the Mâori intellectual tradition therefore remains a 'perspective', to be heard but not necessarily listened to, a Treaty partnership viewpoint for which space might be found in the predominant paradigm but not an independent critique that might bring a different sense of reason to the issue. A Mâori tûrangawaewae of analysis would question the efficacy of GM as a given and would promote quite distinct ways of dealing with it that seek knowledge, not in the hope of profit or even a potential cure but with respect for its power. Technology would be the tool of reason and ethics, not the catalyst for their belated consideration or the driver for a self-aggrandising prophecy about the benefits and allure of what Kawaipuna Prejean once called the "merry mad dance of wayward genes". [P. Kawaipuna, personal communication, Hilo, Hawaii, 3 July 1990.]

There is a very real concern that Mâori people have had neither the time nor the space to properly explore the GM issue in a way that is not constantly reacting to assumptions already made. It is entirely possible that a critique that is sourced within the intellectual tradition of iwi and hapû could bring valuable insights that are currently being excluded from the debate. The rejection or repositioning of that tradition is an ongoing colonisation that does not serve Mâori or Pâkehâ well. At the very least, a non-colonised response would be for the Crown to have extended the moratorium so that such an exploration might occur.

6

The Intrinsic Value of Genes and Organisms

From the perspective of modern biology what defines species is their genes. Species gradually diverge from one another when they stop interbreeding and the inheritance of their genes follows separate paths. This has been the guiding force of biological evolution for three or four billion years, but genetic engineering has put an end to its status as a natural principle. We have found ways to overcome the apparently arbitrary restrictions on what combinations of genes are found in organisms.

It is now possible to take human genes and put them into viruses, bacteria, plants, mice, sheep, cows and other animals. It is also possible to transpose foreign genes into human cells. From a technological perspective there is absolutely nothing special about human genes or cells. They can be analysed and manipulated in the same way as genes or cells from any other organism. From an engineering point of view human genes are just DNA molecules with particular sequences. And now that we know the sequence of the entire human genome, any human gene can be artificially synthesised at will and inserted into another organism.

Actually, we should no longer think of genes as DNA molecules, but as information. Genetic information is transmitted naturally through biological inheritance, but it can also be transmitted and stored artificially in whatever way we choose: as letters written on a page, as digital information burned onto a compact disk or, as is proposed for individuals, carried on a bracelet-chip ready for immediate access as a record of that person's unique set of distinguishing genetic features. The information in the human genome is considered so valuable that billions of dollars and enormous scientific effort have been expended to retrieve it for human use. It has become yet another material resource, a commodity, available for ownership and exploitation according to the rules and agreements of our globalised society.

But what about genetic information in itself, as it has been given to us by evolution and before we retrieved it for our own use? Do genes have intrinsic value? What respect, if any, should we afford human genes themselves? The way we answer these questions will have a profound effect on what it means to be human in the future. Our ability to manipulate human genes poses an existential dilemma of unprecedented proportions. We cannot escape deciding, as if handing down a judgment that will take immediate effect, what intrinsic value human genes have here and now. And when we put human genes into other organisms, the value of both changes irreversibly.

The Intrinsic Value of Humans?

Before we change ourselves and our world forever, we should investigate very carefully the basis on which we identify and value ourselves as human. What is the relationship between humans and our evolutionary relatives, and how has it come about? Are our genes really our own? Do we have any broad responsibility for our genetic relationship with other species and the biological origins of our place in the world? There is a relatively recent point in time beyond which we cannot differentiate ourselves from other hominid species. The genes of all the hominid species have a recent common origin and they differ comparatively little from one another.

After comparing our genes, we can say that the average difference between humans and chimpanzees seems to be only about 10 times the normal difference between two unrelated people. If we go back further through evolution we find that all cellular life derives from an ancient common ancestor. Yet we humans assume a position of enormous privilege above all other species, emphasising our separateness from, rather than our commonality with, other organisms.

Although it is not always recognised in practice, humanity, down to the level of the individual person, assigns itself a certain intrinsic value that is upheld by political and societal principles and institutions. Our genetic information, differentiated through the branching of the tree of life, is what makes us human, so if humans have intrinsic value does this mean our genes have intrinsic value? The prospect is odd. How could information, recorded in the form of sequences of molecules, accumulate intrinsic value, something immaterial, during the processes of evolution?

Science and Intrinsic Value

The idea of intrinsic value makes no sense within the Western scientific tradition. Science deals with general categories of material objects, their interactions and transformations. Even its methodology is said to produce value-free knowledge, dissociated from the details of any particular process of observation. From a scientific perspective values are arbitrarily assigned to things or situations in a way that is completely contingent on the assumptions or perspective of whoever makes the judgment. Scientists think of evolution as a series of events taking place in the material world, governed by dynamic physical processes, which are devoid of any intrinsic relationships to values. The idea of intrinsic value is foreign to science and within the context of science cannot be applied to genes or organisms - either human or non-human.

On the other hand, by applying scientific methods we can reconstruct the patterns of genetic change that have occurred during evolution. Sometimes we can even guess why a particular genetic change has conferred an advantage on some members of a species to the extent that no other members of the species survived. Here is where we must situate any concept we have of the intrinsic value of genes. The value a gene has lies in the selective advantage - the fitness for survival and reproduction- that it confers on the organism carrying it. And the most important feature of the selective advantage conferred by a genetic change is that it is always relative to the characteristics that alternative genetic sequences confer on the organism.

This means that the effect of any characteristic on the survival of organisms depends on the environment they are in, and that environment is at least partly determined by the genetically influenced traits of other species in the organism's ecological system. These complex influences on the mechanisms of genetic change could be described scientifically, but science avoids assigning any value to the coincidences of genetic patterns and historical events that constitute the survival of organisms. For science, value as survival is completely arbitrary. Yes, there are patterns in the genetic information of organisms. So what? Now we can change them and create new patterns.

Scientific knowledge and Matauranga Mâori

Science produces knowledge that makes a legitimate claim to being universal, but it is rarely noted that this 'universality' is restricted to a certain domain of experience. Knowledge derived from non-scientific perspectives does not always have the same limitations and can be a source of wisdom that transcends science. In our own country we have a living example of a non-Western perspective that does not take scientific agreement as the final arbiter of truth or sound decision-making.

Unlike science, matauranga Mâori does not seek the ultimate foundations of reality in abstract principles that describe the behaviour of a purely material reality. Rather, Mâori often express a sense of order and structure that is first and foremost local and historical, contingent on events and relationships established by precedent, not given unalterably and permanently as natural laws. In Mâori tradition, achieving knowledge of something includes arriving at a perception of its proper location in time and space. Knowledge of things and events is concerned with the particularities of whakapapa - layers of genealogy and lines of descent, their patterns and linkages. Everything in the world is related to everything else and the true character of something is dependent on its history. Everything is rooted, not only to its origin in time, but also to its origin in space - the place and tradition of the tangata whenua to which it belongs. The relationship of people and events with the earth and its local geography, evoking the metaphor of an umbilical connection, is of particular poignancy in the contrast between scientific and Mâori explanations of how things come about and what their value is.

We should not be surprised, then, to find that some Mâori have been especially vocal in expressing opposition to aspects of projects that involve the engineering of human genes. The origin of the genetic material that was originally taken from an individual person and then amplified, analysed and transposed into another organism has often been a matter of special concern for Mâori. The Royal Commission on Genetic Modification showed sensitivity to this perspective when it recommended that, wherever possible, synthetic genes or mammalian homologues of human genes should be used in transgenic animals, to avoid the use of genes derived directly from humans.

More broadly, rapprochement with Mâori perspectives requires a renewal of cultural partnerships. We are now in a position to determine together what weight should be given to 'ancient' ways that are linked to a world view that does not give primacy to the scientific prescription of reality, and the 'modern' way that demands that we establish a single lowest common denominator based on narrowly prescribed global standards and specifications. Who, in the end, has the power to decide what ways of thinking will carry weight in our society? We do, if we choose to, and if we are courageous enough to live with the consequences. But shall we base our judgement on standards and processes that have been negotiated through consensual arrangements that follow from the Treaty of Waitangi? Or shall we conform to the demands and imposed force of current international commerce and global political power?

EXPANDING WHAT IT IS TO BE HUMAN

In my opinion, we in Aotearoa / New Zealand should choose a path, contrary to global trends of recent years, that expands as far as possible what it means to be human in a direction that includes, rather than excludes, much of what we tend to look upon as non-human, as other, whether it is genes or organisms we are talking about. It seems to me that the most important genuinely humanitarian changes in recent history have been achieved by expanding the categories that are human rather than by limiting them. For example, being a citizen in a democracy is a privilege that has been extended to more and more humans over the last couple of centuries, encompassing the freeing of slaves and women's suffrage.

Accordingly, when we think of genes and other organisms we should think in a way that emphasises our commonality with other species and extends appropriate privileges to them in recognition of our shared ancestry and the relationships implicit in the tree of life. We should not rely on an antiquated notion that sets what is human above everything else in Nature. On what basis do we completely prohibit any engineering of our own species but allow the genetic engineering of animals after a brief process led by the Environmental Risk Management Authority?

If we decided to assign some intrinsic value to the orderly inter-species linkages that make up the tree of life, then we might want to place greater restrictions on what genetic engineers are allowed to do to other species. This would mean imposing a need to show respect for the precedents that the historical processes of evolution have established. The genetic engineering we currently allow reduces the value of the orderly linkages of the tree of life to pure utility. Our relatedness to other species is exploited for potential commercial gain, as was the case of the Waikato sheep that were used as bioreactors for the production of a human protein, which, it was hoped, might eventually be sold as a pharmaceutical product.

It is part of the methodology of scientific engineering to make use of whatever in the natural order is available without assigning any intrinsic value to it. Considerations of value or respect that should belong to the objects being engineered, or their relationships, are superfluous to the engineering methods themselves. Just to prove that it is possible, humans have put into a rhesus monkey a gene from jellyfish that is capable of making the animal's cells fluorescent green. An engineer can put a human gene into a bacterium in an afternoon; or create cows that graze in a field and for all ordinary intents and purposes cannot be distinguished from ordinary cows except that they carry human genes and produce humanoid proteins.

If we are going to move beyond our current anthropocentric and utilitarian ethics of genetic engineering then we must first recognise that the genes that we call human are simply our versions of genes that also belong to other species - in many cases *all* other species. We could start by exploring how our view of genes would change if we inverted the usual relationship between science and matauranga Mâori. Suppose we decided to subject the scientific conception of genes as pure information, dissociated from any physical or historical associations, to the Mâori conception of phylogenies as whakapapa, bound to the circumstances and conditions of their occurrence and subject to appropriate tikanga. This would be a radical reversal of current trends. We would be saying that genes are to be given a status beyond their scientific, technical specifications.

I would argue that this is exactly the way of thinking that the character of genes requires. There is something in the unity and diversity of biological processes that points to and marks what happens at particular times and places as being uniquely differentiated from everything else, while simultaneously being related to it. Whakapapa gives vibrant voice to the character of Nature's history in a way that leaves science mute in the ethical, spiritual and cultural dimensions of human life. But, like a self-fulfilling prophecy, genetic engineering is refashioning the orderly linkages of whakapapa in its own image, having denied that either genes or organisms have any intrinsic value in the first place.

From an evolutionary perspective, what does it mean to put a human gene into a sheep or a cow? The genetic make-up of domesticated animals has been shaped and moulded by thousands of years of selective breeding conducted by generations of farmers. Much of this breeding is now done using artificial techniques, especially in industrial societies where many aspects of the formerly close domestic relationship with animals have been abandoned. The tendency for the value of these friends of humans to be measured in purely commercial terms has been taken to a new extreme. Sheep, cows and goats have all been converted, by putting human genes into them, into bioreactors for the production of humanoid proteins. I am not completely opposed in principle to every possible instance of genetically engineering an animal, but I do believe it is not something that should be done with impunity, outside of a deep intuition and understanding of the relationship between species. Genetic engineering changes the relationship between our species in an unprecedented way. Is it of no consequence that domestication involves the reciprocity of friendship between species?

What do I mean by reciprocity? It is highly probable that just as humans have altered the genetic make-up of domestic animals, so domestic animals have made a significant contribution to the genetic constitution of humans. We can reasonably surmise that the presence of domesticated animals has produced variations in individual human survivability, and thereby caused biological modification of our species, over tens of thousands of years. Possibly even the emotions that humans are capable of feeling are influenced by genetic features that have been acquired as a result of these selective pressures. If so, the character of what we take to be uniquely human, the conscious identification of the individual 'self', owes a debt to the other species with whom our ancestors formed societies. And we could recognise that debt by extending to other species privileges and rights of the sort that we claim for ourselves as humans on account of our selfhood.

Note that I have not said that we should attempt to extend exactly *the same* rights and privileges to members of other species. But I believe that the right not to be genetically engineered should be extended quite generally to the species with whom we have close genetic and social relationships. And if it turns out that the only way to give life to some humans is to put human genes into some animals, then those chimaeric beings should be given a very special status in recognition of the extreme imposition that we have placed them under, arbitrarily rearranging their very constitution for our benefit, down to the DNA in every one of their cells. Our current laws, conceived primarily in terms of protecting animals from immediate physical cruelty, are hopelessly ill equipped to deal with these realities of genetic engineering.

These brief comments about our relationships with animals serve only to demonstrate some of the considerations that have been neglected in discussions of the ethical, spiritual and cultural aspects of human genes in other organisms. Very different arguments need to be brought to bear on the question of human genes in laboratory mice, in plants, or in micro-organisms, but in each case the perspective offered by inquiring into the intrinsic value of genes and organisms must be adopted at some stage. Genetic engineering starkly confronts us with the question of the intrinsic value of life itself, its entire history and evolution. On the basis of my own respect for the complexity of biology and its historically determined structure, I oppose the release of genetically engineered organisms, including those that contain human genes, from contained laboratory conditions. By introducing the products of genetic engineering into the open environment where they can invade natural genealogies we have started reducing the ordered tree of life to a twisted heap of broken twigs. If we take the process to its ultimate conclusion, future generations will curse us for our arrogance.

A PERSPECTIVE ON THE INSERTION OF HUMAN GENES INTO OTHER ORGANISMS

The Royal Society of New Zealand is a statutory body, charged, among other things, with promoting science and technology, formulating codes of ethics for practitioners of science and technology, and providing advice on scientific matters to the Government and to the public. The Society is an umbrella organisation, which promotes all aspects of science - including mathematics, medicine and social sciences such as psychology and sociology - with a view to understanding our world.

According to the Preamble of its *Code of Professional Standards and Ethics*, which is binding on all members and recommended for all New Zealand scientists, genetic issues have raised more concern than any other new technology, apart, perhaps, from nuclear fission. The Society does not have a formal policy on the insertion of human genes into other organisms, or indeed on genetic modification (GM) in general. However, it has identified what it sees as the key ethical, cultural and spiritual considerations in formulating policy on the use of human genes in other organisms, and it opposes any uses of technology that detrimentally impact on society or on the living or physical environment.

The following discussion provides an overview of the Society's perspective. It is based closely on published statements by the Society. Those interested in a more detailed exposition of the Society's views should refer to the Code of Ethics for the Royal Society and the Society's submissions to the Royal Commission on Genetic Modification.

Proceeding with Caution

The public trust, respect and support that science and technology have enjoyed derive from the way in which science, particularly through technology, has brought hitherto unimaginable benefits to society. This trust can be eroded by various things, including misunderstanding of science. Accordingly, the Society sees its role as providing information - not as telling people what to think about new technologies. Scientific thinking is based on inquiry, curiosity, searching for evidence, challenging current theories, and the ongoing search for better explanations. So while it may not be appropriate for science to tell people what ought to be done, it can continue to inform the debate.

Misgivings arise when scientific applications have been shown to be detrimental to the general well-being of society, and these misgivings can transfer to new technologies. The use of genetic engineering is therefore not just a matter of 'good science': there are ethical and moral aspects that contribute to the well-being of society. As a result, while many of the immediate concerns are for the public health and environmental safety of genetically modified (GM) organisms, the debate has included ethical and moral challenges. Mâori concerns about conflicts with their essential belief systems and the exploitation of indigenous knowledge add a unique aspect to the ethical debate in New Zealand.

In recognition of New Zealand's unique situation, the Society takes the view that we should proceed cautiously, making full use of the opportunities that GM brings, but ensuring that its use is not at the expense of the environment, unnecessary cultural offence or alternative methods of agriculture.

In its submission to the Royal Commission the Society acknowledged that genes and matters of heredity carry with them cultural, spiritual and emotional dimensions. The Society has a duty to consider those dimensions under its Code of Ethics, which states that members "have a duty to respect the values of communities which may be affected by their work".

The Society's commitment to respect the values of communities implies a respect for what the Royal Commission called a "world view", which it defined as "a comprehensive conception or apprehension of the world ... what people do ... to their world depends on what they think about themselves in relation to things around them; all of us hold world views that affect our behaviour individually and collectively" [Report 3.08.]. The Report identified three main (and overlapping) threads of world views within New Zealand: Te ao Mâori (the traditional Mâori world view), an ecological worldview; and Judaeo-Christian religious views. Based on census figures, most New Zealanders subscribe to one or other of these world views. As the Report notes, these three sources of values are fundamentally alike in that they share a holistic world view based on the sacredness and interconnectedness of all organisms and ecosystems.

Te ao Mâori

The Society does not take the view that Mâori objections to genetic modification in general, or to particular applications, should have 'veto' status. However, it places great importance on Mâori concerns and values: about a fifth of its entire submission to the Royal Commission addresses Mâori concerns. This is appropriate because the Society recognises an obligation to respect the Treaty of Waitangi. The submission identifies Mâori as one of the two main groups of people likely to be negatively affected by the risks associated with GM (the other is those involved in the commercial production of non-GM food). The experience of tangata whenua has been that they are the first to suffer adverse effects and the last to benefit from new technologies. Significant intervention is therefore needed to ensure that the impacts of GM technology do not mirror the experiences of other Western technologies on Mâori, such as with guns, alcohol and tobacco.

There are two main risks:

- cultural offence - the mixing of genes between species is an affront to the mauri inherent in whakapapa
- Mâori health risks related to imbalances between metaphysical and physical states (taha hinengaro, taha wairua, taha tinana, taha whanau), where any species has been interfered with in a way that is inconsistent with tikanga.

Sustained breaches of tikanga Mâori have the potential to cause significant long-term impacts on Mâori world views and traditions. This applies to genetic modification both within a species and between species (transgenics), especially where human genetic material is to be inserted into other animals.

Mâori place great value on whakapapa and therefore on genes:

> *... to alter the genes or genetic material is to alter the blood of the ancestors, thereby altering the whakapapa relationship by introducing 'new blood' that may impact on the other rights that are passed down, rights to authority, status, and control.*

A field trial of cows that have been genetically modified to produce a human protein in their milk, to the possible benefit of multiple sclerosis sufferers, is unacceptable to Mâori because it disrupts the line of whakapapa. Moreover, the consumption of medicines derived from animals that have human genes implanted into them, such as insulin, would amount to cannibalism. While cannibalism and, to some extent, incest (as defined by Europeans) were once practised in Mâori society, they are regarded as wrong today.

Insertion of human genes into other organisms is especially offensive to Mâori because it violates the incest taboo: the children of Tane, considered as separate species, are not meant to mate with each other. This issue needs further clarification, though, because in New Zealand agriculture all of the plants and animals were introduced by Europeans and therefore were presumably not created by Tane. However, European livestock and crops are seen as gifts and are the basis of the economy of all New Zealanders, and are just as clearly separate species as are native species, so there is an analogy with the children of Tane. The Royal Commission's report notes that "The incest tapu ... and the injunction against cannibalism meant Mâori made a clear distinction between using human DNA sequences compared with using chemically similar or even identical sequences derived from other animals." [Report 3. 99.]

In so far as protection of whakapapa is essential to the exercise of rangatiratanga, these issues are of concern to the Society because its members have a duty to respect the Treaty of Waitangi and the values of the community, including the prohibitions on incest and cannibalism.

Judaeo-Christian World Views

The Society's Code of Ethics states that "members must ... seek to observe the principles and practices of sustainable management and the needs of future generations both local and international." This obligation includes "the guardianship of genetic information ... and the use to which such information is put". The Royal Commission noted that religious submissions concentrated on understanding the place of humans in the environment and their responsibilities, and that such an understanding gives rise to obligations of stewardship or guardianship for future generations rather than exploitation and ownership. Judeao-Christian submitters affirmed "an interpretation of the Judaeo-Christian tradition as one of care rather than domination."[Report 3.36.] The Interchurch Commission on Genetic Engineering, in its submission, went further, referring to what it identified as: [t]he fear that as a result of manipulating the human genome we may come to see ourselves as commodities able to be manufactured to requirements rather than unique beings whose creation involves a certain mystery.

The Ecological World View

The Society views science as a means of building respect for all living things and for the whole of nature. Its position is therefore consistent with the ecological world view, which is based on "the interdependence and inter-connectedness of all life forms, including human beings" [Report 3.24.]. People's well-being is dependent on the health of the natural world, degradation of which affects the well-being of us all. This implies a commitment to the sustainable management of all our resources - including human and other genetic resources. Changing the genetic structure of an organism is likely to impact on the whole system, although the extent and nature of any impact is difficult to predict given the complexity of nature and our limited understanding of how it works. Decisions on the use of human genes must take account of this position. Such decisions must also be consistent with New Zealand's international obligations under the Biodiversity Convention.

Opposing Views

Not all organisations share the Society's perspective. Numerous submissions to the Royal Commission considered that genetic technology and the medical use of recombinant products (and therefore the research necessary to develop them) are matters for individual decision.

In particular, ethical, spiritual and cultural beliefs were presented as matters of individual and group choice, whose validity does not extend beyond the individual or group that holds them. In support of this position, Lysosomal Diseases New Zealand (LDNZ) noted that the views of Jehovah's Witnesses, "fundamentalist Christians" and animal rights groups do not determine New Zealand policy on blood transfusions, abortion and the use of animals in research respectively. Thus LDNZ argued that:

> *... the personal views of individuals or groups will determine the choices they wish to make for themselves. They cannot be, however, a basis for imposing their view on the opportunities, choices and benefits or rights of others. In the opinion of LDNZ they should be regarded as personal or group advocacy positions, rather than a right to veto.*

Similarly, the Haemophilia Foundation of New Zealand submitted that "it is inconceivable that New Zealand would choose an option of avoiding" recombinant products for treatment and genetic therapies, and "people should be able to make an informed choice as to what is right for them personally." Diabetes Youth New Zealand, noting that "Human insulin of rDNA origin" [The production of which involves the insertion of human genetic material into the bacterium E. coli.] is a much superior product to insulin derived from pigs and cows, argued that what is right for individuals is determined by a treatment's effectiveness - it is "not a moral or ethical issue, it is simply a question of access to a better life". The New Zealand Organisation for Rare Diseases submitted that "religious and cultural beliefs and personal ethics are not valid reasons for denying opportunities, choices and beliefs to others", which implies that scientific knowledge alone is "rational" and "objective" and should therefore determine policy. The LDNZ argued, similarly, that "objections to GM technology are often not based on rational or objective information" and that "these concerns should be addressed by public information and education campaigns that include science better explaining itself".

The Society does not support the belief advocated by LDNZ. In its submission to the Royal Commission it emphasised that "questions of morality, ethics and religious opinion" are issues that "arise from within the everyday pursuit of scientific endeavours, but pose questions that science no longer has the ability or legitimacy to answer".

The issue of responsible and ethical behaviour also needs to be addressed. An IBAC (Independent Biotechnology Advisory Council) study found that "the majority" of respondents wanted the development of moral and ethical leadership and debate in the arena of biotechnology, and argued that a legal and regulatory framework for biotechnology is required. [Submission para 20.]

Indeed, our largest newspaper, *The New Zealand Herald*, has been a consistent and staunch supporter of GM technology, blaming opposition on public ignorance and scare-mongering. However, the Society criticised the view that blames uninformed citizens and irresponsible mass media for creating public hysteria over genetic engineering. It rejects the view that the response to public concerns should be to educate the uninformed consumer, arguing instead that consumers are not passive or uncritical recipients of media information, that they are not as uninformed as is often assumed, and that there is little or no empirical evidence to support the alleged bias in media coverage of biotechnology.

The Society also expressed its concern that 'laypeople' or 'the public' (as defined by scientists, policy-makers and industry representatives) are rarely consulted at any stage from the conception of a research project to the successful introduction of a product derived from that project, and that as food consumers, patients, residents and citizens, most people do not come in contact with GM products until they are ready to be used. By then, of course, it is too late to raise any issues and the only form of objection available is to reject the product for personal use, and perhaps to try to organise a boycott. Insofar as the public has concerns about the insertion of human genetic material into other species, it is too late.

Conclusions

The Society does not have a formal policy on the use of human genes in other organisms. However, its *Code of Ethics* contains principles applicable to such use. In particular, it imposes a duty on members to respect the values of communities, the needs of future generations and the natural environment, and the Treaty of Waitangi. Any proposal to use human genes in any manner must be subject to these value considerations, and must not compromise the well-being of society or the sustainable use of the natural environment. The welfare and the needs of the community must take precedence over responsibilities to clients, colleagues or other interests.

HUMAN GENES INTO OTHER ORGANISMS: ETHICAL, SPIRITUAL AND CULTURAL DIMENSIONS

The Bioethical Framework

The Bioethics Council is to be commended for the approach it has taken to its very challenging charter. Life Sciences Network members have often mused about the difficulties inherent in trying to bring sense and a shape to society's consideration of the wide and seemingly intractable differences of opinion that surround questions of bioethics. The Royal Commission appropriately identified a suitable framework for the consideration of such issues within the common values we New Zealanders share.

In choosing to start with the issues surrounding the transfer of 'human' genes into other organisms, the Bioethics Council has touched the issue that is very close to, if not at the heart of, the New Zealand debate on genetic modification. As such, the ensuing discussion should draw out the wide variety of strongly held views, all of them sincerely held.

The task for the Bioethics Council in guiding the subsequent dialogue is to ensure the appropriate balance is achieved between the right to hold a view and the desire to impose that view on others. It appears to the Life Sciences Network that the outcome of considering the spiritual, cultural and ethical dimensions, while of interest in itself, will be most relevant when applied by decision-making bodies such as ERMA. And in a liberal, democratic, pluralist society the ethics of denying the benefits of the knowledge science has revealed are going to be just as important as the ethics of undertaking the activity.

So, the history of activity in the area will be an important consideration. But historical support or opposition will only take us so far. Perceptions about what is acceptable are dynamic. There is wide variability between societies and between groups within a society. The Life Sciences Network firmly believes that the seven values identified by the Royal Commission, within a utilitarian framework, provide the best basis for ethical consideration of the balance of rights among individuals, groups and society.

Gene Transfers

Having said all that, there is a sense in which the discussion about the transfer of 'human' genes into the genomes of other organisms may well be moot. For many years manufacturers of human insulin have modified bacteria and yeasts with the gene that expresses human insulin to produce the purest and most economic source of human insulin available. Prior to this development diabetics had to use insulin derived from the pancreases of pigs and cattle, and more than 20% of patients then rejected the insulin or suffered severe side-effects.

In this case the ethical and cultural issues seem to have been remarkably easily disposed of, and there is no indication spiritual considerations were even considered to be a factor. The benefits of the new process were evident and clearly outweighed any negative considerations. Having transferred 'human' genes into other organisms for many years without objection, doesn't that indicate the practice is ethically acceptable?

The fact that a gene was taken from a human being and implanted into a micro-organism to create a treatment for a genetic condition in a human being appears to have occasioned only excitement. There is no evidence Mâori or Polynesian communities (or others for that matter) have raised cultural or spiritual objections to a treatment that has such special benefits for them. Muslim and Jewish communities are also likely to be much more accepting of insulin that is not derived from the pancreas of a pig.

What has also been frequently overlooked in the debate about the transfer of 'human' genes into other organisms is the further fact that this is a transfer of genetic material between species (human to micro-organisms) that could hardly be further apart on the spectrum of living organisms. There is no possibility this transfer could occur through normal sexual reproduction.

The ethics of this cross-species genetic transformation appear to be very clear. It would clearly be unethical to deny people with diabetes the best treatment available. The rights of diabetics to an efficacious treatment outweigh any scruples we may have about the consequences on a bacterium of the insertion of a gene from another organism, especially when we have been modifying the genomes of micro-organisms for human use for a very long time indeed.

Contrast the reaction to the modification of micro-organisms with the modification of other species such as cattle. The insertion of 'human' genes into the embryos of cattle to produce proteins that have therapeutic value for humans has been subject to considerable opposition. Objections have been raised - and addressed by the regulator - on cultural, scientific and environmental grounds.

But the ethical issues appear to be just as clear as those that apply to micro-organisms. The proposal has been approved by an Animal Ethics Committee and the potential benefits for humans with multiple sclerosis, cystic fibrosis or other genetic dysfunctionality could be substantial. It must also be noted that this is a research project to develop the treatment as well as the technology. Thus objections based on the current utility of the technology, or the product, are premature since without the research it will be impossible ever to realise the benefits.

'Human' Genes

The question then arises: Is there a defining line between acceptable transfers and non-acceptable transfers? If there is, where should that line be established? At the risk of being reductionist (and the very nature of this dialogue invites us to do just that), we do need to understand what it is that constitutes a 'human' gene.

After all, all genes in all living organisms are made up of the same four base nucleotides (adenine, cytosine, guanine and thymine). These bases are then arranged in groups to create genes, which produce proteins and enzymes. These combinations of proteins and enzymes are the building blocks of all organisms. Recent work with the genomes of humans and the fruit fly, for instance, shows that about 60% of genes are conserved between the fruit fly and humans. That is, 60% of the genes have been retained since the evolutionary path of fruit flies and humans diverged. Estimates of commonality between the human genome and some plant genomes get as high as 40%.

So, what is a 'human' gene? Our closest species relative is the chimpanzee, which shares 98.8% of the same genetic code. Therefore it is reasonable to conclude there are very few genes we humans can claim as distinctly our own. Current estimates of the size of the human genome (about 40,000 genes) would give us about 800 genes we could truly call our own - and even then we may share some or all of those genes with a species other than our closest genetic relative - the dolphin, perhaps.

Whether or not there really are genes we can truly claim ownership of as humans is likely to be established in the next few years as more and more of the genomes of other organisms are characterised and cross-referenced with our own. And if, as we suspect, this approach leads to the conclusion that there is nothing new in the spectrum of genetic material, we will then need to start looking elsewhere for what it means when we say we are human. The science indicates the answer is likely to lie in the way in which our genes are arranged and the combinations and sequences that have evolved over the past 150,000 years to make the modern human being.

In light of these already established facts, what is it about 'human' genes that make them special? Any consideration of cultural, spiritual and ethical dimensions of the transfer of so-called 'human' genes into other organisms necessarily implies there is something special about our genes which no other species has. But the empirical facts deny that distinction. We are merely another organism on the planet. There is nothing special about us humans at the genetic level, and it may be that we will find every gene of interest to us somewhere in some other organism.

To take that a step further then, doesn't it mean that the deliberate insertion of a 'human' gene into the genome of another organism will be nothing more than an expeditious route to an effective outcome - like the production of therapeutic proteins? Which brings us back again to the point of the debate - isn't it all a bit moot? Knowledge, and the role of science in increasing our understanding of the world we live in, has a habit of making yesterday's deep questions irrelevant, based as they usually are on an imperfect understanding of the context within which they occur.

Therefore, if we can accept there is nothing *intrinsically* unethical in our ability to work with genes at the molecular level, then the real questions about cultural, spiritual and ethical dimensions exist at the point where we consider the purpose of the manipulation rather than the manipulation itself.

Managing the Debate

Existing structures that examine the ethical dimensions of scientific and medical research are well versed in the appropriate frameworks for balanced decision-making. On the other hand, there are no specialist structures for examining cultural and spiritual dimensions within the regulatory context. While the Environmental Risk Management Authority (ERMA), the Minister for the Environment and the Bioethics Council all have opportunities to canvas spiritual and cultural dimensions, the difficulty is that those dimensions tend only to be discussed within the context of cultural or spiritual objection. Other than the core values identified by the Royal Commission there are few grounds for a wide consensus.

This clash between the sincerely held values of a minority and the values of the majority is highly unlikely to be able to be reconciled through an institutional process outside the political framework. A facilitated process of dialogue may develop greater understanding and, over time, greater acceptance of the validity of difference but without changing differentiation. The extent to which views about what humanness means are central to cultural differentiation will determine whether or not those views are reconcilable with the views of other cultures.

All societies exist in a state of constant tension between competing cultural and spiritual values. The strength of a successful liberal, pluralist democracy is the ability for competing values to find sufficient accommodation and room to live and let live.

At the point where minority values are imposed on the majority a society will fragment, often with fatal consequences for other minority points of view. To preserve the interests of the wider society it is therefore vital that cultural and spiritual objections to the transfer of genetic material from human beings to other organisms be considered within the context of the specific purpose of the proposed transfer.

In a liberal democracy, therefore, individuals (or a group) who have spiritual or cultural objections to the transfer of genetic material should have the right to elect not to participate in the proposed activity. Along with this right is the obligation not to withhold from others the right to follow their own conscience and choose to participate in the same activity.

The question then is whether cultural and spiritual objections are sufficient, of themselves, to prevent an ethical proposal to transfer 'human' genes into another organism from proceeding? It is clear to the Life Sciences Network that those objections, unless they are widely held and expressed through a political decision, would not constitute grounds for a regulator to decline an application for an otherwise ethical proposal.

Are there transfers of human genetic material that may be objectionable to the value systems of a wide proportion of the population? A partial answer may lie in the current high level of objection to human cloning shown in public opinion. By extrapolation it is likely there would be widespread objection to transferring genetic material that would give human physiological characteristics to another organism. While many would express their objection on the basis of sincerely held cultural or spiritual beliefs, it is much more likely the objections would actually be of ethical origin.

Part of the challenge we face today is sorting out the possible from the improbable. It will be important for the Bioethics Council to ensure the dialogue it guides New Zealanders through concentrates on what is *likely* to happen rather than extending to everything that *could* happen. The chances of any scientist wanting to manipulate another organism to make it look, sound or feel like a human being are remote - especially in New Zealand. But there is activity that falls far short of that description, which we are already engaged in and which will continue to trouble some groups in our community.

The Life Sciences Network does not seek to diminish their concerns or their right to engage the rest of us in a debate about them. What we do plead for is an informed basis for that discussion and the careful facilitation of the dialogue by the Bioethics Council. It is the nature of our genome that enables us to consider these issues at all. Let's not fail in our duty to be guided by knowledge and intelligence. The resulting challenge for us all is to engage in a dialogue around those proposals that will emerge in the years to come and to assess them in terms of the benefits they will deliver to the wider community. Our objections to them, if they are to prevail over the choices of others, must be based on careful, scientifically sound analysis.

The Interchurch Bioethics Council (formerly the Interchurch Commission on Genetic Engineering) was instituted by the Anglican, Methodist and Presbyterian churches to address Christian values as they relate to the use of genetic modification (GM) in New Zealand. The beliefs on which these values are based are described in the Preamble of our submission to the Royal Commission on Genetic Modification. These include a sense of reverence and humility in God as Creator and an awareness of our responsibility to/for the whole of creation.

Love is the underlying principle for Christians, and in expressing this love the Church has concerns for the humble and needy of this earth. Faith and hope are ever-renewable and powerful motivators for Christians. For the scientist, the company or the country working with GM technology, hope can guide and motivate so that decisions are made for good rather than evil. In this paper we discuss the issues of transgenics as they relate to these values.

Transgenics is the name given to the technology whereby genes from one species are inserted into the genome of another species. Any area of transgenics is a cause of considerable unease within the community, because it is seen as transcending naturally occurring species barriers in a way that does not work organically with natural processes and their inherent checks and balances, which have been in existence for millions of years. It makes the creation radically subject to the will and limited reasoning of mankind. Therefore for some it is seen as contravening the natural order of things, or going against the wishes of God, or the creative force that rules the universe. When the species from which the genes are derived is the human species, the concerns within the community are increased dramatically. For this reason in this paper we will focus on the transfer of human genes into other organisms.

The Purposes of Transgenics

In order to look at the ethical, spiritual and cultural dimensions of the transfer of human genes into other organisms, we first need to consider the purposes for which transgenic technology is used. The most widely practised transgenics is in medical research and development. By inserting specific human genes or DNA fragments into an animal such as a mouse, medical researchers can obtain information that is of prime importance in elucidating disease mechanisms and that will assist in attempts to diagnose and treat human disease. In other examples, drugs such as insulin are obtained by transferring the gene for the desired drug into yeast or bacteria, which are then used to produce large quantities of purified drug.

In consultations the Interchurch Bioethics Council held throughout New Zealand with church members and the general community, it appeared that the extent to which there are reservations about the spiritual, ethical and cultural issues in transgenic technology involving human genes is influenced by the purpose for which the research or development is being carried out.

Medical benefits of pharmaceuticals produced by transgenic technology (such as insulin) are potentially acceptable to most people, including Mâori. Research into a gene encoding stomach cancer was undertaken in a joint project between a Bay of

Plenty Mâori family and the Cancer Genetics Laboratory at the University of Otago. The isolation of a gene that causes a predisposition to stomach cancer has led to the identification and understanding of the condition, which would not have been possible otherwise. In this instance, GM was used to develop a diagnostic tool, and any proceeds from the outcomes of the research will be shared equally between the Mâori family and the University of Otago. It is significant to note that there was full consultation between the researchers and those involved, specific health benefits will accrue to Mâori, and any financial proceeds will be shared.

Out of our beliefs and our cultural context come our ethical values - our understanding of right and wrong. Ethics must reflect both belief and context in order to determine what we as a society deem acceptable on both individual and societal levels. Barbara Nicholas writes:

We could reduce ethics to utilitarian or pragmatic calculations of risks and benefits, but gene technology pushes us to examine the wider frameworks within which we construct our ethics - what does it mean to be human? how do we create meaning and value? against what 'horizon' do we understand the choices that we can now make? Gene technology is requiring that we construct a new ethics, building on what is recognised as of central importance to us, but taking into account the new possibilities that are now with us.

Our spiritual and cultural traditions can provide the basis on which to develop a Christian response to the challenges raised by new biotechnologies. From the perspective of Christian beliefs we have a role in caring for the creation that God has provided for us. The term 'stewardship' has often been used to describe our role in creation. From this concept several ethical principles can be derived.

1. Considerations should be other than economic, and should take into account the purposes of biotechnological endeavors, and the expected benefits in terms of the relief of human suffering and the well-being of the community.

2. Justice is central to Christian ethics and follows from the command to 'Love your neighbour as yourself'.
3. The concept of unconditional love is central to the Christian gospel. The Christian message has a particular emphasis on caring for the poor, the helpless and the vulnerable.
4. There is an understanding that we should 'Do good without doing harm', in contrast to a utilitarian approach where harm may be permissible if it is for the greater good.
5. There is also a principle of respect for the integrity of the earth and its creatures and restraint in our use of power to achieve what we think best without regard for traditional safeguards and mysteries (indicated by the Pâkehâ word 'sacred' and the Mâori word 'tapu').

The practice of using animals for medical research raises questions about our responsibility to treat all species humanely. The dominion and stewardship we are said to hold over the created order is seen by Christians to include caring for the environment and for all God's creatures. The development of transgenic technology has allowed the introduction into animals of human genes and, in the process, human diseases, which may cause suffering and disease. The extent to which this is permissible in the framework of caring for the whole of both humanity and other living creatures is contentious.

As created beings we have a role of stewardship in caring for the creation that God has provided for us. As part of creation we also understand that we are connected with the created world, so that what affects this world will also affect humanity.

Mâori express this as the importance of protecting the mauri of all things, and by practising a holistic system of management termed kaitiakitanga, meaning the exercise of guardianship by the tangata whenua. The mauri of any living thing is its essence or fundamental integrity as a fellow creature with us in creation, and it is this essence that is locked into the genome of the species and in the individual in a way that protects its integrity.

On the other hand, we have a duty to use our God-given abilities for the good of humankind and "to have compassion for those in need and to help in the healing mission" [Matthew 9:35.]. If medical research is seen as directed at healing and at preventing disease and suffering, and if transgenic technology can be used for these purposes, it would seem to be in the realm of Christian activity.

It is not the purpose of this paper to discuss the scientific risks of transgenics, except as far as they raise ethical concerns. However, the possibility of transgenics playing a role in the development of new viruses is against our sense of stewardship in safeguarding the well-being of our planet. Xenotransplantation, which is the transfer of living cells, organs or tissues from a non-human animal source into a human, is currently under discussion in the public arena.

The ethical, spiritual and cultural issues that are important in xenotransplantation include the risk of xenosis (a virus from the donor being changed as a result of its implantation into a human), whereby new viruses may be developed, leading to the creation of new human pathogens. These are also important in the reverse situation of the transfer of human genes into other organisms. There is a risk of reverse xenosis in transgenics, in that the transfer of human genes into other animals could similarly initiate the development of new viruses. These scientific concerns raise ethical issues related to our responsibility to care for the creation that God has provided for us.

Cultural Dimensions

Culture can be seen as the contextual expression of beliefs particular to groups of people. Within New Zealand we have a multicultural population and a bicultural commitment through the Treaty of Waitangi, so our context is very diverse. To some extent we are determining a new cultural context that holds together the tension between progress and the diversity of beliefs. Some of the concepts we have expressed in terms of sanctity and stewardship would in Mâoridom be seen as an awareness of mauri and a concern for kaitiakitanga. It is the responsibility of the Crown to listen to the traditional views of

Mâori groups concerning GM issues. The Treaty of Waitangi also protects the rights of non-Mâori, and the cultural and spiritual values of both parties to the Treaty need to be respected.

In Mâoritanga it is a cultural offence to mix genes of different species, constituting an affront to the mauri inherent in whakapapa. Genetic manipulations, especially between species or those involving the use of the human genome, are seen as culturally insensitive. Mâori beliefs regarding transgenics are discussed in a paper elsewhere in this publication. Those involved in GM technology have a responsibility to have meaningful discussions with Mâori and to work within parameters that take into account their cultural beliefs

In considering the cultural and spiritual beliefs of the whole New Zealand community, it is important to give recognition to the widespread intuitive unease about the transfer of human genes to other organisms, especially to higher animals. The extent of this concern is related to the purpose for which the work is being done, as discussed earlier. The nature of the organism and its position in the animal kingdom are also important factors. Thus it is possible to describe a continuum of organisms, with single-celled organisms such as viruses, bacteria and yeasts at one end and highly developed organisms with obvious similarities to humankind at the other end. The beliefs of an individual would tend to determine the position on this continuum at which the transfer of human genes is acceptable. For many, the point of acceptability might be found somewhere closer to mice and not as far along as primates. It seems that the closer we get to simple organisms the more applicable are the reductionist views according to which scientific reason tends to look at organisms as merely being complex biological mechanisms.

A significant issue here is whether the organism into which human genes are to be transferred is part of the human food chain. In recognition of scientific and cultural concerns, the Royal Commission on Genetic Modification recommended that, wherever possible, non-food animals, or animals less likely to find their way into the food chain, be used as bioreactors rather than animals that are a common source of food. There are important reasons for this stance.

Firstly, to many people the possibility of eating an animal into which human genes have been inserted is unacceptable for spiritual and cultural reasons. The term 'symbolic cannibalism' can be used to describe these concerns. From the Mâori perspective, if human genes are inserted into an animal, the animal then has a particular relationship to humans. This is evident in the concern about what happens to discarded animals or animal offal in the Ruakura experiments related to the production in cows' milk of human proteins that may be useful in multiple sclerosis research. The claim that human genes are not in fact used, and that synthetic copies of human genes are inserted, does not allay these concerns. While such a claim may be scientifically accurate, opponents of transgenics see such claims made by the scientific community as being merely manipulative. What is at stake is the intermingling of that mauri which is distinctly human with that found in other creatures.

Secondly, there is concern that the human genes transmitted into animals may produce proteins that will be harmful if introduced into the human food chain. The role of prions in variant Creutzfeldt-Jakob disease is an example where cannibalism through feeding and rearing practices affected the whole food chain. There is a perceived risk that bioreactors that are part of the food chain may become available for human consumption. This may happen inadvertently or by deliberate intent, perhaps for financial gain, and there is evidence in the literature that the sale of transgenic animals for food has occurred. We do not know the full implications of these sentiments for public policy. However, the transfer of human genes into higher animals should only be approved where a very specific benefit is expected and after consultation in depth with the New Zealand community. Serious consideration should be given to restricting the use of organisms as bioreactors for producing human proteins to organisms that are not part of the food chain, in keeping with the recommendations of the Royal Commission on Genetic Modification.

Spiritual Dimensions

The term 'spiritual' relates to a set of beliefs held by an individual or group. In practice it is extremely difficult to separate cultural and spiritual dimensions in writing about this topic, and some of the comments that could be made under this heading have already been covered in our discussion of cultural input. In the context of Christian spirituality, the core belief is in the existence of God, who has revealed himself in scripture, tradition, reason and experience. Humanity was created 'in the image of God', being both unique and yet part of God's creation. That we are created in God's image provides purpose and meaning to our existence. It also creates special responsibilities to attend to the mysteries and symbolism of the faith, knowing that some things can be taken by faith to be important because we are not omniscient.

There is a general belief that the distinctions between species, although not absolute, are very deep-seated and represent major biological divides that define us as beings. This is supported by biblical references to species reproducing "according to their various kinds" [Gensisis1:11-12; Genesis 1:21.]. The extent of concern at the mixing of genes between human and other species by the transfer of human genes into other organisms is magnified as the extent of the transfer increases. It is reported that "the current trend is to insert more and more human DNA into an animal of another species." The transfer of a single human gene into a non-food-chain animal to produce one particular protein is not as large a concern - although still significant - as the transfer of many genes.

The transfer of genes that cause phenotypic (observable) changes so that the organism shows human characteristics is completely unacceptable to many people, and is against Christian and Mâori spirituality. At the extreme end of the spectrum is the production of hybrid organisms by the fusion of human and non-human gametes. This would be seen as an affront to Mâori in terms of their concept of mauri and as problematic in terms of the Christian belief that humans are created in the image of God, which implies that humans are distinct from other animals. There is a common agreement that spiritual values require that the production of any human-non-human hybrid embryo should be prohibited by statute.

There is a sense of awe at the conservative pace of change in nature and the stability of inheritance which is the basis of embryonic development. These dynamics reflect a very delicate balance of many factors, and a slight modification may have a profound effect. There is a concern that transgenic studies and the potential modification of our own gene pool by transgenic engineering threaten inter-species boundaries in ways that compromise the distinctiveness on which much of our thought and attitudes are based. Many people believe that roots, origins or lineages have their own integrity and contain the basis of our belonging to families, groups, societies, and indeed our own history. We have a responsibility to keep the treasure/taonga we have been given or inherited intact for future generations.

Our being and all of creation are grounded in God. Traditionally that grounding is seen to be in the fact that we are called into being by God, and this is related to the creating and sustaining activity of God through Christ. For Mâori the Creator plays an active part in our world, and our spiritual values are acknowledged through our recognition of the many atua (gods) in our realm. Mâori perceive the environment in a holistic way and see themselves as an intrinsic element of that environment. The holistic approach can achieve a balance and harmony conducive to abundant life. The harmful effects of physical wrongdoings and spiritual transgressions might cause problems among their people now and in future generations.

Christians can echo many of these sentiments in respecting the hand of God and the limitations of human knowledge. Within this context we need to consider what types of action and intervention in our world are consistent with the vocation of humanity, and the Church in particular, to be faithful stewards of that which we have received in trust.

Emotion and Evolution in Science and Ethics

Genetic engineering and medical research

A controversial AgResearch project aims to place a synthetic copy of a human gene (the myelin basic protein gene, or hMBP) into the genome of cattle. The aim is for the resulting transgenic cows to produce hMBP in their milk. The milk is not intended for consumption, but for research into the treatment of the degenerative disease multiple sclerosis (MS), a fatal condition that afflicts approximately 1 in 1,000 people. The process of removing a gene from the genome of one organism and splicing it into the genome of a second organism is known as recombinant DNA or, more popularly, genetic engineering (GE).

Although this case has received a great deal of publicity, it is not the only example of human genes in other organisms. Until recently the Scottish company PPL Therapeutics has been developing transgenic sheep containing a human gene. The purpose of that project was to produce drugs to treat cystic fibrosis and emphysema. Human genes have also been placed in pigs in order to create pig organs (for example, a heart) suitable for transplantation into humans.

The insertion of human DNA into micro-organisms such as bacteria has been used in the production of pharmaceutical drugs for almost two decades. Since the mid-1980s it has been the favoured method for producing human insulin, for use by millions of diabetics around the world. The human gene responsible for insulin production is spliced into a host organism (for example, E. Coli bacterium) and the host organism effectively becomes an insulin-producing factory.

Recombinant techniques using human genes have also been used to produce a range of other drugs to treat debilitating human diseases, including:

- factor VIII, for males suffering from haemophilia A
- factor IX, for haemophilia B
- human growth hormone (HGH), for short stature and anti-aging
- erythropoietin (EPO), for treating anaemia.

Unlike the hMBP cattle project, these examples have received little publicity and have entered almost unquestioned into the regular practice of medicine.

From the controversy surrounding the AgResearch hMBP cattle project it is clear that the placing of human genes into other organisms arouses strong emotions - both for and against. Having the power to profoundly affect the lives of people and animals, it is a technology that raises many arguments about a wide variety of cultural, spiritual, ethical and scientific issues.

Two Types of Arguments in the GE Debate

Two main types of argument dominate the GE debate: intrinsic and extrinsic arguments. Intrinsic arguments are concerned with whether the technology or its applications are good, neutral or bad - irrespective of their consequences. Either the technology fits or doesn't fit with an individual's cultural, spiritual or ethical beliefs. For proponents of the technology it usually fits, or is not an issue; for opponents, it is often the primary objection against the technology.

Intrinsic objections are based on cultural, spiritual and ethical beliefs about humans' relationships to each other, to non-human nature, and to God. Examples of such objections include 'GE is playing God' (God made us special, different from other animals, and we have no right to interfere with His plan of creation by mixing our genes with those of other species); 'GE is disrespectful to or against nature' (human genes in other organisms crosses boundaries that nature cannot); or 'GE interferes with the whakapapa, mauri, life force, telos or rights of an organism'.

Such statements are beliefs about what is right or wrong, acceptable or unacceptable. They are 'ought' statements - neither true nor false, and not open to direct scientific investigation.

Extrinsic arguments are about consequences - effects in the physical, social or spiritual worlds. Yet they have an ethical/ spiritual component as well as a scientific component. The scientific component relates to physical and social effects. It is concerned with statements of fact. The truth of statements about effects is open to investigation by science. One responsibility of research organisations is to determine, as accurately as possible, the physical and social effects of their developing technologies.

However, these physical and social effects still need to be evaluated in terms of what is and is not important. This is where the ethical/spiritual component of extrinsic arguments comes in. In Western society the moral principles (beliefs or values) most commonly used to evaluate consequences are the four principles of bioethics or common morality: benefit, non-harm, justice and individual autonomy. Usually, non-harm (safety) and benefit dominate extrinsic arguments about GE, with autonomy and justice receiving less attention.

Other cultural values might equally be used to evaluate effects; for example, Mâori cultural values such as whakapapa, kaitiakitanga and mauri. The principles used to evaluate consequences are culturally derived, intrinsic moral and spiritual beliefs. Therefore, intrinsic arguments are also a crucial part of extrinsic arguments. A major ethical issue in the application of extrinsic arguments is the choice of moral principles used to evaluate the consequences. For this reason the focus of this paper is on intrinsic arguments rather than questions of scientific fact.

Culture, Religion, Science, Ethics and Emotion

Culture, religion and science develop our understanding of the world and preserve knowledge about ourselves and nature (philosophy, art, literature, mythology and music also play a significant role). They provide the ontological (what is) and axiological (what ought to be) basis for our interactions with each other and with the non-human environment, in terms of both physical survival and aesthetic pleasure. They do not exist as separate islands of knowledge, but are strongly interrelated and interdependent.

Individuals growing up within a culture are educated to adopt that culture's intrinsic moral and spiritual beliefs from an early age. These beliefs form an individual's core value structure in which their self-identity and personal meaning are imbedded, and through which they examine and evaluate their world. As a core part of their identity and self-image, people have strong emotional attachments to the intrinsic moral and spiritual beliefs of their culture.

Recent psychological and neuropsychological research provides support for the view that moral judgement starts as an intuition, strongly linked to an emotional response to something in the environment, and that much moral reasoning is a rationalisation of this initial response. The point is not to deny that reasoning contributes to moral judgements, but rather to argue that emotions play an important role in moral judgements.

Some science advocates of recombinant DNA technology claim that opponents' arguments are based on emotion, and are therefore irrelevant to decision-making about science or technology. This argument is simplistic, because it ignores the importance of emotion, morality and spirituality in people's lives. It is based on a lack of understanding of the role emotion has in moral judgement, and of the relationship between science and society. Technologies such as GE are developed by people, people use the products, people enjoy or suffer the consequences. Technologies intimately affect the lives of people. To be human is to be both rational and emotional. To deny either of these components is to be less than human. Without emotions our moral sensibilities would be severely limited.

When it comes to public acceptance of the effects of a technology on society, therefore, it is essential to consider how the technology will impact on people's emotional, moral and spiritual sensibilities, as well as their rational reasoning. Responsible science is obligated to acknowledge, respect and appropriately incorporate the cultural, spiritual and moral beliefs of society. Indeed, this may well be necessary for science to gain and maintain the trust and co-operation of society. A science organisation that does not do this cannot be considered in-touch.

The emotional component of moral judgement helps to explain why splicing human genes into other organisms invokes greater moral concern than recombinant DNA involving transferring genes from, for example, one plant species to another. Generally, we feel greater emotional attachment to humans than to either animals or plants, attributing higher moral and spiritual status to humans.

The connection between emotions and moral judgement also helps explain another phenomenon, anecdotally observed, regarding AgResearch's hMBP cattle project. Strong emotional support for the project comes from the Multiple Sclerosis Society, sufferers' families and medical advocates. Theoretical arguments and empirical evidence both suggest that the social proximity (in terms of kinship and community) of a person to the beneficiary or victim can affect their moral judgements about an issue.

Emotion and social proximity may also help explain why inserting human genes in cows receives significant opposition and yet inserting human genes in bacteria has been readily adopted. Humans feel greater social proximity and kinship to cows than to bacteria. Cows, like us, are mammals. They have similar sense organs and the ability to suffer pain and distress. Manipulating the genome of cows produces greater emotional and intrinsic moral concern than manipulating the genome of bacteria.

Science in Society

Intrinsic moral beliefs about what is acceptable or unacceptable differ between cultures and societies, and between groups within a society. Some moral beliefs enjoy almost unanimous support (murder is wrong), while others are more controversial (abortion is wrong). Cultures change and evolve over time, and so do their intrinsic moral beliefs. Some practices that were once morally acceptable have become less acceptable in modern societies, such as slavery, child labour, drink-driving, environmental pollution and the death penalty. Similarly, practices and beliefs once unacceptable have become more acceptable, even enshrined in law, such as religious freedom, freedom of speech, birth control, homosexuality, children born outside of traditional marriage, and divorce.

New scientific knowledge and technology can actually contribute to the emergence of new spiritual and ethical interpretations and cultural practices. It can hardly be denied that science has played a major role in Western cultural development since the enlightenment. Two historical examples are Galileo's empirical proof of the Copernican heliocentric world view and Darwin's theory of evolution.

Demonstrating that the earth revolves around the sun, Galileo removed humans from the physical centre of the universe. Darwin's theory of evolution continued this revolution in thought, removing humans from the spiritual centre of the universe. These scientific theories changed our understanding of our place in nature. They have implications for the moral status of humans, non-human animals and the environment.

Galileo and Darwin not only challenged the received scientific wisdom of their time, but also the cultural, spiritual and moral norms. Both theories caused moral and religious outrage. Today they are received wisdom. These cases represent examples of ethical dissonance between scientists' and society's spiritual and ethical beliefs at a particular point in time. With hindsight we can see that Galileo's and Darwin's beliefs were ahead of the rest of society. These are great figures in history partly because they had the courage to challenge not only contemporary scientific beliefs, but also the cultural, spiritual and moral beliefs.

An essential criterion for scientific progress is that the propositions and theories of science be open to challenge and revision in the light of new evidence. Perhaps an important criterion for the evolution of cultural, spiritual and moral beliefs is that they, too, be open to challenge from new knowledge and new ways of thinking about the world, including scientific progress.

Earlier it was argued that it is important for the science community to acknowledge, respect and incorporate the cultural, spiritual, and intrinsic moral beliefs of society. Here the argument is that, since such beliefs are not immutable, but change over time, it is important that science has the freedom to challenge them. As the above examples show, this is an important way in which these beliefs change. Perhaps, this is an important responsibility of science in society. The issue then becomes one of finding an appropriate balance between these two occasionally opposed objectives.

Not every scientific challenge to the mores of society will eventually be accepted. Science does not necessarily know better than culture or religion. Rather, the argument indicates the need for openness and debate and an ongoing dialogue between science and society about the directions of science and society's cultural, moral and spiritual imperatives. By being open and transparent and engaging in public dialogue and debate about leading-edge scientific research, such as the hMBP cow project, science organisations and the science community not only demonstrate social and moral responsibility, but may also be at the leading edge of the cultural, spiritual and ethical evolution of society.

A necessary part of respecting and incorporating cultural, spiritual and ethical norms into the scientific agenda is to try to understand these beliefs and their prevalence. It is also important to try to determine how they are changing over time. Without an understanding of the direction of change, it is hard to see whether the ethical dissonance created by leading-edge science is leading moral evolution or is swimming against the moral tide. Seeking to understand these things through dialogue and social research is an important aspect of what it means for the science community and science organisations to be socially responsible and in touch.

Returning to the question of recombinant DNA and human genes in other organisms, which applications will be accepted and which rejected is still evolving. Two surveys of the New Zealand public conducted by AgResearch, one in May 2001 and the other in May 2003, suggest that intrinsic moral beliefs about GE may in fact be moving towards acceptance.

What New Zealanders think about GE

Table 1 shows that, although public intrinsic moral beliefs are still weighted against GE, there has been a considerable degree of change towards acceptance in the past two years.

Table 1. Levels of agreement with intrinsic moral beliefs about GE technology*

	% strongly agree or agree		% neutral		% disagree or strongly disagree		% don't know or no response	
	2001	2003	2001	2003	2001	2003	2001	2003
Using GE technology fits with my spiritual and cultural beliefs	8.8	25.1	26.7	33.4	59.3	36.8	5.1	4.5
Using GE technology fits with my basic principles	11.9	31.5	22.3	27.1	61.2	37.5	4.6	3.9
It is acceptable to genetically modify cows for the benefit of humans	20.6	30.3	16.0	21.2	58.3	43.1	5.0	5.3

* The data are derived from two random surveys. The 2001 survey was of 3,000 New Zealanders aged 18 and over. There were 1,682 respondents, giving a 56% response rate and a margin of error of ± 2.5%. The 2003 survey was of 2,000 New Zealanders aged 15 and over, with 969 respondents, giving a 48% response rate and a margin of error of ± 3%.

Table 2 shows that the public are still more opposed to GE food than supportive. However, in the last two years support has increased and opposition decreased. For medical GE applications, support and opposition were about equal in 2001, but in 2003 support is four times as great as opposition. Perhaps most importantly, for both applications at both times, circumstantial support was over 50%. The majority of the New Zealand public were neither strongly supportive nor strongly opposed to GE. They were either undecided or considered it necessary to make judgements on a case-by-case basis.

Table 2: Support for and opposition against GE for food and medical applications								
	% total support		% circumstantial support		% total opposition		% don't know	
	2001	2003	2001	2003	2001	2003	2001	2003
GE food production	3	8	52	60	36	25	8	4
GE medical applications	16	31	62	57	14	7	8	3

Conclusions

In some cases the use of human genes in other organisms has been quickly accepted with little debate or questioning (insulin). In others, it has provoked considerable controversy (hMBP cattle). However, the two surveys summarised above suggest that the gap in ethical disagreement between the public and the practices of molecular biologists appears to be closing.

It is likely that acceptance or rejection of specific technologies will be strongly related to intrinsic moral beliefs and extrinsic moral perceptions of benefits, harms, distributive justice and individual autonomy. However, other cultural values such as whakapapa, kaitiakitanga and mauri need to be acknowledged and considered too. Further social research is needed to determine more clearly the nature of the circumstances in which the splicing of human genes into other organism is acceptable and when it is not. Such knowledge can help science organisations to choose recombinant DNA research projects that fit more closely with the current cultural, spiritual and ethical norms of our society. It is already clear that medical applications fit this criterion better than food applications.

Science must not dismiss the emotional side of human nature in its deliberations about the directions of the scientific agenda. Cultural, spiritual, and intrinsic moral beliefs must be acknowledged and respected by the science community if science is to act responsibly and maintain the trust and support of society. Finally, in order for society to continue evolving, there is an imperative for science to be free to challenge not only its own received wisdoms but also the received wisdoms of culture, spirituality and ethics. However, it is a responsibility of science organisations and the science community to do this in an acceptable manner, through a process of ongoing dialogue and engagement with society.

Bibliography

Anne Sayre: *Rosalind Franklin and DNA*, New York, W. W. Norton, 1978.

Chambers, K. L.: *Biochemical Coevolution: Eugene*, Oregon State University Press, Biology Colloquium, 1970.

Ernst Baumler: *Paul Ehrlich: Scientist for Life*, New York: Holmes & Meier, 1984.

Francis H. Crick: *What Mad Pursuit: A Personal View of Scientific Discovery*. New York: Basic Books, 1988.

Herbert Morawetz: *Polymers: The Origins and Growth of a Science*, New York, John Wiley & Sons, 1985.

Linda J. Lear: *Rachel Carson: Witness for Nature*, New York, Henry Holt, 1997.

Martha Marquardt: *Paul Ehrlich*, New York, Schuman, 1951.

Peter H. Spitz: *Petrochemicals: The Rise of an Industry*, New York, John Wiley & Sons, 1988.

Raymond B. Seymour; Roger S. Porter: *Manmade Fibers: Their Origin and Development*, New York, Elsevier Applied Science, 1993.

Robert Olby: *The Path to the Double Helix: The Discovery of DNA*, New York: Dover, 1994.

S. T. Mossman; Peter J. T. Morris: *The Development of Plastics*, Cambridge, Royal Society of Chemistry, 1994.

Vivian Ovelton Sammons: *Blacks in Science and Medicine*, New York/London, Hemisphere Publishing, 1990.

William F. Furter: *A Century of Chemical Engineering*, New York, Plenum Press, 1982.

William H. Brock: *The Norton History of Chemistry*, New York, W. W. Norton, 1993.

Index

G

H

I

J

L

M

O

P

R

S

T

W

□□□